"How to" guide

Tried and Tested Ideas

for local fundraising events

3rd edition

incorporating
**Organising
Local Events**

Sarah Passingham

DIRECTORY OF SOCIAL CHANGE

Published by
Directory of Social Change
24 Stephenson Way
London NW1 2DP
Tel. 020 7209 5151; Fax 020 7391 4804
E-mail books@dsc.org.uk
www.dsc.org.uk
from whom further copies and a full books catalogue are available.

Directory of Social Change is a Registered Charity no. 800517

First published 1994
Second edition 1997
Third edition 2003
Reprinted 2004

ISBN 1 903991 37 4

British Library Cataloguing in Publication Data
A catalogue record for this book is available from the British Library

Cover design by Lenn Darroux
Text designed by Sarah Nicholson
Typeset, printed and bound by Stephen Austin, Hertford

Other Directory of Social Change departments in London:
Courses and conferences 020 7209 4949
Charity Centre 020 7209 1015
Charityfair 020 7391 4848
Publicity & Web Content 020 7391 4900
Policy & Research 020 7391 4880

Directory of Social Change Northern Office:
Federation House, Hope Street, Liverpool L1 9BW
Courses and conferences 0151 708 0117
Policy & Research 0151 708 0136

Contents

Acknowledgements

I can hardly believe that I have been preparing guides and advice for the voluntary sector for over 10 years. In all that time the same group of people has supported me and checked my facts. I am profoundly grateful for their patience and good humour. Philip Norton is the Charity Law specialist at Hansells, Norwich, and he has borne the brunt of the tax, lottery and charity law aspects of this latest edition; his colleague, Kathryn Hirst, was kind enough to steer me on the health and safety section, and Owen Warnock, of Eversheds, has advised me on food safety matters.

Many thanks also to Simon Barnes from the International Spinal Research Trust, whose wise words have largely made up the section on disabled people; to Alison Baxter at the Directory of Social Change for her confidence and understanding and to Dennis, as always, for his editing skills and text suggestions.

About the author

Sarah Passingham has been creating, directing and supporting events and their organisers since 1985 and has been writing for the Directory of Social Change since 1993. The voluntary sector has always been her area of interest, along with cutting the red-tape of bureaucracy and this, her fourth publication for DSC, aims to give non-professionals the confidence to be anything but amateur.

In recent years she has made a deliberate decision to develop interests in other areas, studying the work of Mother Julian of Norwich and writing the libretto for a new oratorio, *Mystical Revelations*, based on Julian's writings and recorded for a CD released in 2002.

Dedication

For both my indomitable parents.

PART ONE

CHOOSING YOUR EVENT

Why hold an event?

The first thing you should consider as you ponder your local fundraising event is ... why run it at all? Running an event is one of the more risky ways of fundraising. It is time and labour intensive and you almost always have to make a financial investment up front. Have you considered that perhaps you might be able to raise money another, less painful, way?

This chapter will discuss the following topics:

▶ Making a decision to hold an event

▶ Involving the community.

Making the decision to hold an event

You need to be reasonably certain that holding an event is the correct thing to do. Begin by thinking through what it is that you are trying to achieve.

Working out your objectives

You need to decide on your actual objective in holding an event. Sometimes you may decide on two or more objectives to aim for, but it is a good idea to put these in order of priority. Work it out on paper if it helps you to clarify your thoughts.

Bear the following in mind:

- All organisers for charity events will at least wish to cover their expenses and most will put forward fundraising as their prime objective. But it doesn't have to be. A community event may not be so concerned with raising cash as bringing together different groups of people in an area, celebrating a special date or finding an excuse to have nothing more than a cracking neighbourhood party.
- Occasionally organisers have something more specific in mind, such as raising the level of awareness for some previously under-appreciated service or activity. This sort of event is often more of a showcase or exhibition and is frequently of an educational nature.

Often the most successful events are a mixture of all these elements.

Getting other people on board

Remember that, except for the very smallest of events, you will need help – and this means asking other people to join you in the planning process. And if you involve other people early on in the project, getting together to work out aims and ambitions, you will find that everyone will be moving in the same direction when you finally decide to go with an idea. This group may well go on to become your organising committee; it helps to have a few people around who were in on the decisions from the very beginning and therefore know why that initial decision to run an event was made.

Preparing the priority list

When you have decided that an event is appropriate, and considered the size and feel of your event, prepare a priority list that might include such headings as:

- Raise level of awareness about ....
- Raise funds for charity.
- Involve the inhabitants of a certain area of the town.
- Put on some entertainment to encourage those who don't usually get out much.
- Break even on expenses.
- Help community relations between X housing estate and Y neighbouring block of flats.

Finally, don't forget to list and prioritise your own personal satisfaction or needs to be met from taking the lead in the big idea.

Involving the community

Once you are certain that you want to organise an event you can really start to get creative. Involve your local community and listen to what they would like to do. You will always find it easier to recruit helpers and find an audience if your idea is popular locally.

Or look at it another way. Which members of the community are you keen to involve? For instance, you would not expect a knitting marathon to attract many young men. Conversely a competitive athletics meeting will be largely confined to those under 25 years old. The village fair will attract lots of young families but perhaps fewer teenagers.

In other words, you need to decide on the size and 'feel' of your event by considering what the people you are interested in attracting would really like to do.

For example, imagine that a man called Bill Pincher works for the RSPCA in a large town. He is concerned at the way dogs are used as presents during the Christmas period and the high numbers that are later abandoned or cruelly-treated by families who didn't realise what owning a full-grown dog would entail. Bill knows that ignorance of dogs' requirements is the main cause of such problems and would like to promote greater awareness of these locally. He knows of one large local housing estate which is rather run down, but the people are lively and community-minded although at times not quite seeing eye-to-eye with the local police. Bill's idea is that all on the estate could be offered the opportunity of having a bit of fun, while benefiting dogs and the RSPCA.

Bill might arrange his priorities something like this:

- Raise level of local awareness about the needs of dogs.
- Break even on expenses.
- Involve the inhabitants of the estate.
- Put on a 'bit-of-a-do' for those who do not usually go out for their entertainment.
- Make some money for the RSPCA.
- Help community relations between the estate and the local police force.
- Get some personal satisfaction and enjoyment out of organising an event.

The next stage after deciding on the priorities is to choose an event, and make some decisions about its venue, date and audience. This is discussed in Chapter 2.

Key points:

- Work out your objectives before you decide on an event.
- Decide on your priorities.
- Decide if you will bring in help at the early stages of your planning, or if you can manage the event on your own.
- Match your priorities to the different elements.

—

2

Using the decision ring

There are four decisions that you, or you and your committee, have to make before you start getting down to the nuts and bolts of planning your event.

You do not need to make these decisions in any particular order, and you may already have one or more answers but you cannot proceed until all four elements are in place.

Until you have made these four decisions there can be a horribly insecure feeling of having 'all the balls in the air' at the same time. Don't worry, this is normal. In fact I have come to enjoy this moment when things could turn out in a number of different ways. It is best to envisage the decision-making as a circular thought process, rather than a linear one. This is your 'decision ring'.

This chapter will cover the following topics:

- Choosing an event
- Deciding on a venue
- Deciding on a date
- Deciding on the expected audience.

What sort of event do I choose?

In Chapter 3 of this book you will find 56 ideas that, given the right environment, have a proven track record for raising funds. I have had a go at most of the ideas on the list – some are a lot harder work than others but don't let that put you off. Do some spade work yourselves, research your own area and find out which ideas are overworked, what is the up and coming fad or discover a new group who are itching to show off their shepherding skills on motorcycles or the latest techniques in kickboxing. Make opportunities for other people and they will make opportunities for you.

The most important thing to bear in mind about any event you choose is that it should be condensed; it is better to have eight activities packed into two hours than six dragged out over four. Children and many adults will start to drift away if they sense that the next activity on the programme is not just around the corner.

If you feel unable to decide on an event, go back to your objectives and priorities to help you decide on an idea. More often than not your first aim will be as simple as 'to raise as much money as we can from as many people as we can attract'; and that often means a family event held during the summer and usually in the open air.

But do not be deceived. Community events are not the easy option they might appear despite the lack of pressure to raise huge sums of money. It can be as difficult to get people to part with their time as their money and you will have a great deal of organising work to do in the preliminary stages. On the other hand, with more enthusiastic volunteers available by the time the big day arrives you may well have less to do at the end.

In general if you have tradestand owners involved you will make more money than by working just with volunteers, but you must be professional in your approach to them: they are trying to run a business and the tolerance levels are lower. If you want a relaxed, gentle event, you might want to leave tradestands out.

When you have satisfied your objectives list you may find you want to hold a 'mix and match' event where you run several ideas concurrently or one after the other. This can work well, often adding extra interest to an otherwise rather stark programme, but avoid the temptation to get too carried away; remember your target audience and stick to a theme. Fragmented shows are hard to control, even harder to market and the public does like to know what it is getting.

Checkpoint

The best piece of advice I can give is: having decided on an idea, go and see as many similar shows as you possibly can and observe their good points so that you can copy them. Decide why other ideas irritate or confuse you. Have a good look at the structure of the site and ask yourself if it works. How have the organisers managed the signage or the parking of cars?

If you are interested in making money, study the ways that the public are parted from their cash and where the largest crowds are, even at what times of day it seems to be most popular. You can read a guide to running an event from back to front again and again, but there is nothing so informative as going to look for yourself.

Who do I expect to come?

Many organising groups do in fact have a clear idea of what their event will consist of. As a rule of thumb, however, you should never lose sight of the fact that any event, however lavish and carefully planned, is only successful if it attracts an audience.

Specialist events will suggest their own target groups or, looking at the matter from another direction, specific groups of audience will only be interested in a narrow band of events. (See Chapter 7 for more information on target groups and target marketing.)

However, it is worth bearing in mind that although it is hard to devise events that involve all members of the family directly, an event which considers all of the family members' needs is often greatly appreciated. Nothing is more trying on a hot afternoon than attempting to enjoy a 'family fayre' with a bored toddler. Try to offer some variety to any main attraction or present a wide range of entertainment at the 'fayre' type of event. For instance, at the risk of gender stereotyping, give Dad a chance to show off at the coconut shy or Mum an opportunity to buy someone else's cooking.

Make sure those who are not so good on their feet will be able to feel entertained while sitting down even if it is only enjoying a cup of tea in a pleasant tea tent. I say 'only' but often that life-saver for them can be a money spinner for you. Without being cynical, try not to waste an opportunity to make a few more pennies. If you offer seats next to the show ring, ensure there is someone selling programmes and that a doughnut stand is on hand to tempt folk.

> **Key points:**
>
> **To choose an idea remember:**
>
> - Make a considered choice of event and think of the specific groups you may wish to attract.
> - Pack several elements into a short space of time rather than being tempted to spin things out, but make the various parts relevant to each other.
> - Visit other events to study them at first hand.

When shall I hold my event?

So which of the 365 days of the year are you going to pick? Often the date and the venue you chose are mutually dependent. It may be that the field you want to hire or the hall you plan to book is only available at certain times. Often they are booked years ahead for popular dates such as New Year's Eve.

Sometimes the nature of the event means that some of your deliberations are already *fait accompli*, due to an event traditionally being held during the summer bank holiday weekend or perhaps because you have chosen a midsummer ball as your fundraising idea. Try not to compromise your event by taking second best. If you have planned an open-air evening party event you must make it during June or July; don't settle for May when it is still cold in the evenings and it gets dark too quickly. If you expect 70 specialist cars and 3,000 people to turn up (lucky you!) for a vintage car weekend don't agree on the local recreation ground if the city's park is unavailable. At best the event will be uncomfortable and at worst it could be dangerous.

In choosing a date, think about the time of year. Weather is important, and not only for an outside event; people don't want to turn out in freezing conditions only to have sit in a draughty church hall for hours to listen to a concert. Nor would anyone feel moved to spend a boiling hot afternoon watching a film in a hall with no ventilation.

When considering an appropriate time of the year and the time of day for your show don't forget the problem of long daylight hours if you plan to hold, for instance, a *son et lumière* or a firework display for school children, especially in the north of the UK. The Queen's Jubilee celebrations suffered from some of these problems and other organisers have discovered that laser shows don't always work well in cities where there is a high level of light pollution, or on a day when there is little cloud cover.

Meal times are worth consideration particularly where families are expected. Fetes and fairs are generally busiest between 2pm and 4.30pm, in other words between lunch and tea. Of course you can open in the mornings and you will catch a different crowd but it might be a good idea to save your most spectacular attractions for the afternoon.

School holidays may be important to you and these dates are available in advance from your local education authority (LEA).

Don't clash with other people's events . . .

Make sure that no other organisation is having a similar event on the same date in your catchment area. If you live in a remote community *any* event may prove to be competition. You can check for conflicting events with your local tourist information centre, from events listings in your nearest library or by ringing your local radio station. In some areas the local arts authority may hold a clash diary – get your event listed as soon as possible to prevent competition when you have firmed up your date. If you are holding a specialised event, for instance a horse show, then the local specialist clubs and societies will be able to advise you if there are any clashing dates.

. . . and check TV schedules

One other suggestion; it is always worth checking the television schedules if at all possible. I remember one fateful evening when I booked a famous Russian pianist to play an equally illustrious programme and confidently waited for the 'sold out' sign to go up. Only 26 people turned up. I had forgotten that it was the final of the Leeds piano competition and my audience was at home watching their televisions. These sort of coincidences are hard to predict, but the final of the FA Cup is published well in advance!

Equipment availability

Make sure that all the important equipment you need is available for your chosen date before you firm up on a day, including mobile WCs, crowd barriers, marquees, etc. Similarly, fields or some other space for car parking must be available, (after harvest in the country is always a good bet) and that your potential site-personnel are not all planning a coach trip away-day.

> **Key points:**
>
> **To choose a date remember:**
> - Probable travel conditions.
> - Conditions of site or hall associated with that time of year.
> - Traditional dates.
> - Other local events in competition.
> - Major national events e.g. football, Wimbledon, elections or even popular TV programmes.
> - School holidays.
> - The advice of specialist organisations.

Where shall I hold it?

If finding a date is difficult, getting the right venue may be easier. Often there is only one obvious choice and if this is not available you might do better to go back to basics and choose a different event or wait a while. Whatever you do, make sure you chose appropriately; if you have a smallish event you could do worse then to borrow a large back garden or front meadow and save your money rather then hiring a huge school sports field where you would all be rattling around. If you do have a large space available, keep your small event compact in one particular area of it.

Voluntary organisations are in the enviable position of being able to choose anywhere they like. I hated having to turn away shows I just knew would be successful because they would not fit into my theatre. When I moved on to running outside events I had every council (and much privately) owned slice of land potentially at my disposal. What riches! I ran hundreds of events in parks and gardens, as you might expect, but I also experimented with roads (closed to traffic, of course!), river banks, the waterways themselves, cathedral grounds, market places and car parks. You name it and I have probably held an event on it; it was a wonderfully vibrant and exciting time with big companies providing sponsorship or other help.

The culture has changed in the past decade but you don't get what you don't ask for and, in my experience, people are often very generous in the name of charity. If you see the perfect venue behind closed gates, write a letter or go to see the owner; they can only say yes or no.

Consider all possibilities . . .

An inside event usually has to take place in a public hall, but you might find a sympathetic farmer or business person to lend you a barn or a warehouse. You might even find you could use a church for something suitable. I have used marquees even in winter, and provided that there are no gale-force winds and you use plenty of modern hot-air heaters they can be very successful. It is worth negotiating a good rate for winter hire of marquees and you can often get them at short notice as they are usually readily available from October to March.

Then there are those more outlandish venues. Partner up with the local authority to close the city centre for a few hours on a Sunday afternoon. Try holding an event on a boat, or on a steam train if you have a revived railway near you. Some railway companies are interested in alternative uses for their stations, as long as it doesn't restrict the flow of passengers. You could even try putting something traditionally held indoors outside in a field or on the beach, such as a sculpture exhibition or a dance workshop. At Norwich City Council, we once hosted an acclaimed national sculpture exhibition in a disused Norwich cemetery. Contrary to some fears, and despite some astonishing pieces, it was a respectful, well attended yet very peaceful event.

If your choice of indoor venues is restricted you might find that some town councils are prepared to let empty office space or shops for a limited period if they are sympathetic to your cause. Ask the local authority's estates officer or planning officer well in advance, as you might need temporary planning permission for change of use.

General factors to keep in mind

- Are public WCs available or do you need to hire mobiles?
- Have you suitable access for disabled people – or mothers with pushchairs?
- Do you need water, electricity or gas? Some parks have all-weather electrical points and may even be able to provide a three-phase supply if necessary; it is always worth asking.
- If your event is staged you may need a building with a lighting rig or at the very least a structure that is capable of taking one. Some shows come with their own hydraulic rigs that rise up out of their own travelling boxes. We are talking serious money here, mind you.
- Is there shade for animals and will the grass will need mowing before the big day?

Checking the local bye-laws

You should always check local bye-laws. You may have exceeded the number of days that entertainment can be held in a particular venue, for instance. And you most certainly will not be able to hold an event on public land or in a building where there are concerns over safety or where the neighbours run the risk of being disturbed. Look at the section on risk assessment in Chapter 8.

Remembering the needs of caterers

Finally remember your caterers' needs at the venue. They may seem the most picky and demanding of all your hired hands but they are responsible for people's health and are governed by strictly enforceable laws. Their business could be closed down, or they could be prevented from working at your event, fined or even imprisoned if they do not comply with statutory guidelines. If you are planning to feed the public in any way other than just tea and a biscuit, please read Chapter 11 carefully.

Car parking requirements

You need to be certain that there is ample space to park cars safely – this is a vital consideration unless your event is very small and you only expect people on foot.

The importance of easy access

Your biggest problem may be access – it is no good having all your equipment ready to bring onto a park if the only way in is up a narrow lane between two rows of houses that you cannot even squeeze a car through.

Having said that, some parks or grounds with apparently tiny gates offer a removable section of fencing for access purposes and the groundsmen are often quite used to making a second entrance for vehicles.

Public land is often protected with locked barriers or posts. Make sure you make provision for them to be unlocked on the day, or have a key made available.

Checkpoint

An indoor venue might well have better facilities, especially if it is a licensed public building. The secret is not to be afraid to ask if you don't see what you need. I have usually found managers or council officers to be most helpful as long as I have made it clear that I feel it is a favour they are doing me and not my God-given right. After all you are the one who is breezing in and about to turn their peaceful, easily run venue upside down!

Key points:

To choose a venue remember:

- Suit the site to the event.
- Car parking availability.
- Access.
- Availability of facilities.
- Unusual venues are a possibility.
- Safety.
- Neighbours' comfort.
- Check licences and bye-laws, if necessary (see Chapter 6).

3

Fifty-six good ideas that work

 ART IN THE PARK
A celebration of art of all kinds held outdoors

Operating requirements: Depending on how large you make this event, you could get away with one coordinator and a treasurer but you might need more helpers for the day.

Equipment needs: Again this is going to depend on the scale of your event and the venue that you choose. At the very least you will need a coordinator's base – an open boot of a car, a table and chair or a small tent will do, an entrance sign, you might need some fencing and an entrance gate if you charge an admission fee, and some litter bins.

Lead time: You need to allow yourselves three to six months to set up.

Initial cost: £75–£250. If you can find some land or a park donated free of charge, your only major outlay will be publicity. If you need to pay a hire fee you will have to work out your budget very carefully to see if this event is worth the price. On the other hand it is an attractive idea and good for sponsorship.

Suitable for: Fundraising for hospitals, art centres, community groups, schools, colleges, rag-week at universities, children's organisations and other city or town based groups. Probably not right for holding in the country unless as specifically part of a rural art scheme.

Expected return: If you are charging an entrance fee you might expect over £300–£500 but if your main way of raising funds is to hold a collection, your proceeds might be less. You will need to weigh up your location versus your audience. A city-centre park will attract crowds of casual shoppers and they may be willing to give to a collection and pay a small fee for individual activities, but would be less happy at being charged an entrance fee as their time is limited. A university campus based event may be better off charging admission but leaving all the attractions free of charge; you could also charge for parking as space and helping hands are not at a premium.

What's in it for the contributors: You are offering a bright, colourful, busy event that appeals to all ages. People have a chance to show off their talents and creativity and many will welcome an opportunity to learn or try out something new.

Frequency: For the casual low-key event you could be looking at a once-a-week exhibition from art exhibitors all contributing a percentage of sales. For a larger scale event you will be restricted to an annual show.

Special requirements: If you are including music as a major feature of your show you may need to apply for a Public Entertainment Licence from your local authority. If you include a booze tent you will need a Liquor Licence from the local magistrates court and if you include food, other than tea and buns, you will need to get advice from your local Environmental Health department to ensure that you comply with the current Food Safety Acts. You may also need a collection permit if you intend to rattle tins at visitors: this is also available from your local council. Think seriously about obtaining insurance cover especially if you might be including something potentially dangerous such as fire-eating.

Variations on a theme: Sculpture exhibition. Open air painting sale.

What is Art in the Park?

As the name implies, it is a collection of artistic (I use the term loosely) endeavours all taking place in the open air. Some aspects may consist of an artist selling work on a stall or stand. Other areas might include teaching people to juggle or letting them try their luck at unicycling. You might charge people to listen to an open air concert or you might have a band in a bandstand adding to the atmosphere. One event I organised included hourly kite-making and origami workshops. The 'how-to' leaflets were an additional and popular source of income. Another popular and rather more serious activity would be to have an exhibition of sculpture in the open. Not a lot of scope for fundraising there but you could apply for a grant from your regional arts board or try to get sponsorship from a local company or local branch of a national company, and then sell literature to go with it or make a collection.

So how do I raise money from this event?

Decide if you will work on an entrance fee basis. This is only possible if your area is adequately fenced. Think about charging for car parking. Consider a collection or donation boxes. For a long term display or exhibition you could protect your boxes permanently within a brick pillar. You could charge a fee for commercial stall pitches. Or ask for a percentage of the take from amateurs, but since you cannot keep control of this type of payment you are really asking stall holders to make a donation if they have had a good day.

Volunteers might be prepared to club together over the preceding weeks and make things to sell. Volunteers with special skills can offer workshops or trial sessions (at a price) in circus skills, face painting, cycle and splatter painting – à la Jackson Pollock, no-fire pottery, you name it, the list is endless.

How do I get started?

Form a group or committee. Work out your venue and the type of show you wish to promote then check that your benefiting charity are happy for you to use this idea.

Contact the local college or art school well in advance and enquire if they would be interested to design posters and organise the printing as part of their course work. This approach is often very successful as students are usually delighted to be working on something 'for real'. You may have to contribute towards the cost of paper as education establishments are frequently as strapped for cash as you are.

Try to make a decision as to whether you are going for serious art and high culture or if you are just organising a bit of fun. It is probably best not to mix the two as you might trivialise artists' work on the one hand or become too elitist on the other.

If you are going for the serious angle, consider contacting your regional arts board and asking their advice. They may well be able to put you in touch with local artists, give financial aid or assist in the marketing. This approach is particularly relevant if you are fundraising for an arts organisation.

Prepare your marketing plan according to the style of your event and your potential audience and put your publicity where the right people will see it. Try not to use the scatter-gun approach. It wastes money and materials and is not effective.

Possible problems

Local residents or shops may take a dim view if you are noisy or they perceive competition. If you irritate people you may not be able to hold the event again, so be considerate. Find out what legal requirements you need to cover before you plan your contents. Someone else may have booked the same collection day or the park you have chosen might be barred from holding events requiring a Public Entertainment Licence.

Handy hint

If you have a city centre location, advertise on the day by using a couple of people dressed up to drum up trade from the main shopping areas. Erect a few direction signs to ensure that interested people can find their way easily.

Plus... and minus:

- Very flexible event.
- Very atmospheric.
- Family event.
- Excellent PR for arts groups.

- Can get a bit out of hand unless strictly controlled.
- Not a great money spinner for the work involved.
- Relies on good weather unless you hold sensitive areas in a marquee.
- You might need to apply for licences well in advance.

EVENT 2 BARBECUE PARTY
Selling food cooked outside

Operating requirements: Small committee consisting of coordinator, treasurer, publicist and head chef. Consider asking someone to be in charge of arranging some entertainment for children.

Equipment needs: Venue, commercial barbecue, fuel, fire lighters or fluid, cooking utensils, plates and cutlery – disposable or otherwise, food and drink, tickets, a few tables and chairs, plenty of fresh water, means of keeping food cool and lights, if you are planning an evening event.

Lead time: 2 or 3 months.

Initial cost: Allow 75p – £1.00 per head for food and 30p for a soft drink or more if you choose to sell cartons. Food would include a burger in a bun or a vegiburger or a drumstick, some sauce and salad. If you plan to make it simpler or to add ice cream or lollies, adjust the price accordingly. Do not over-cater. Tickets will cost you about £30 to print and you must not forget advertising costs.

Suitable for: Local or national appeals.

Expected return: If you sell everything you should make three or four times your initial outlay.

What's in it for supporters: A chance to get involved with a local cause, meet friends and have a bit of a party.

Frequency: One-off.

Special requirements: You need to be aware of the current regulations (see Chapter 11). The regulations covering the selling or supplying of food apply to everyone preparing food other than in a domestic situation. If you were found to be supplying unfit food, even for charity or gratis you would still be liable for prosecution. Read all the government guidelines carefully or persuade someone in the catering business to organise the cooking side of your barbecue for you. If you plan to have a bar you will need to apply for a Liquor Licence (see Chapter 6).

Variations on a theme: A beach party. Vegetarian food. Historical fancy dress, try Neanderthal man! Have a 'cook-out' from the Wild West. Try a night-time barbecue or mix any of the above. Giant hardboard cacti floodlit from below would give a quick and impressive atmospheric touch. You could even throw a posh cocktail party with barbecued nibbles; especially good if you have a large and impressive setting.

How does it work?

Basically you are selling barbecued food for profit in a party atmosphere. There are probably many ways of organising a barbecue, but you really need to choose a system that will be safe, fun and won't leave you with plates of wasted food.

The simplest method to ensure that you achieve all three is to hold the event at midday, in a large private garden with access to a fridge, running water and WCs. If there is a large garage or barn to actually cook the food in if it turns wet, so much the better. Spread the word amongst friends and the local community, lay on some entertainment for children and sell tickets in advance.

Once you have sold your tickets you will know how many children and adults to cater for, give or take a few latecomers. You will have cash in hand to buy your essentials and will be in a position to ask for discounts if you intend to feed 50 or over.

How do we get started?

Decide on your venue and a date. Choose a venue that has a firm flat space for the cooking area, preferably sheltered from the wind. Watch for overhanging branches or vegetation and set up your grills well away from danger. Consider holding barbecues out of the usual summer period. Hot food is equally welcome on bonfire-night or even in the snow!

Get two or three quotes from local suppliers to give you an idea of what your costs will be per head. If you can ask friends and helpers to donate some of the food, so much the better. Reckon to sell at least 50 tickets (hopefully you will do more) and make enquiries at the time with regard to obtaining a large commercial barbecue. Some butchers are prepared to hire these at a nominal rate or even free of charge if you buy enough from them. Don't try to make do with domestic barbecues, they won't stay at a constant heat for long enough and you will still be cooking when the sun goes down. Look in *Yellow Pages* for a gas barbecue if you are desperate.

Decide if you need some entertainment for youngsters, a bouncy castle, a magic show, or perhaps every participating family could agree to bring a bike or a ride-on toy, maybe there already is a sand pit or you could provide a story corner. If you expect very young children ensure that dangerous areas such as sheds, farm animals, ditches or ponds and roads are inaccessible.

As soon as you are sure of your budget (restaurants tend to treble or quadruple the cost of ingredients to arrive at the sale price), get your tickets printed. Remember to publish the date and time, the address, the appeal and what is included in the price. Tickets will probably work out to about £4–£5 for adults and about £2.50 for children. They should include one plateful of food and one soft drink. If people would like more they have to pay extra for it. And if you want to include a cash bar you will need to apply for a Liquor Licence at least three months before the date, although people could bring their own booze.

Advertise your event by asking your children or grandchildren to colour photocopied A4 posters. Display them in local shops, pubs, community halls or leisure centres. Run a paragraph or a small ad in the Parish magazine or community news. If you ask as many friends as you can to each sell ten tickets, you should have a good crowd in any case.

Plan to supply a few picnic tables and chairs for those who find it very uncomfortable sitting on the ground, but in my experience you really don't need to worry much about seating arrangements, people often bring their own or stand about in groups.

Make sure you think about a car park or tell people where they cannot park. For a big party and where visitors are unfamiliar with the house and garden, make a few signs to point the way to the car park, WCs or entertainment. You might need to hire a mobile WC if you expect a good crowd.

How do we cook the food safely?

Try to avoid buying frozen food. If you have to freeze it yourselves or you have no option other than to buy pre-frozen make sure that you defrost very thoroughly in a fridge for 24 hours.

Some people advocate pre-cooking food. You really need not pre-cook burgers. In some cases the act of cooling the food and re-heating is more dangerous than cooking it from the raw. Caterers will occasionally cook drumsticks or chicken joints in boiling salted water prior to barbecueing; but again, you must cool your meat quickly and keep it below 4° C before you heat it again.

Simple guidelines for barbecues

- Use clean utensils and equipment.
- Make sure that you wash them frequently and that you have separate facilities for washing hands.
- You need an adequate supply of hot and cold water.
- A thermometer is recommended to check the temperatures of cooked food.
- Make sure that your barbecue is really hot. Ideally you should light the charcoal 1 hour before you use it. After 20 minutes rake the embers into an even layer, cover with more charcoal and leave for another 30–40 minutes to ensure there are no cold spots.

- Keep all raw food as cool as possible and eat cooked food as soon as it is ready.
- Ensure that food is thoroughly cooked all through, use thin cuts where possible.
- As soon as you finish cooking remove the grills to prevent grease from becoming burnt on.
- Do not transport the barbecue until it is absolutely cold.
- Always follow the golden rules for food hygiene as outlined in the government produced Food Sense booklet PB 0549 and in Chapter 11 of this book.
- Barbecues have been known to blow over in strong winds or be knocked over, so keep the general public away from the cooking area as far as possible.

How do we organise the day itself?

Prepare salads the evening before, or in the morning if you have lots of helpers. Collect the meat at the last minute, unless you are pre-cooking, so that you don't have to worry about keeping quantities of raw meat cool in a domestic fridge. Keep stocks in a cool box beside the barbecue so that you can cook as it is ordered. For that special touch make up a large pan of barbecue sauce. It is inexpensive to make and really adds a home-cooked feel to the meal.

Put out trestle tables with paper plates, paper napkins and plastic cutlery, salads and sauces if you are using them. Have a clean dustbin with a liner nearby for rubbish. Use a separate table for drinks, in plastic or paper cups. Tickets are exchanged for a plate of food and a drink. To prevent accidents and crowding make sure that there are enough helpers to serve the food. Keep the cooking area behind the serving tables and you shouldn't have a problem. Extra hungry people can buy second helpings by paying the servers; in this way you won't be dropping coins onto the barbecue and the cooks won't be forced to handle grubby money.

If you put a start and a finish time on the tickets, say, 12pm to 3pm, people will come in dribs and drabs and you should be able to cope with demand. If you only publish the start time you may find you have a hungry crowd at the beginning and too many people to feed within a reasonable time. Try to keep tabs on how many tickets have been redeemed (clip them into bundles of ten) and you should be able to judge how much more you should be cooking as you come to the end.

You could swell your funds by holding a raffle or a tombola or by selling tea and coffee.

As the last satisfied customers are going, collect all the rubbish and plates of any uneaten food, tie them into black bin liners and, unless you have a rubbish collection within 24 hours, take them to a tip or you will attract vermin.

Remember to publish your proceeds so that the people who supported you can see the results of your efforts. If you have a large cheque to hand over to a national charity extend your PR by having an official presentation with local media present.

Handy hint

For the purposes of budgeting allow six glasses of wine or orange juice from a 70cl bottle and eight glasses from one litre. Beer and lager is obviously sold by the pint and half pint or by the can. It is probably better not to sell spirits at all at a lunch time party and your licence might preclude it.

Plus... and minus:

- Good popular family event.
- No need to hire a venue.
- Sell tickets in advance so cash in hand for initial outlay.
- Can budget fairly accurately.
- No need to supply chairs, etc.
- No expensive advertising needed.

- Reliant on good weather.
- Do need a reliable barbecue.
- Quite labour intensive.

EVENT 3 BLANKET COLLECTION
Spectators throw money into a moving blanket

Operating requirements: Coordinator, treasurer, 12 helpers.

Equipment needs: 2 large, not too good, strong blankets.

Lead time: A couple of weeks, but in practice you will need as long as it takes to find the right venue.

Initial cost: Nil.

Suitable for: Local and human interest appeals.

Expected return: Over a hundred pounds but with a packed stadium and a popular charity, it could be much more.

What's in it for contributors: Instant amusement, following the crowd.

Frequency: Any sporting event.

How does it work?

Two teams running around the perimeter of a playing area, usually a football pitch, catch money thrown into the blanket from the crowd.

How do we get started?

Everything hangs on the organiser of a big crowd-pulling event allowing you to belt round a pitch or arena exploiting their audience.

The obvious place to try first is the local football club. You could also try any other arena-held sports meeting. Aim for a date where a large crowd is expected and ask to take the blanket round at half time, when the crowds are excited but not leaving to go home.

For safety's sake you should also arrange for a private room where you can sort the money, count it and bag it prior to banking it. As the sporting event may well take place on a Saturday or in the evening you might need permission to store the money in a safe on the premises until a more convenient time. If you have completed your count by the end of the match, announce the figure collected.

How do we get the most from this idea?

Inform the commentators all about your appeal and your target figure. Ask them to announce your cause and with any luck they will keep encouraging the crowd to contribute.

Arrange two teams to travel round the pitch, one team travelling clockwise, the other anti-clockwise, thereby getting two bites at the same cherry. Use four people for the corners of each blanket and two to follow behind picking up all the coins that didn't quite make it. You could arrange a bucket collection at the same time along the back rows to maximise the potential and organise another collection at the exits when the match finishes.

You can liven the activity up a little and prolong the collection potential by marching to music and including a band to parade at the same time. If you have trouble obtaining a live band you might be able to persuade the commentator to play some music over the PA systems.

Do we need a Public Collection Licence?

We are in a state of flux when it comes to new acts and laws covering this area. Regulations have still not been published, despite these having been put on hold since 1993, but they are expected 'soon', so we shall be a little clearer by then. Certainly a football ground during the course of a match used to be exempted under the grounds of the previous regulations and general agreement is that it will remain so by virtue of the fact that access to the ground has only been granted because of payment for a ticket.

It has been specifically stated that interiors of shops and theatres are to be exempted from the need to obtain a licence and I feel that a football ground will be treated in the same way. But if you are in any doubt, contact the licensing department of your local authority.

Possible problems

Flying coins can hurt and could be dangerous. Suggest that your teams wear fancy dress and cover their heads, alternatively they could all wear hard hats.

Handy hint
Use old sheets instead of a blanket and paint the charity logo in the middle.

Plus... and minus:

- Needs very little organising, just one person with some tough persuasion skills.
- No financial outlay.
- Good result for the time it takes to operate.

- Just one opportunity, so you need to brief commentators very well.
- Might find it hard to find the right venue.

BUY A BRICK
Build a local facility

Operating requirements: Coordinator, treasurer.

Equipment needs: Nothing special, just a good filing system.

Lead time: 1 month to set up. A year, or more, to run.

Initial cost: Low level advertising costs.

Suitable for: New buildings, redevelopments or extensions.

Expected return: Several thousand pounds.

What's in it for contributors: Kudos in being listed in the book of sponsors and satisfaction of seeing a project or building take shape which they helped to fund. PR opportunities and advertising in the case of larger company donations.

Frequency: One-off.

Variations on a theme: Buy a theatre seat. Buy a school desk or other equipment.

How does it work?

The idea is to motivate sponsors to contribute to the funding of a building or part of a building. It works especially well where there is already a good feeling of community spirit and where the core population remains fairly static. Village halls, theatres, community centres and sports pavilions are all typical of the kinds of premises that can benefit from this kind of appeal.

Sponsors are invited to pay for a brick at a time – usually £5.00 or £10.00. Their names do not go on each brick but notes are made of all the contributors and a special book listing every donor is drawn up on completion of the building and kept on public display.

For an area that could be tiled internally you might be able to obtain wall tiles that can be decorated by each sponsor or named in their honour. Handmade bricks are probably too expensive to name individually but tiles might not be prohibitive. Alternatively, a good mural can be attractive as well as informative.

How do we get started?

If at all possible divide your project into stages. Perhaps you need an extension to house new kitchens and changing rooms. Plan to raise enough money to build the extension first of all. Then start another appeal for the kitchens and after they are complete go for the changing rooms. People do like to see results and £90,000 just might seem too daunting. Three £30,000 tranches will seem more attainable.

Initially advertise amongst current members or users or, if this is a new venture, to potential users. Send appeal letters, get the press involved to start the appeal and use your community or parish news letters to start the ball rolling. Hold parties or receptions for members or supporters, give talks to groups or organisations, use Rotarian lunches, WI meetings, church groups all to get your message across. Campaign house-to-house in person if you are really brave, or by leaflet drop if you are short of time or courage. In short, invite absolutely everyone you can think of to 'buy a brick'. Of course they are not really buying a brick as such, but it helps to put the appeal into perspective and they feel good about their contribution being recorded.

Make sure all contributors are given a receipt; for large appeals this might be a postcard printed to look like a brick with 'Thank you' engraved on it and some information about the cause, along with a form to make a further contribution, on the back.

Try for commercial donations, perhaps you can persuade a local business to buy a whole wall or fit out the bar or gym. In this case have a plaque professionally prepared and displayed in the appropriate place.

Other generous groups could have rooms named after them or, in the case of a theatre, have a plaque on the back of a seat in the auditorium.

In the case of individuals, you are trading on their vanity; for companies, they will see it as a PR opportunity, so remember to word the invitations accordingly.

What about when the project is complete?

Throw a party, of course! You can even take the opportunity to make this into another fundraising event with the addition of a raffle or a competition to guess the weight of a pile of bricks.

Ask everyone to bring something to eat or drink, persuade someone popular to do the official opening, make a big 'thank you' speech and hand over the sponsorship book. Invite a journalist so that it can be written up for the local paper, and start the next appeal with the money that you raised at the party.

Finally, make sure that you keep all the names and addresses of those kind enough to have contributed the first time around, they just might give more for the next stage.

> **Handy hint**
>
> Start a 'friends' association' to which every donor automatically becomes a member. After the building is up and running other people can become 'friends' by paying a contribution. 'Friends' benefit from perks, such as special discounts, a week's prior booking for entertainment or entry to special 'friends' nights'.

Plus ... and minus:

- You need no infra-structure, no venue and no cash.
- You need very few helpers.
- You don't even need to work to a deadline, although the quicker you reach your target, the sooner you can start the first stage.

- You do need someone very punctilious to collect the donations and make notes of all the contributors.
- You need to keep finding new ways to inject enthusiasm and interest into the project. Momentum can easily die away after the first rush.

EVENT 5 CAROL MARATHON
Sponsored carol singing

Operating requirements: Coordinator, treasurer. A choir of volunteer carol singers. Musicians are optional but welcome.

Equipment needs: Collecting tins, several carol books.

Lead time: 6 months if you need a Street Collection Licence, only a few weeks if you don't.

Initial cost: Nil, unless you need to hire song sheets.

Suitable for: Any charity but particularly good for Christian organisations or schools and church fundraising.

Expected return: Depends largely on where and when your marathon takes place, how big your choir is and how many sponsors they find.

What's in it for contributors: Enjoyment of the Christmas spirit.

Frequency: A one-off at Christmas.

Special requirements: If your event is to take place outside on public land (roads, pavements or a park) you will need to apply for a Street Collection Licence (see Event 22).

Variations on a theme: 1. A sponsored church or school choir sing on their own premises. No collection permit is needed, the space can be warm and comfortable and seats are available for supporters to enjoy the performance. 2. Same idea, different music; barbers' shop to Oasis at all times of the year. 3. Same idea, different activities; knitting, dancing playing chess, etc. 4. Any of the above played as a competition; the last person still doing the activity is the winner.

How does it work?

Each member of the choir arranges their own sponsorship, perhaps so much per hour or a flat fee if they get to a certain time. The choir sings in a popular area and, in addition to funds raised through sponsorship, a collection tin is regularly handed around the audience.

How do I get started?

Decide on the date and area that you need to sing and apply for a Street Collection Permit from your local authority. You might well have to apply six months, or more, in advance to get the day you want for the busy Christmas period. Contact your chosen charity to borrow some collecting tins and make sure that they are not planning any national collections too near your date. If they are, perhaps you could coordinate your appeals. Once you have booked your date you can relax until about a couple of months before.

Organise some sponsorship sheets. Type one up and get it photocopied, it's probably not worth getting them printed unless you have a huge choir and plan a marathon each year.

If you have not already amassed a choir, now is the time. Of course, the bigger the choir, the more sponsors you will get and you may want to take turns, so plan to sign up at least 20 or 30 singers and musicians. Get a firm commitment from each member for the minimum that they will collect and give them a sponsorship form to start using immediately.

When you have your choir complete, hold a meeting and decide how long you are going to aim for. A 6 to 12 hour marathon really means that you will have to sing in shifts. Three to six hours, and you might make it with the whole choir singing at once, although they are going to be pretty hoarse. You might decide to sing in fancy-dress, it will certainly get you noticed. Perhaps you could devise a novel container for collecting money, say, Santa's boot or a doll's crib.

Start practising as soon as you can, unless you all sing on a regular basis anyway. Vocal chords are like any other parts of the body, use should be increased gradually. You wouldn't dream of playing an hour of squash after you had 'couch-potatoed' for the last 20 years, or if you did, you should not be surprised if the men in white coats came and took you away, that's if you weren't being scraped up by the men in black first!

So, practice at least twice a week and decide on a programme. Scores that are tricky to sing should be avoided; you don't want to do yourselves permanent damage.

Plan your route too, unless you are intending to stay in one place, but consider the neighbouring residents and shopkeepers; you don't want to drive them to distraction, think how aggravating buskers become after an hour or two!

Remember that December can be pretty chilly so choose places that are not windy and take it in turns to stop and have the occasional sit-down. For a long marathon, arrange a ready supply of thermos flasks of hot coffee and soup. Chocolate bars are a great pick-you-up and milk is thought to be good for the vocal chords, so have supplies on hand.

Do we need to advertise?

Not really unless you plan a static performance within a building. A bit of pre-event PR will do no harm at all and you might find your sponsorship forms fill up faster; it's good for the cause too, especially if it is not well known, but you don't need to have posters printed or take an ad in the paper. You are collecting from passers-by, not trying to attract an audience as such. Remember to send a press release out to say how much was raised after the event.

What about afterwards?

If your singers are not too shattered it would be nice to arrange a small party in someone's house or a pub nearby. Organise something hot and easy to eat and drink. Don't expect too much from people, they won't want to stay long, but it is good to extend the feeling of camaraderie a little longer.

Suggest that the singers have two or three weeks to collect their sponsor money and arrange one more meeting to announce your final total and present the cheque to the benefiting charity. Don't forget to thank everyone personally.

Handy hint

Plan your date to coincide with a late night shopping day so that you can benefit from an extended shopping crowd.

Plus ... and minus:

- No need to hire a venue.
- Very little organisation.
- Negligible outlay.
- Shorter marathon suitable for children over 10 years old.

- Might find difficulty in recruiting members.
- Seasonal if using the carol singing idea.

EVENT 6 — CAR WASH

Car owners pay you to wash their cars

Operating requirements: Coordinator, treasurer. Volunteer helpers (one adult and several responsible older children who want to earn some pocket money are ideal).

Equipment needs: Buckets, squeegees and sponges etc. Forget expensive shampoos, washing up liquid is fine. Money apron.

Lead time: 3 weeks.

Initial cost: Say £25 for sponges, etc.

Suitable for: Very good for Scout groups but suitable for anything.

Expected return: In a busy car park you could make £500 plus.

What's in it for contributors: A nice shiny car and an opportunity to reappraise their opinions of 'the youth of today'!

Frequency: Every Saturday. Especially near Christmas.

Special requirements: A reliable and easily available water supply.

Variations on a theme: 1. House to house washes. 2. In rural areas, an advertised car wash in the car park of the village hall or local surgery.

How does it work?

There are two ways to work this idea.

- Park and Wash: In towns or cities where car parking is at a premium on Saturdays you may be able to find a town centre based company that has it's own car park which is normally used only during the week. Negotiate permission to open the car park to the general public at the weekend and charge for parking (say £3.00 or less if it is not a town centre) and extra for a car wash (£2.00).
- Car Wash only: Here you can ask permission to use NCP or local authority car parks. You won't be able to have a slice of the parking fee but you can offer a car wash service to those who park.

How do we get started?

Your hardest problem will be to find a suitable car park to use. You must have a supply of water unless you know a very accommodating farmer or parks officer who can leave a full water bowser on site all day.

Many local authorities have a policy of not allowing any sort of trade to operate on their car parks. Councillors may be a little more flexible if they know it is for charity and only a one-off. They could get some publicity out of it and if there is one thing politicians cannot refuse, its the promise of some good PR.

A privately-owned car park might be a little easier to find, especially if you agree to hand over a percentage of the parking fee. Offer them some publicity too; company directors like the opportunity of being seen in indulgent roles in the local news. Don't forget to erect signs to a private car park. You may have to obtain temporary planning permission for this, although not always if your signs are up for less than 12 hours. Check with your district council.

So now you have your site sorted out. What about a workforce? Children, 10 years old and upwards, will often be willing and enthusiastic workers, especially before Christmas. Ring round all your friends, put a note up in the school, or speak to youth club leaders, and offer a small wage. You need two people per car and they should be able to wash each one in five to ten minutes, depending on the dirt factor.

Make it easy by supplying some decent equipment. You need large buckets, gentle detergent, squeegees (for the windows), big sponges and absorbent, synthetic drying leathers. Really dirty cars will also need a soft hand brush for wheels and in really cold weather it might be kind to offer each helper a pair of rubber gloves. Ideally each team will need one each of all the above, but you might be able to pool resources if your park is not too big. Arrange to meet before you open to the public for some basic training and to ensure that each person knows exactly what is expected of him/her. Plan rest periods to eat or get warm, or cool down. Suggest two-hour shifts, or shorter, if you are working with young children.

How do we advertise?

Don't persuade the public to come to you by using costly advertising. You go to them. People going shopping are only concerned about parking their cars as quickly as possible. It is a rare breed who will seek out a new car park especially for the chance to have their car cleaned. By all means advertise with a couple of signs on the car park you plan to use, for a couple of Saturdays prior to your wash day. You could send a press release to your local radio station or newspaper, they might wish to come and take a photo' or two or interview you at the end of the day to see how much you made. Don't bother with leaflets or news ads; it's not worth it.

How do we organise the day?

Display a sign at the entrance explaining that this is a 'charity wash day' and proceeds are going to whatever cause or project. You are more likely to get customers and less likely to risk complaints if people know that you are not a commercial operation.

If you are taking a parking and a wash fee, make sure that an adult is taking money at the entrance. Wear a money apron so that there is less danger of theft and arrange for cash to be collected and taken away regularly. Start with a £30–£40 float.

Make sure that all members of the wash team are wearing a brightly coloured waistcoat displaying the charity for whom you are working – you can cut these from thin vinyl, sew on some ties and stick a logo on the front and back. It also adds to visibility and makes the team safer in a busy car park.

Don't bother with parking tickets unless you want a record of how many cars you attract, just charge a flat fee for the day and adjust the suggested fee to compete with alternative car parks. Shoppers rarely park for more than three hours. Offer the wash at the entrance and if you have an interested customer take for that too. Keep the money separate so that you can tell how many cares have been parked and washed, or if you have to give a percentage to the owners of the site.

Put something obvious under the windscreen wiper (a square of red paper, for instance) so show the wash team that a car needs washing. As the team get round to washing the waiting cars, they remove the 'flags' and return them to the cashier for re-use.

This system of marking cars is also useful for large public car parks where you are washing only but are particularly busy. It means that your wash team do not have to keep an eye on incoming cars or carry money.

Keep a supply of fluids (for human use!) available and beware of the power of the sun in hot weather. Observe the Australian slogan: 'slip, slap, slop' – slip on a T-shirt, slap on a hat and slop on some sun protection cream.

At the end of the day, clean or mop any areas around the water supply, especially if you have had to go indoors. Rinse out all the equipment and make sure that it goes back to the right owners. Pay the wages and any site fees. Suggest a date when all the children can meet up to find out how much money they made. Give loads of praise and thanks, children (and most adults) need to feel appreciated and you might want to use them again.

Possible problems

Charity car washes have had a mixed reception in the past. Owners have had cars damaged, i.e. aerials snapped, paintwork scratched, etc. so be aware that not all potential customers will be enthusiastic about the idea.

If you are using children, especially, give a certain amount of training and stress the importance of quality rather than quantity. Try to build a good reputation.

Unfortunately you cannot obtain Public Liability insurance cover for the thing you are working on, i.e. the cars themselves. However if a bucket is left in the way of a pedestrian and he falls over it and breaks a leg you will be covered if he sues. Insurance companies consider that if you are offering a service for payment you should be professional enough to be able to carry it through without causing damage. In any case the car is already insured by the owner, you hope, and companies notoriously dislike insuring anything twice.

If the weather suddenly gets very cold, abandon the idea. A slippery car park is very dangerous and the owners are not going to love you for sloshing water about to provide a skating rink.

Handy hint

Borrow from friends if you can, or commercial cleaning equipment companies might lend you materials or sell them at a discount. Look up Janitorial suppliers in the *Yellow Pages*.

Plus ... and minus:

- Very little outlay.
- Needs little or no advertising.
- No need for lengthy organisation.
- Great for children over 10.
- No sophisticated equipment needed.
- Good potential earning power.
- Can be used in private or public car parks.

- Can be tricky finding a suitable site.
- Seriously consider Public Liability insurance cover, but you won't be able to insure for damage to cars.

EVENT 7 COIN PAINTING

Coins are collected to create patterns on the pavement

Operating requirements: Coordinator, treasurer. Artist and at least six helpers – possibly children.

Equipment needs: Washable paints, chalks or huge area of blank newsprint. Cones and ropes.

Lead time: 2 months.

Initial cost: Less than £30.

Suitable for: All types of charities. Needs to take place in a safe pedestrian area, a security protected shopping mall is ideal.

Expected return: Over £100, possibly considerably more.

What's in it for contributors: An opportunity to take part in a unique and transient piece of art.

Frequency: One-off.

Special requirements: You need a reliable venue, this idea is particularly vulnerable to theft and vandalism.

Variations on a theme: Draw the outline of a giant dinosaur in the playground, children cover the lines with 2 pence pieces.

How does it work?

An artist paints a reasonably simple design onto the ground. Passers-by are encouraged to place a coin in the appropriate place for its denomination to build up the picture. The picture is 'painted' until it is finished or for the whole shopping day, whichever is the shortest. It is unrealistic to try to go beyond about 5.30pm. At the end, photographs are taken for posterity and all the coins swept up and taken to the bank to convert into a cheque for the benefiting charity.

How do I get started?

First find your artist – someone well known adds to the news-worthiness of the event. In the absence of a home-grown Jasper Johns, try offering the idea to the local art school; tutors might like to run a project and choose the best design.

Whilst finding your designer, look for a suitable venue. It may be that your area doesn't have a Mall or an Arndale Centre to offer. You could use a large floor space in a sports hall or a cathedral but I feel you really need a continuous stream of people walking by to make this idea work well. Consider the possibility of a pedestrian precinct or a well-used park in the summer, but you must be reasonably sure that your helpers are not going to get mugged or the whole design mown down by vandals on cycles.

Explain that you will be using temporary paints or chalks that can be washed off easily. If you agree a venue in principle, but the owners cannot be convinced about the materials, you will have to lower your sights a little to beg a quantity of newsprint from a local newspaper. Failing this you will just have to get out the lining paper and some glue! Or ... you could stick the outlines of the design onto the ground using coloured tapes ... but make sure that whatever you do, it is BIG.

If you have a large space to fill, consider just drawing outlines. Coins of all denominations can be placed all along the lines to create the design. For a smaller space solid colours should be used and the coins placed over each colour to build up individual blocks. This is explained in more detail below.

Do we need to advertise?

Well, maybe not using leaflets or posters. I would go for something a little more subtle. Suppose you have a student at the local art school geared up to be your creative input and you have an agreement to 'paint' your coin picture in the local shopping mall which just happens to be owned by a large insurance company.

If you were the director of that company could you see some good PR mileage in making a picture based on the theme of your company's work or, more prosaically, the company's corporate symbol? Too right you could! It's manna from heaven and you'd be a fool not to grab the idea and milk it for all it's worth.

Having got the company PR department interested, all you may have to do is be available while they organise media releases. If you have a famous artist involved you could even get TV coverage. On the other hand, it could be part of the bargain that you do the running around.

Some companies might even be prepared to meet, pound for pound, the amount raised, providing a form of sponsorship.

Finally, whilst not strictly advertising, you need to warn the surrounding businesses a week or so in advance so that they can prepare themselves with additional quantities of small change as people will want to change notes so that they can be take part.

How do we organise the day?

On the Saturday prior, display some signs explaining the event for the following week.

On the morning of the day, pace out the area that you will need and surround it with cones (or stools) and ropes to keep the space clear. Lay down a few caps or hats so that people can contribute as the artist is preparing the ground.

At this stage she/he is operating rather like a pavement artist. The work should be built up using just three colours (large areas will be in just two colours) to coincide with the brass, copper and silver colours of our coinage. As she/he completes one area you can invite the public to start to fill in the space with coins. Use the money collected in the hats to start off a patch. Hopefully the artist will have used one colour to paint small but very important parts of the picture, such as eyes or jewellery. These areas should be reserved for pound coins; there will be some people who would only contribute 10p in the normal course of events, but faced with the opportunity to 'paint' a mouth or other unique part of the picture, will happily contribute several pound coins just so they can say 'I did that'.

If a crowd develops, or as the picture gets bigger, you will want to prevent people stamping about over the area. Now your helpers come into play. Keep the barriers up and use your boy scouts, or whoever, to place the coins for people. Put your helpers in uniform or coloured waistcoats marked with the charity logo or ask them to wear all the same colours. It helps contributors find someone to give their money to quickly and easily.

As the picture draws to completion, contact the local radio station and newspaper office and give your local TV newsroom a ring to say that you will be finished in about an hour. Work out a very rough estimate of how much the picture is 'worth'.

Arrange for a professional photographer to take some pictures at the end and suggest that the mayor or company chairman might like to be photographed placing a final rosette of 'fivers' to make the finishing touch.

Be ready with your brooms to sweep everything up and don't forget plenty of buckets or money bags to carry your spoils away; coins are incredibly heavy.

You may be able to leave the painted design on the ground until it wears off but you must be prepared to wash and scrub it all off there and then, if required.

Possible problems

Paint looks much more striking than chalk but some paints wash off some surfaces better than others. Take advice from a commercial paint company (they may even supply the paint free of charge). Try a small area first and prove to your, and the owner of the venue's, satisfaction that it will come off easily. Chalk may take a few showers to completely disappear but some scrubbing brushes should do the trick fairly quickly.

Handy hint

Contact your regional arts board to explain your project, they just might be able to think of an artist who would be prepared to help you.

Plus ... and minus:

- Very little outlay.
- No need for a committee.
- Children can be involved.
- High profile event.
- Attracts many contributors

- Coins will almost all be small denominations.
- Big commitment to find the right venue and artist, probably needs good negotiating skills.
- Need several helpers, especially if you have to scrub the area clean at the end.

EVENT 8 CREAM TEAS
Home-made teas for sale in the garden

Operating requirements: Coordinator, treasurer and helpers.

Equipment needs: Trestle tables, picnic tables and chairs, insulated cool boxes, crockery and cutlery, hot water urn, electrical supply and a couple of catering sized tea pots.

Lead time: 4–6 weeks.

Initial cost: Under £40 for advertising, plus costs of ingredients.

Suitable for: Local fundraising. Churches, village halls, hospices etc.

Expected return: As in the barbecue, aim to make three or four times your ingredients costs. If scones and cakes are donated, so much the better.

What's in it for contributors: An event particularly suited to retired and elderly people although it by no means excludes families. A taste of yesteryear Britain.

Frequency: Two, or at the most three, times during the summer at different venues.

How does it work?

There are three ways to operate your cream tea.

- Cream teas are offered to passing trade in much the same way that you might expect a tea garden business to work in the West Country, the difference being that this event relies on publicity to bring people in on a one-off occasion. You will need signposting and advertising to make this work well.
- You can sell tickets to the general public. This gives you a good opportunity to judge the quantities of provisions needed and puts money in the kitty before you open (see Event 2 Barbecue party). As for the barbecue, you will need a good advertising campaign although, because you have a longer period of time in which to sell your tickets, word-of-mouth will be a valuable asset.
- You can sell tickets through invitation only. If you have a small town garden or appeal to a very small potential customer base fundraising for a very specialised organisation, you might find this is the option for you especially if you invite a celebrity or several VIPs. Everyone can do something and you are really holding a private party for which you ask a small contribution. But you are not going to make pots of gold.

I favour the first variation, unless you are forced into the third, because firstly, in the second variation you have the additional expense of the tickets themselves and secondly, when confronted by plates full of goodies you may well find that your customers will be tempted to buy more than they had intended, which will enhance your profits.

Charging £2.50 or so for a ticket may seem quite expensive for a cup of tea, a scone with cream and jam and a piece of cake and you might put some people off. However, the individual cost of two delicious scones, oozing strawberries and cream, a slice of chocolate cake and a flapjack washed down by a couple of cups of tea, all mounts up.

How do we get started?

First decide on your venue (probably a beautiful garden but don't rule out an accessible river bank, a pretty barn or even a churchyard or hall if you are in an urban environment) and a date that does not coincide with any other local summer activity.

You should also decide for whom you are planning your cream tea. The people who really enjoy this type of event are the older age groups, so make it their event with tranquil surroundings, chairs to sit on and china cups to drink from; however you need to make sure that you have a supply of squash and biscuits for children.

Confirm a supply of chairs and folding tables. A couple of trestle tables covered with clean sheets or cloths are useful also. Don't forget to book your supply of crockery and some spoons and knives well in advance. You may be able to hire these from a village or church hall or a community centre. The same source might be able to supply an urn and some tea pots although many commercial catering suppliers have everything for hire, even for quite small quantities.

Advertise your event in local shops, at the over-60s club, the doctor's and dentist's surgeries, libraries, in the local paper or anywhere where retired people, in particular, visit.

If the garden where you are holding your event is very special, you might consider asking a nominal entrance charge. It all helps to swell the funds. You might also think about holding a croquet tournament at the same time. This is often extremely popular and some players are very competitive and might bring a number of spectators.

By now you will have a good idea how many people are likely to come and you will have to work out how much food you need. Buy some catering packs of good quality tea, sugar and strawberry jam. It will always keep if you don't use it all. Ask volunteers to make scones, cakes and biscuits or order them from the local baker, although your profits will dwindle quickly if you have to buy your goods. If you have some left over you can freeze them or sell them off at the end. Or you could hold a raffle for all the leftovers. Reckon on getting nine slices out of an average-sized cake. Buy whipping cream on the morning of the event, but order it from the dairy first to be sure of having enough. If you live in the South West, you might choose to use clotted cream instead although be aware that cream is a high-risk food and you need to take care in keeping it cool. Have plenty of butter available in case people don't like cream or if you run out.

How do we run the day?

If you are charging an entrance fee, station your collector near the gate a good ten minutes before you officially open. Make sure they have a chair and someone to relieve them after an hour or so. It helps to have a sign up showing the logo and name of your charity and what is going on. Fly some bunting if you have some, it all adds a bit of atmosphere.

Arrange an area for people to park their cars safely although most people will come on foot.

Keep your serving tables all together, probably near an electric socket for your urn and preferably in the shade. Ensure that all trailing flexes are covered with mats or, ideally, string them up at least 7ft above the ground. Wrap plugs and electric sockets in plastic bags in case of sudden downpours. Keep your route to the house away from the flexes.

If you have enough helpers, keep one person to collecting money only. It is not very hygienic to be handling money and food.

Although tea, cakes and biscuits are not particularly high-risk foods, fresh cream is, so to be on the safe side keep only small quantities of cream and cream-filled cakes or scones on the table. Use cool boxes or the fridge in the house, if it is not too far away, to store supplies until they are needed.

How can we maximise profits?

You might need to do something more than just sell teas to make your efforts worthwhile. Don't be tempted to add too much in the way of entertainment though; in my experience the most memorable events, however humble, are those that have a special identity and don't just seem like the ubiquitous fete.

- Make more cakes than are needed to raffle at the end or just sell whole for freezing. (Don't fill these with jam or cream. Butter icing is ideal.)

- Have a 'Guess the weight of the cake' competition (see Event 24 Stalls and sideshows).
- Hold a raffle for an appropriate donated prize.
- You could have a plant stall or garden produce stand, especially if you know your visitors are keen gardeners.

Handy hints

To get nine slices from a round cake: first cut out a very slightly smaller than usual slice by eye and remove it. Cut the cake in half from the centre of the cake out to the edge exactly opposite the middle of the missing slice. Now shift one half round slightly so that you have two thin slices missing on either side. Cut the cake in half again to form four large triangles which you half again into eight slices. With the slice you first removed you now have nine slices from an eight-slice cake! Sneaky? Who, me?

Fill cakes with fresh cream and jam, or fresh fruit, only as you use them. Any left over will not be wasted and can be frozen safely. You can freeze cream to use for cooking also. Pour it into ice-cube containers so that you can defrost small amounts at a time.

Plus ... and minus:

- Not difficult to organise.
- No expensive venue to hire.
- Small capital outlay.
- Not very labour intensive on the day.

- You do need to mobilise lots of volunteers to bake the goodies.
- Not a great money spinner.
- Limited appeal, but absolutely right for some areas.

EVENT 9 CUSTOMISED SCHOOLKIT AND CABOODLE

Selling school items designed by the students

Operating requirements: Coordinator (member of the school staff), treasurer, sales people.

Equipment needs: Customised produce as detailed below. Stall, or semi-permanent base within school.

Lead time: 3–4 months.

Initial cost: Entirely dependent on the amount of stock you order. Usually payment not required until 30 days after receipt of goods so take payment with orders so that you can be sure of paying the bills.

Suitable for: Schools, large play groups or nurseries, special needs centres.

Expected return: Usually you charge two or three times what it costs to buy.

What's in it for purchasers: Seeing their children's drawings in print – the 'Goo' factor! Good quality useful items, professionally produced.

Frequency: Continuous.

Special requirements: Needs to be run like a business, with accounts and possibly VAT.

Variations on a theme: Home-designed Christmas cards (not to be confused with selling charity cards) and other stationery.

How does it work?

Children prepare drawings of themselves, their chums or their school. The drawings are professionally printed onto various items – tea towels, kit bags, shoe bags, laundry bags, peg bags, T-shirts, notelets, table mats, calendars, mouse-mats, etc. These are sold for profit. You could have a stall at the school fete or, at larger schools, there may be a semi-permanent 'shop' available.

How do we get started?

Find a printer who is prepared to print from your designs. Make sure that the quality of products is good enough; some T-shirts are very cheap but poorly made.

There are a number of national companies who are used to working with schools from all over the country and provide clear instructions and template sizes to achieve just what you want. The quality and variety of goods is excellent.

Contact your printers at least three months in advance (more if you need things before Christmas) and find out what lead time they need to print your items from the time they receive your finished art work.

To make the whole idea a little special you can arrange a project for members of the whole school or group to each produce a drawing on white paper using a new black felt-tipped pen.

Make sure that you see a sample before printing the whole run, or at least visit the works to agree the artwork.

It is a good idea to bag up all the goods individually which helps to keep everything clean as well as looking professional; some companies will do this automatically. When you receive your items you will have to price them and decide how to sell them if you haven't already done so.

Market your stall or shop, prior to opening, with A5 leaflets showing a price list and where the goods are available. Give a phone number or contact name so that people can discuss orders that they may wish to collect on a specific day. You could even take orders before you go ahead with the printing, although the products are so attractive they usually sell better where customers can see them. Remember that there will be a minimum order.

Possible problems

Make sure that your organisation is registered as a charity if possible as this will give you certain grant and tax advantages. See Chapter 6 for a discussion of possible VAT issues.

Handy hint

Give children frames or squares of paper so that they all produce drawings roughly the same size. You can use signatures but 'portraits' are far more appealing.

Plus ... and minus:

- Potential for making large profit.
- No special venue required.
- Initial drawing project involves children of any age and could be run as a special event in itself.
- Very attractive products that every member of the family and friends will be queuing to buy.
- Companies specialised in this service already set up.
- Few helpers needed.

- Need school's cooperation and site for shop if 'going permanent'.
- Has to be run as a business. May involve large quantities of cash.
- Possible VAT registration. Charity status and bank account advantageous.

EVENT 10 DUTCH AUCTION
All the thrill of an auction without the expense

> **Operating requirements:** Auctioneer and/or coordinator, treasurer, collector, two or more stewards.
>
> **Equipment needs:** Venue preferably with a stage, if not you will need a podium of some sort. Chairs for the audience and room to display items to be auctioned. Collecting box or plate. Timer.
>
> **Lead time:** A month to six weeks to set up the event but you might need several months to collect all the items.
>
> **Initial cost:** Usually a Dutch auction takes place as part of another event; perhaps a dinner, wine and cheese party or maybe an art exhibition and will cost very little to stage. If you have managed to collate some really splendid items to be auctioned you should hold the event in its own right, print catalogues, market it well and attract a really large audience. This could cost you £50–£150.
>
> **Suitable for:** Particularly good for local causes when used as an added attraction to something else. When holding a Dutch auction as the main event it will need to be for a popular, current or nationally known cause.
>
> **Expected return:** Your return will depend largely on the size of your audience as well as the quality and popularity of the goods offered. For a large event you could make £1,000 or more.
>
> **What's in it for contributors:** The opportunity to buy something for considerably less than its real value and to experience the excitement and thrill of a real auction with none of the risk.
>
> **Frequency:** Annual.
>
> **Special requirements:** It helps if you produce a celebrity auctioneer.

How does it work?

- **Variation 1**: The auctioneer offers items for sale as in a conventional auction. At the first bid s/he will start the timer which is kept secret from the audience. The first bid will come in at, perhaps, £1.00 A steward will collect the pound from the bidder in a collection box. The next bid may be £1.50 and the steward will collect 50p; this being the balance to make up the £1.50 in the box. The next bidder might bid £2.25 but will only have to pay 75p and so on.

The bidding continues until the timer rings and stops the bidding. The person making the last bid has the goods.

You could arrange for the steward to just make a record of names and amounts, if everyone is known to the stewards or auctioneer, payment can then be made in a lump sum at the end of the evening.

- **Variation 2**: The auctioneer opens the bidding himself and lowers it in stages until a buyer is found. I feel some of the excitement is lost using this variation as you are not bidding against anyone else. However, there is an element of anticipation in case you lose a coveted item to someone else.

If you print catalogues before the event they can be sold to use as tickets or numbered, to hold a raffle, or sell advertising space to raise more funds.

You can run a Dutch auction with just one or two really special items for sale, such as a holiday or a television, and, if you are using variation 1, it is the auctioneer's responsibility to see that he gets at least one bid from everyone in the room. The timer should be set to allow one bid every 20 seconds, to allow the stewards to collect the money, or three bids a minute. Multiply the time by the number of guests, give or take a minute or two, and you should be able to run up some serious bidding. At this type of event most contenders will up the bidding by at least £5.00, so with 100 guests you might expect to make £500 in just over 30 minutes.

If you have plenty of smaller goods people will raise the bidding by pence rather than pounds but everyone will have fun bidding several times for lots of different goods. Add a few surprises in kind such as for the promise auction (a couple of hours gardening or an offer to cook a meal). It is surprising how much can be made on really popular items so judge the timing appropriately. Put a couple of really short times in – sort of loss leaders – to inject some excitement whenever you feel interest is flagging.

How do I get started?

You might need to get together a small committee and delegate special duties. It can be very time consuming collecting goods for sale or finding someone prepared to be auctioneer. You may have to store goods for sometime also so you need to consider somewhere secure. Obtain a logo from your benefiting charity for use on publicity.

First you need to collect your sale goods. For special prizes try non-chain stores for donations and some holiday companies are prepared to help so long as you can guarantee good PR and publicity; which is where your VIP comes in.

If you know an artist or sculptor who is particularly sympathetic to your cause you could ask if they would be prepared to offer an original piece of work to be auctioned.

The celebrity personality and the prizes are a bit of a chicken and egg situation. The VIP might be more prepared to help out if s/he feels that you have some big 'prizes' to offer and the stores are more prepared to make donations if they know you have a big name to add weight to potential media interest.

For smaller auctions you will have to ask for donations locally. If people can't find something in their attics that will do, ask them to bake a cake, give some vegetables or plants or make something special. Get a specific commitment out of people if you can without being pushy. The local pub, shop or restaurant might give a free meal or a voucher.

Next, decide on a date and venue, or if your auction is to be part of a larger event, and check that it is convenient for your auctioneer.

Now you have to work out how you are to market the event. You have two choices. Either you advertise as you would for a theatrical show or you send invitations. If you advertise to the general public it is probably helpful to sell tickets in advance. The hall you hire will hold a fire certificate which dictates how large your audience can be. It would be very sad to have to turn away people on the night if your auction was very popular and it could be tempting to sell more tickets than you should.

Don't forget to involve all the media. Send press releases to newspapers, radio, even television if your celebrity is a really big name. Advertise carefully or give due consideration to your guest list.

Tickets can be free or paid for but you do need them, if only to work out how many people are coming. If they are paid for, you could use the entrance money to buy the sale goods if you are not successful with donations, or to hire a stage personality from an agency.

Lastly you need to ensure that there is enough car parking for your patrons. If you expect a really large crowd in a small village or a part

of town that does not provide enough parking it is a courtesy to inform the police. They will be happy to advise you and might wish to control the area.

What happens on the big day?

Set the hall out like a theatre, that is with the chairs all facing a stage area. Provide a separate room for viewing the goods if necessary or place them round the auditorium. They need to marked with lot numbers.

After the main attraction (in the event of a dinner people remain seated where they are) or at the appointed hour, the auctioneer starts the bidding in the manner described above. S/he will work from a numbered sheet and ask stewards to bring the lots forward or pass them along the rows for people to examine where appropriate. In the event of a few very special lots this will not be necessary.

The more charismatic and persuasive your auctioneer is (and if you have chosen someone local it helps if they know most of the people present) the more bids you are likely to get.

Most people will come to the auction planning to spend a fixed amount and towards the end more and more people will sit out of the bidding because they have reached their ceiling. Of course you want to make as much money from the event as you can, but it is unfair to shame people into spending more than they wish. To keep everyone interested and to let the auction end on a high note save the best lot until last but let it be known from the start that this is planned. You don't want to be left in a situation where bidders are 'all spent out' and you have very few bids for your star item. Everyone can join in one more time and after it is all over they know it is time to go home.

Is there anything we should do afterwards?

Thank everyone profusely for supporting the event and arrange for a bouquet or something special to thank your auctioneer (to be presented in front of the audience). Make sure that you have planned for some help in tidying up and if it is very late, leave it until the morning if possible.

It will always be appreciated if you write a letter of thanks for all large donations and include the final figure for your proceeds. Write an official letter of thanks to your auctioneer, as it is a very stressful job. People do like to know how things turned out and they will be more willing to contribute or attend again if they feel you were grateful and the event was a success. Send another of the ubiquitous news releases saying how brilliant the auction was, how many people came and include a quotation from your auctioneer if possible. Tag on a date and invitation to attend an official paying over of the money raised to the charity.

Possible problems

It just might be that people are not sure what happens at a Dutch auction. If you begin to sense that people are in the dark as to what is expected of them, prepare an A5 photocopied sheet of 'How it works' to send or give to those who ask. If you are organising variation 1 as a small local affair without invitations, add a line saying something like, 'bring plenty of small change' or 'all cash bids under 50p', to all the posters.

Plus... and minus:

- Can piggyback another event.
- You can raise funds from entrance tickets, the sale of advertising space in catalogues and the auction itself.
- Needs little in the way of special equipment.
- Flexible. Could be all over in 20 minutes or take a couple of hours.

- Can be time consuming in the organising.
- Audience might need explanation of what is expected of them.
- Not suitable for children.

EVENT 11 FAST PARTY
People pay not to attend a dinner

Operating requirements: Just two people can organise this non-event! Actually one could do the work but, as with all fundraising, it is as well to have two heads checking money.

Equipment needs: Some really beautifully designed invitations and someone with a witty brain.

Lead time: A couple of weeks.

Initial cost: Just the cost of the invitations (unless you can get a friendly printer to sponsor the event for a little advertising on the reverse of each invite). And postage.

Suitable for: Well known organisations, either local or national. Especially good for aid charities; if the event is taken seriously it can show solidarity with victims.

Expected return: Well the sky's the limit. Keep your 'tickets' to about £2.50–£5.00 per couple or family and you will find it surprisingly successful. This idea works best if you send invitations to people you know personally so if you combine your efforts with a couple of others you can widen your guest list. Add a donation leaflet from your chosen charity for more generous givers.

What's in it for contributors: First, they don't have to respond at all if they don't like the idea. Second, lots of people like to support a particular group but they often don't like an 'organised' social event; they may have small children, not have a car or are elderly and not be able to get out much; they may not be able to afford £20–£25 for a special dinner. A 'fast party' allows them to show support at a relatively low cost without having to give up valuable time and effort. And no one can be 'busy on the night'!

Frequency: A 'one-off' event. It might be better to restrict your use of this idea; it is amusing and clever once but some people might feel it is a bit of a con if you use it too often.

What is a fast party?

It is not a party held in double-quick time! No, 'fast' is as in not eating. Sounds pretty strange. How does it work?

Guests are invited to a party that will not take place. They are asked to go without one meal on a particular date and to contribute the cost of that meal to the proceeds. They may or may not take part in the spirit of the event, but many are happy to contribute anyway.

What's my starting point?

Find two or three other people to help write a guest list and pool some ideas for a witty invitation. Work on the premise that 'guests' might like the chance to show off a very flashy invitation on their mantelpieces, even if it is for a bit of a laugh. Something like this might do, but I'm sure you can think of something better:

MR AND MRS ......

(Your name or organisation)

have pleasure in not requesting your presence at a

FAST PARTY

in aid of

BARKSWORTH DOGS HOME

not to be held on Saturday 20th June

not at Growl'n'snap Grange

The guests of honour will not include
HER MAJESTY THE QUEEN'S CORGI
THE LORD MAYOR OF BARKSWORTH

RSVP	Tickets in advance
[address.......]	£2.50 per couple
	[Cheques payable to......]

Guests are invited to give up one meal on the date above for this worthy cause and donate the cost to Barksworth Dogs Home. Send your cheque to the above address.

Have the invitations printed on a good quality card and of a standard size to fit into an envelope and include a self-addressed envelope to encourage the cheques to roll in. (The printer will probably supply envelopes cheaper than at a retail stationers.) If you think you might repeat the 'event' annually, you can have extra printed at very little extra cost. Remember to leave the date line clear so that you can write in the new date next year.

What if I get very few replies?

You should get at least 50 per cent of invitees donating something. If you think you should have done better you could try a follow up call and offer to pop round to collect, without being pushy. Some people may not wish to contribute for whatever reason and you should respect their decision but others may have just forgotten and welcome a call to save them going to the post box.

Should I do anything after the date is past?

Well, apart from handing the proceeds over, it is a nice idea to send a short thank you letter. This could be photocopied to keep costs down – keep a note of any specially generous donations so that you reply personally. To add to the theme you could print a revolting menu on the back to show what they would be thankful to have missed! Remember to add the cost of the thank-yous and the postage to your budget.

Possible problems

It may be better to have cheques made out to the charity itself as personal cheques are easy to abuse. Contributors may be happier writing cheques direct to a cause that they know and trust. Check with your benefiting group as to how they would like to receive the money.

Handy hint

This idea could work well as a form of PR. Make sure that you prepare a couple of good press releases, before and after, for your local newspapers, radio stations and charity newsletters.

Plus ... and minus:

- Very little organising necessary.
- No venue, no nothing!
- Surprisingly effective.
- Very little outlay.
- Fairly easy to obtain sponsorship.

- Limited use.
- Best used on friends and family but you can only ask them once. Try to give them a good laugh for their money.

EVENT 12 GARDEN OPEN DAY

Open your garden to the public for an entrance fee

Operating requirements: Garden owners prepared to have hordes of nosy people tramping over their property. One or two organisers. Stall holders, and refreshments stall holders if required.

Equipment needs: Table and chair for entrance fee collector. Tables for stalls, tea and buns paraphernalia (see Event 8 Cream teas) if required. Signs.

Lead time: Two or three months, or longer if a series is arranged, to allow for advertising.

Initial cost: £40–£60

Suitable for: Just about anything. The beauty of this idea is that it is infinitely flexible. For a WI fundraiser add a splendid tea tent and produce stalls. For a mums and tots group add a teddy bear's picnic and a supervised paddling pool. For the gardening club add plant stalls. For the school add a treasure hunt or quiz stalls; the list is endless.

Expected return: This might depend on the weather and the amount of additional attractions. Charge 50p/£1.00 entry, children under 10 free and nearly all your takings will be profit.

What's in it for visitors: An undemanding few hours out and an opportunity to catch up with a few friends. For the keen gardener it can be a time to get some ideas or buy some new specimens. For others … well, never underestimate the curiosity of folk. If the local 'big hoos' – as they say in Scotland – can be persuaded to open its gates, doors, swimming pool, tennis court, etc. you might be amazed at how many people will come out of sheer curiousity!

Frequency: This idea is perfect for a 'summer series' of gardens open in the area, or it can be just as effective as a one-off. It is perhaps best not to open the same garden more than twice a year.

Special requirements: If you are serious about making this a real gardening day then a couple of knowledgeable horticulturists on hand to answer questions is a must.

How does a garden open day work?

Very simply, you are charging an entry fee for people to see around someone's private garden. You will need to make sure that there is not another entrance where visitors can get in without paying. It is unlikely that you will get gate-crashers at this type of event but visitors do make genuine mistakes. You may or may not have added attractions to supplement the entrance money.

How do I get started?

Form a little group of organisers (it need only be two), decide on a garden and persuade the owner that they won't mind their private space invaded for a day.

Contact the group for whom you are fundraising to make sure that they are happy for you to use this idea and are not in competition with another of their events. Then check with the local tourist information centre and central library that you are not opening on the same day as another garden in the same area.

You may have other objectives than just raising money. If so, work out what else you wish to achieve (e.g. to give patients from the local hospice a day out, or to teach teenagers about looking after the countryside). Whatever it is make sure that you theme your additional activities to your objective or to the 'flavour' of your benefiting group.

What if I want to open my own garden in a good cause?

There are at least three organisations that run garden open days throughout the country: the Red Cross, St John Ambulance and the National Garden Scheme. The address of the headquarters of the latter can be found at the back of the book and you will find the regional headquarters for the two first aid organisations listed in your local telephone directory.

How do I publicise my event?

Decide if you want your garden day to be a strictly local affair or if you would like visitors from far and wide. Of course if the garden is only small or you are fundraising for a very local charity it would be better to restrict your publicity to the surrounding area.

Always adjust a general approach to your particular needs. Remember, the further afield your audience is, the more advertising time you need to allow.

Advertise in local garden centres. You might be able to persuade a journalist to interview you for the gardening section of the local paper or on local radio. Advertise in your chosen charity's newsletter or at other events. How about organising a gardening quiz for the local paper with the winner becoming the VIP to open the garden day? Or meeting the 'personality' booked to open the event.

Don't waste money having huge A1 posters screen printed. A4 or at the most A3 posters are all you need. Just black on a colour or outlines on white paper for children to colour in are effective. You might find A5 leaflets are all that is needed. You can photocopy a few large sizes for shops or notice boards.

Distribution is everything. Place them where they are most effective. Try getting an insert service with the community newsletter or parish magazine. See if you can obtain a list of gardening club members and deliver leaflets direct or advertise at one of their shows. Members of local heritage and conservation groups may also be interested.

For larger events, use the tourist information listings and the 'what's on' features in all the local media. Teletext and Oracle will list local attractions also.

Always make it clear for whom you are fundraising. Remember, date and time, place, what the event comprises, a contact name and telephone number and the price.

What do I do about parking cars?

If your event attracts people from out of the immediate area you will have to think about where to park cars. The ideal is a field or a long drive but there are not many places that can provide this. If you are relying on cars parked on the road it might be a good idea to contact the police for their suggestions. They might want to put a line of cones in sensitive areas. Don't forget to signpost the car park.

You could charge for car parking, but in my experience, for a gentle event like this, you would be best advised to cut your losses and let the parking look after itself free of charge. You probably don't want two or three people tied up all day collecting money and parking cars.

If the weather has been wet or the grass is rather long you may find a well-used path from the car park to the entrance gate becoming slippery and dangerous. Preclude any accidents by pegging down wire netting securely over any problem areas. It helps stop people sliding and it protects the grass underneath.

What else can I have in the garden?

This rather depends on the space you have available but try to keep activities limited or to a strictly gardening theme or you might as well be holding a fete.

The following are just a few ideas that you might include.

- A leaf or flower quiz: leaves or flowers from the garden are stuck onto a board and numbered. Contestants pay to enter and are given a sheet of paper on which they write their names and telephone number and list the numbers with the corresponding names of the trees or plants from which they think the leaves or flowers have come. The winner is the first correct list drawn at a certain time or at the end of the day. A prize should be donated.
- Garden produce stall.
- Home made produce stall.
- Plant stall.
- Wickerwork, corn dollies or dried flower stall.
- Treasure hunt: contestants pay to enter and are given a list of items to find. They can either look for numbers stuck on the objects (to prevent damage or removal) or write down where they have seen them. The winner is the first correct entry drawn as before.
- Teas or barbecue: see separate chapters.
- If the garden has a swimming pool, tennis court, croquet lawn or other facilities make a charge to use them.
- Have some music and make a charge for requests.
- 'Garden answers' stand: Customers are invited to bring specimens from their own gardens or ask questions for help from an expert or experts. Make a small charge for each answer.
- Blade sharpening stand.
- Secondhand or reconditioned gardening tools stand.
- Raffle for a donated piece of garden equipment or perhaps a painting of a countryside scene. Remember raffles have to be drawn before the end of the day if you want to avoid being registered for a lotteries licence.

Handy hint

Ask the owners of the garden to present prizes, join the panel of 'experts' or be involved in some way. It helps them to feel part of the day and prevents the impression that your organisation has in some way 'taken over'.

Plus ... and minus:

- Venue is free.
- Very flexible, making the idea suitable for all groups.
- Family event.
- Can use on-site facilities as added attractions.
- Can operate with very few organisers but you might need more if you have a lot of additional activities.

- Relies on the weather.
- Needs to be fenced, but most gardens are.
- Needs arrangements for car parking.

EVENT 13

HOST-A-SALE
Shopping at home

Operating requirements: One host.

Equipment needs: Nothing other than you will have available at home.

Lead time: 2–3 months.

Initial cost: Nil, unless you send invitations by post and provide a few refreshments, in which case you will have the cost of the stamps and tea and biscuits.

Suitable for: Making a donation to any charity. Particularly good for women (probably) at home during the day or evening.

Expected return: £100. You could earn substantially more if you use a public hall or hold a coffee morning or cream tea at the same time.

What's in it for contributors: Opportunity for a bit of a get together and to buy things without having to visit the shops.

Frequency: Best kept to a couple of times a year.

Special requirements: Suitable party plan company.

How does it work?

This is how Tupperware started in the US. A representative of the company comes to your house to demonstrate or display items for sale to a group of invited friends. It is usual to offer refreshments and a party atmosphere.

The rep will bring a set of display items and takes orders to be delivered to you to distribute. Payment to you, for the use of your home and friends, is a percentage of the value of the orders taken in goods or cash.

You may be able to persuade the company to give you cash, but if they insist on goods you can then hold a raffle at the end of the event.

That seems a lot of work for a pretty small return, I hear you say. Well, maybe, but if you can offer the company a large potential market (i.e. you ask 20 to 25 friends) or a group of you club together and hire a room in the local community centre at an off-peak time and pool an invitation list so that you can expect 50 to 100 people, you will be more successful in negotiating for cash, especially if you explain the cause.

How much organising is there?

It really won't be much work, I promise you, and you should have some fun. The company supply all the invitations and all you have to do is fill them in and give them to your friends. The representative will arrive about half an hour before you start and if you clear a table for her use she will do everything else.

If you plan to hold your party during the day and you invite young mums or dads, make sure that you allocate a play space for preschool children and delegate someone to look after the 'creche' if you invite a good crowd. Make it clear to people that there is no obligation to buy.

If you are worried about the amount of distribution work you will have after the party, ensure that you only invite people that you see regularly or who you see in a group, such as when you collect your children at school.

So who are all these 'Party Plan' companies?

You will find your local distributors, from whom you can book a demonstrator, listed in *Yellow Pages* under Party Planners; don't forget to browse the internet for more party plan companies.

There are also numerous local companies, usually 'cottage industries' manufacturing clothes, jewellery, cosmetics or furniture. Try putting an enquiry advertisement in your local paper and see what you come up with. Local and privately-owned companies are more likely to bend company policy to give you what you want. Traditional companies might be helpful but you will probably have to wait for comments to arrive from head office.

Plus... and minus:

- Needs very little organising.
- You can hold the party in your own home.
- No need for other helpers.

- Probably not going to make much more than a token donation, but it's a good excuse to have some friends over.
- The party plan company might insist on you being paid in goods.

EVENT 14 — 100 CLUB

One hundred people contribute to a fundraising club

Operating requirements: A minimum of 2; promoter and treasurer. Additional invited monthly assistance in drawing the numbers. It helps if 10 contributors agree to be responsible for collections.

Equipment needs: Box of 100 small cubes (usually wooden) each numbered clearly 1 to 100.

Lead time: 2–3 months

Initial cost: £50 setting up fee (£35 initial registration with your Local Authority and basic advertising costs). £17.50 annual renewal fee.

Suitable for: Small-time, ongoing fundraising where there is a reasonably static population and a perennial need to raise small amounts of money for maintenance, refurbishment, rent, etc. Village halls, medium-sized monthly meeting groups, churches, sports groups, community centres, etc. Not suitable for children.

Expected return: 50 per cent of cash collected. i.e. £600 per annum for monthly £1.00 stake from 100 club members.

What's in it for contributors: 50 per cent of cash collected given in prizes.

Frequency: Ongoing with monthly prizes.

Special requirements: Permission to run a Social Lottery. Recognised charity to raise funds for. See Chapter 6 for details on lotteries.

Variations on a theme: If you confine your 100 Club to members of a club or society e.g. the PTA for a school or members of a Sunday cycling club you are exempt from registration; you can only advertise within the confines of your clubhouse or building or private premises of the members but there is no limit to the size of the lottery or on the price of each number.

How does the 100 Club work?

One hundred members pay a joining fee of, say, £2 (or less). The joining fee pays for administration and stationery. Each month they pay a regular amount of £2.00 (the maximum fee that you are allowed to charge under the restrictions of the present regulations) which entitles them to enter the current month's draw. So far so good.

Now comes the clever bit. The prizes are fairly modest for ten months of the year; £20 for the first prize and £10 for the second. But twice a year, perhaps in June and December the club pays out larger prizes; first prize – £100, second prize – £50. This keeps members interested and prepared to stay in the club for a year or more which makes collecting the contributions easier as you can encourage members to pay six months in advance, and saves the work of finding more members to replace those who fall by the wayside.

How do I start the 100 Club?

First you need to obtain permission from the group for whom you wish to fundraise that they are happy for you to be doing this and, assuming they agree, then write a short constitution. This will outline your objectives and the rules. This can be very simple but must include:

- A statement recognising the need for registration under the Lotteries Act.
- Details of the rules of the collection should be included – who is eligible, the prize money offered, the stake required, when draws will take place, etc.
- An address for the promoter should be incorporated and, whilst perhaps not strictly necessary, details of the charitable objects should be outlined.

Next you must register with the local authority to enable you to run a Social or Societies' Lottery (see Chapter 6). This will cost you £35 for initial registration with a further £17.50 annual renewal fee. This fee has been fixed for several years and is correct at the time of publication but it is likely to increase a little in the future.

At this stage you should work out a marketing plan to attract your hundred contributors. It needn't be complicated. Set a timescale, work out your target audience and plan your attack!

Let's look at the three elements. Your timescale could be realistically set at two months, but you can adjust this as you go: you only need to collect your first month's contributions and draw your first prizewinners when you have about 75 per cent of the numbers allocated. (Just leave the spare numbers out of the draw and remember to reduce your prizes accordingly or you will find you are short of funds. You must tell your members that you will be changing the prizes, however.)

Your target audience will be people living in the locality; all in one village, one parish, or a specific area of a town or city. They will probably be active members of the community and might well be users (or potential users) of the organisation or premises which your 100 Club represents. Don't waste time and effort on people too far from your area or those whose main activities are out of the locality.

Your main attack should make use of several weapons. Posters (these can be handmade) in shops, pubs, community centres or village halls, column inches in local newsletters or even the local press, possible door-to-door mail shots in the form of a letter. And last but by no means least, the good, old fashioned grapevine. Word of mouth is one of the strongest local advertising media you have available. Start a rumour and see how quickly it gets repeated back to you!

Do I have to be fundraising for charity?

Yes. The terms of the Lotteries and Amusements Act specify that you must be an established group and raising money for charitable purposes and this has not changed within the boundaries of the National Lottery Act 1993.

Are there any other restrictions in the terms of the Act?

Indeed. The total value of chances sold must not exceed £20,000 for any one lottery or an annual accumulation of £250,000. Effectively, although the arrangements are exactly the same for each draw, you will be running a separate lottery each month so (sadly!) you will be well within the limits. You do not have to accumulate your proceeds until, say, the end of the year. You may not allocate numbers to children under the age of 16. Perhaps most restrictive of all is that £2.00 is the maximum price that you can ask for each monthly contribution for each number. Finally you will have to make a return, on a form provided, at the end of each year to the local authority.

Is the above information correct under the new regulations of the National Lottery Act 1993?

Yes. Small changes are now in effect. The new regulations are very detailed and complex. If you have any worries, speak to the licensing department of your local authority.

Is the joining fee an annual fee?

Because there will inevitably be people dropping out for any number of reasons you will probably find that the small but steady flow of joining fees will cover the very minimal costs of membership cards, stationery, etc. If you are not covering costs you might have to consider increasing the initial fee or making it an annual one.

What if people are late paying up?

You should make it clear in the rules that accompany each member's card, that numbers will not be included in the draw if funds have not been received PRIOR to that draw taking place.

How is the club and its promoters kept free from suspicion?

You should have two operators – though this is not required by law; the promoter and an honorary treasurer is the usual set up. You will probably be a branch group from a larger organisation (the one for whom you are raising funds) and will benefit from a committee overseeing your activities.

The draw should take place on a completely separate occasion, perhaps a monthly meeting of another local group, involving people who are not members of the 100 Club.

Your accounts should be brought up to date each month and be available for examination at any time if required.

It helps if winners' names are published, perhaps quarterly. The list could be made available to contributors only, but if it can be displayed on a notice board of the local community centre it will act as a powerful marketing tool if you need more contributors.

Possible problems

You may not be able to use this method for raising church funds as many church groups do not like the idea of gambling. The 100 Club is certainly a game of chance and so by definition is a form of gambling. By the same token you may be restricted from advertising the club in the local parish newspaper or on the church hall notice board. You may be unable to hold the draw at a church function.

If you cannot find your full quota of members within a reasonable time and you are forced to start your draws giving reduced prizes, make sure that all the members know in advance that this might happen by including this option in the rules. You don't want to be accused of changing things as you go along.

Handy hint
A contributor could, of course, hold two or more numbers and still be legal. But you might like to put your own rules on this to make the chance of a win more even.

Plus ... and minus:

- Continuous source of funding.
- No venue necessary.
- Advertising not usually needed after the initial drive.
- Your monthly income is a known quantity.

- Relies on continuous help from several people.
- Can't operate if too many people drop out.
- Might not be suitable for certain groups due to gambling associations.
- Need licence.
- Late payments from collector to promoter mean some contributors' numbers will not be in a draw (or the draw delayed if this is allowed in the rules).

EVENT 15 JUMBLE SALES
Second-hand clothes sale

Operating requirements: A coordinator and a treasurer. Somebody or some people who are prepared to collect or have jumble delivered to their homes for weeks prior to your date. On the day you will need at least one helper for each table and two others to take money. If you have loads of extra jumble you might need another 'floating' helper to keep adding to the piles from a stock kept elsewhere.

Equipment needs: A hall or room. Trestle tables according to the size of your sale. Wheeled clothes rails, if possible. Somewhere safe to keep the money. Large quantities of carrier bags for variation 2. Blackboards or sign boards for variation 3.

Lead time: At least a month, possibly two.

Initial cost: Cost of hire of room and publicity.

Suitable for: Every type of organisation.

Expected return: Probably not much more than £100.

What's in it for customers and helpers: Customers get a chance to buy, often very good, clothes at silly prices and they don't have to go into town for them. It's a chance for a bit of a chin-wag and gives people an opportunity to get rid of stuff that they feel is a sin to throw out. Jumble sales appeal to our consciences. Actually I hate jumble sales so I have to be severely pressured to help, but there are those who like nothing better than to see a pile of clothes disappear in a mad rush of elbows and handbags. And there are, of course, helpers' perks which mean that they get the pick of the stock before the doors open (for a price, naturally). I did once come by a beautiful woollen winter coat in this way.

Frequency: As long as you weed the real junk from your jumble you can hold a jumble sale as and when you have enough for a sale. If you keep turning out the same grotty clothes every time your customers will soon decide that there is better to be had somewhere else.

How does it work?

Old clothes are donated regularly to a known collector. When enough is collected, a sale is held, usually in a public building. Nobody really needs to be told what happens at a jumble sale; there can't be anyone in the country who has never been to one. Except, possibly, the Queen. I bet even she would like one visit, if only to see who bought her Hermes head scarves! However, there are three variations on running a sale. You might find one idea more suited to your needs than the others.

How do I get started?

First check that the group or charity that you are collecting for isn't holding a rival event in the locality. Send the word out that you are collecting jumble; you can decide on a date for the actual sale at this stage or later if you wish.

The easiest method of starting the grapevine working is to pin a notice in a couple of local shops or newsagents. Put a couple of lines into the community newspaper or get the charity or group themselves to pass the word at a meeting or gathering.

Book a date at the hall you plan to use and start to advertise your sale within about two or three weeks of the date. If you have a mountain of clothes to shift you might consider placing a small classified advertisement in your area's newspaper, otherwise you can rely on local posters in the school, the hall itself or shops. These sort of events do tend to sell themselves, especially once you have established a reputation, but you can't rely on it. Most independent radio stations have a free listing of all local charity events, so make sure you drop them a line giving all the salient facts and not forgetting to include your name and contact number in case they want more details.

As it arrives, sort your jumble into different sections; shoes, hats, outdoor-wear, sports clothes, jumpers and men's and women's clothes. Children's and babies' clothes should be sorted by age or size. You may decide to keep all obviously summery or wintery clothes aside until a more suitable season. Another popular section is a dressing up box where really dotty items can go, all for 10p each. Make sure the clothes are clean. Some people donate jumble in a truly appalling state. Decide if it is worth washing and if not, chuck it away. It is rarely worth having something dry-cleaned unless you are saving it for a 50/50 sale (see 'nearly-new sale' section below).

Variations

- **Variation 1:** The traditional jumble sale involves bargaining with a helper, agreeing a price and handing over the money. It helps if all the helpers taking money are wearing money aprons. They won't have the time or space to keep searching for change in a communal box and they should keep their eyes on the tables at all times.

- **Variation 2:** I favour this method and it is a real cracker for jumble that has been around a while or is seriously out of fashion. As each customer enters they are given several carrier bags and told that they can fill the bags with anything they like. All carriers are charged a fixed price at the exit.
- **Variation 3:** This method is good for difficult areas (see 'problems' below). Work out a pricing structure prior to your event i.e. jumpers and skirts – 50p; trousers – 75p; babies' clothes – 25p, etc. Display the prices on blackboards around the room so that helpers and customers can see them. As customers leave the hall they are fed through a funnel made from two or four tables where the goods are priced and charged. There is no debate and no arguments. You may be left with quite a lot of grot but you can hold a pound-a-bag sale for the last half hour if you feel brave.

What happens on the day?

Make sure that you have lots of helpers available. Start in the morning and lay your room out slowly so that you are not under pressure. Ask, at this stage, for volunteers to return after the sale is over to help pack the remainder away and tidy up. Let them know how long you think it will take. Provide some refreshments for your helpers and lock up securely when you all go to lunch. If you can't secure the hall or room, you will have to leave a couple of people to look after things until you return.

Traditionally jumble sales start at 2.00pm, so make sure your table helpers and money-takers arrive a quarter of an hour before opening. Run through your plans so that everyone is clear what to do and give them an idea how long they will have to stay at the end.

Sales in my area tend to be short and furious; usually everything is all over in about an hour or an hour and a half at most. I'm sure other parts of the country are the same. Don't drag the thing out unless you have very good items and provide a crèche. (You can advertise this as a 'nearly-new sale' – always publicise added attractions such as a crèche or tea.)

Arrange your tables in two lines using two further tables to join the lines at top and bottom to form a long rectangle. Pile your jumble in sections around the table. Place the clothes rails, if you have them (they are sometimes available for a nominal price from department stores), around the end of the room furthest from the door. People tend to browse through these and you don't want to cause a bottleneck near the entrance. Where there is a stage and you are short of space, this is where to put the hats, shoes and dressing-up box. In each area ensure that you have at least one helper per table or rail. On the main table, helpers work inside the rectangle; from here they can keep a good eye on what is going on.

You can charge an entrance fee but I feel it is better not to. On the other hand you might have a tradition of charging for entrance in your area, in which case it is probably better not to rock the boat by changing things.

Nearly-new sale

A nearly new or 50/50 sale is run largely on jumble sale lines so I feel that it doesn't really warrant a whole chapter to itself.

The main difference is that instead of the price for each item being recorded as profit, you are committed to returning a percentage of the sale price to the original owner. In effect you are charging commission to sell something on behalf of someone else. You are likely to receive clothes in much better condition than for jumble sales, but they will be priced correspondingly higher. You can insist that all clothes are freshly laundered or cleaned and intact with buttons and fastenings firmly secured.

Usually the percentage is 50 per cent, but it could be anything you choose. In our area we find that we can only get a reasonable quantity of good quality clothes if we offer a 60/40 split – donors keep the 60 per cent. And, of course, it doesn't have to be restricted to clothes. No-longer-needed baby equipment is always popular, it has such a short period of use that, unless you go in for vast families, is unlikely to wear out. Gardening tool and equipment nearly-new sales are also popular, especially at fetes. Toys, household goods, curtains and furniture are all worth thinking about.

But how do you know who owned what?

For garden tools which sell reasonably slowly over the counter you can keep a written record and tick things off as you sell them. This is obviously totally impractical when you are selling clothes in a village hall in the scrum as described above.

The simplest method is to get all owners to price up their own goods. The sale price is written on the front of a square of paper and the name is written on the back (it could include a telephone number if owners are not well known to the organisers) and pinned to each item using a safety pin (dressmaker's pins come off and can injure people) or string.

The sale is conducted in exactly the same way as Variation 3 above except that each item is now priced individually by the owner. When the cashiers take the money they remove the labels and drop them into a tub. When everything is all over, the remaining clothes are sorted into piles according to the owner, while the labels from the sold clothes are also sorted into piles. Sixty per cent of the accumulative value of those items sold is given to the owner when they come to collect any remaining clothes. In this way you sort out all the finances there and then and are not left with piles of items to return.

Possible problems

Loads of 'em! Jumble sales attract a unique type of customer. You will find them lined up at every sale at least half an hour before opening time. They seem to possess more than their fair share of elbows, carry huge bags, and move like lightning.

Beware though, although most of your customers will be genuinely looking for bargains, and some may be in dire need of anything that you can offer, there will be others who come to steal. I have been told of people who arrive with bags ready prepared with false bottoms! When challenged they are abusive, obnoxious and deny everything. They will look at you with an eye as unnerving as a goat's and let forth a stream of personal comments that make you want to give them everything you have just so they go away. That is their plan. If your sales habitually attract this 'element' as my Granny would say, you might be better off using Variation 3 or you will begin to lose volunteers and a good proportion of your customers.

A further problem is what to do with the piles of real junk that you cannot sell. Oxfam, Age Concern, or Sue Ryder will not be interested in them any more than you are, so don't embarrass charity shops into having to refuse your rubbish. If you have any out-of-style, but good condition, men's suits or outdoor coats that you just can't get shot of, they might be interested.

You can try any recycling companies that you find in your local telephone directory, but you will have to deliver and they will probably only give you about a couple of pounds per hundredweight. You might think it is worth it. Some rag companies take duff jumble but only if you remove all buttons, zips etc. Most supermarkets have a recycling centre and take textiles. If this is not an option, you may be left having to take it to the municipal dump, which seems criminal but could be the only other option.

Handy hints

Go in for a bit of home-made security. I'm not suggesting that you employ Securior, but a tall man dressed in dark trousers, a blue shirt and sporting some very shiny shoes does wonders for morale!

If you have heaps of serious rubbish to get rid of, bag it all up yourselves, put a £10 note in one bag and advertise the fact and, as in Variation 3, sell each bag for £1.00.

Plus ... and minus:

- Great way to get rid of old clothes.
- All over fairly quickly.
- Doesn't need serious marketing or costly publicity.
- Nearly-new sales can be successful fundraisers.
- Needs no special equipment other than tables and possibly a clothes rail.

- You will need to hire a room or public building.
- Jumble sales can attract some intimidating people.
- Jumble sales are not very lucrative unless you establish a real reputation for quality.
- You will almost certainly lose a certain amount due to theft.
- You need space to store jumble and might be left with piles that you have to get rid of.

EVENT 16 KARAOKE NIGHT
Volunteers sing-along to a backing track

Operating requirements: Coordinator, treasurer. Compere and road crew who should come with the equipment.

Equipment needs: Screens and sound system, risers or stage area. Video camera and blank tapes.

Lead time: Three months, depending on the availability of the equipment.

Initial cost: Under £100, unless you plan to hire a hall and do your own event from scratch.

Suitable for: Any charity; more and more people want to have a go at Karaoke.

Expected return: Karaoke is not a guaranteed fundraiser. If you judge your market carefully and exploit every angle the idea has good potential.

What's in it for contributors: A chance for a really good laugh, companionable entertainment and an opportunity to participate rather than retiring to the usual position of anonymous spectator in the dark. Particularly good in villages where there is little else in the form of live entertainment.

Frequency: The more often the better. Appreciation and confidence grows with experience.

Special requirements: Your venue must be licensed for public entertainment. Unless you are aiming at under 16s you will also need a Liquor Licence (see Chapter 6).

What is Karaoke?

Karaoke came from Japan about 20 years ago, where participation entertainment is much more part of the culture. It provides an opportunity for ordinary people possessing no musical background, to get up in front of an audience and sing live whilst being accompanied by pre-recorded music.

Ten years ago a Karaoke evening consisted of a microphone and some instrumental-only records of popular songs, often as part of a disco. It has come a long way since then and you should not consider hiring any Karaoke equipment that does not provide several TV screens, use video discs with sophisticated sound equipment and have enough microphones to cover a group of six or more.

It is unusual to find Karaoke other than in a pub or club these days, but if you choose to hire a public hall you will be well advised to have a bar as well. We Brits are known for our reserved behaviour and a good slug of alcohol is often needed to lubricate the vocal chords ... at least at the beginning of the evening. You might find it difficult to draw the evening to a close, however, once your participants have shaken off the manacles of shyness ...

How can I use Karaoke to fundraise?

Karaoke is not cabaret, although it can be used to complement a cabaret evening, but unless you are brave enough to organise a whole cabaret show you probably should not consider hiring a hall and selling tickets. After all, why should people pay to take part when they can have regular Karaoke entertainment in their local for free?

No, the way to maximise your proceeds from Karaoke is to go to the places where it is already taking place on a regular basis. Fundraising is achieved by exploiting the evening without spoiling the informal atmosphere and there are several methods that you can use, but for all ideas you should aim for the following elements.

You need an audience that you can rely on and one that has already conquered inherent inhibitions. You need a venue that is used to hosting the evening and already holds the various licences that you are required to have by law. And you need a popular Karaoke compere who uses modern equipment. Spend a few weekends travelling around experiencing different Karaoke pubs until you find one that you like. Then start cultivating the landlord!

Raise money by adding to the entertainment rather than detracting from it or changing the original idea. Try selling videos of the singers. Buy or cadge video tapes (they need only be about 15 minutes in length) find a camcorder hot shot to record each singer and sell the tapes for £10.00 at the end. Make sure that you put every 'turn' from each singer onto the same tape.

Hold a raffle, for donated prizes. A collection taken two or three times during the evening can be successful, as can a permanent box left on the bar. You could also try negotiating a percentage of the bar take over and above the average return. Your extra publicity should help to swell usual numbers.

If you find someone very talented that the audience really likes listening to, you could run a Dutch auction (see Event 10) to 'buy' a selection of songs.

Ask to speak to the regular compere at your chosen venue. Pick his brains for ideas and get him on your side. He (or she) will know the audience best of all and might well be very enthusiastic if s/he is involved at the planning stage. He might even be prepared to run a competition (paid entries, of course) for the best compere if he doesn't feel too threatened. The winner gets to compere the next half-hour or whatever.

A word of warning: some organisations have tried to fundraise by running Karaoke competitions. 'It don't work', as I was informed succinctly by one Karaoke compere. It fundamentally changes the atmosphere from one where a singer can make a fool of himself and the audience are good natured enough to take it all in good part until the next turn, to a feeling of serious competition, often from outsiders, all aiming to win cash or a holiday. People complain of unfairness, claim that they need another go or just won't even bother coming if they feel they are not much good.

Will I need to advertise?

Although the pub will undoubtedly have its own marketing policy, you should offer to undertake some additional publicity.

Find out where they already advertise (you don't want to duplicate efforts) and major on the fact that you will be offering something special such as the videos, for instance. Sell the event to the press by using the charity angle. If you know someone in the business, consider persuading a well-known singer to open the evening or to sing along with people. You will sell many more videos this way. Even a popular footballer or other young sports person might be willing to help.

So, yes, you need to publicise. Though maybe you need to look more at PR than straight advertising.

Is it all songs from the charts?

There is a good selection of golden oldies, such as Frank Sinatra and the Beatles which many older people enjoy singing to. There are also some traditional folk songs and a good choice of country and blue grass music that can all be used to theme an evening, although it has to be said that the main selection is contemporary.

However, tucked away in some videodisc catalogues you can find 'Roll out the Barrel' and other war time classics. You could try putting together an over-sixties Karaoke night using all the old songs. If you are old enough to remember singing round the pub piano or have seen smoky pub sing-songs in all those old Elstree studio movies you'll know that there is a great untapped talent out there who are used to community singing and might be longing to have a go.

Possible problems

The beauty of using a Karaoke pub is that any problems that there might be are not yours. The landlord should sort out any rowdiness and the compere is there to direct the singers. All you have to do is exploit the situation. In the best possible taste, of course!

On the other hand, if you get a pub full of people like me, you'll never persuade any of them to get up and sing. And you wouldn't want to anyway!

Handy hint

Look in the What's On column of your local newspaper to discover which pubs feature Karaoke.

Plus... and minus:

- If you use a pub you will need very little outlay or help.
- It is one of the few fundraising ideas that really appeals to the 18–25 age group.
- Could be good at changing the image of a largely middle age, middle class charity to give it a broader appeal.
- It can be held on a regular basis.
- You take advantage of a ready-made audience.

- Bit hit and miss when it comes to raising money.
- Not suitable for children.
- No good if you are looking for an event without alcohol.

EVENT 17 PROMISE AUCTION
A sale of promises of duties

Operating requirements: Coordinator/auctioneer, treasurer, steward/clerk, cashier/s.

Equipment needs: This activity is most successful when held on the back of another event (see Event 10 Dutch auction) since equipment and furniture may already be available. Chairs for the audience and a podium/soap box or stage. A means of making a record of the bids and collecting cheques or cash. About 50 'promises': this will take just over an hour to get through. You could hold the event in its own right and sell catalogues (see Event 10 again), sell refreshments or have a bar.

Lead time: A month or 6 weeks for a small auction, up to 12 weeks if you anticipate a grander show.

Initial cost: Very little outlay. A contribution, perhaps to the publicity of the main event.

Suitable for: Very local events for local causes. Ideal or raising money for schools, churches, local groups or issues.

Expected return: Over £100–£500, depending on the quality of your promises and the generosity of your audience.

What's in it for contributors: Opportunity to buy a service that might otherwise be unavailable or prohibitively expensive. Adds to the enjoyment of another event. Donors have an opportunity to support a special cause in a way other than financial.

Frequency: Annual. Choose a time when people feel flush or in need of some help. Christmas time or the start of the summer holidays, perhaps.

Special requirements: An experienced and lively auctioneer. If you have a bar you will need to be licensed.

Variations on a theme: Slave auction, Surprise auction, Silent auction, Sealed-bid auction. Details below.

How does it work?

The auction is run on identical lines to a conventional auction. It is the lots that are different. Each lot is a 'promise'. These promises are usually typed on individual sheets of paper, signed by the person making the promise and sealed in an envelope.

Just use your imagination, ask around, collect donations from commercial companies, leisure centres, farmers, your local MP. The list is endless. Make sure you have a good choice from handmade goods, special opportunities, offers of help and donated items.

How do I get started?

Gather a small group of helpers or form a committee. Decide on a date and a venue and apply for an occasional Liquor Licence if you are to have a bar (see Chapter 6).

Your next priority is finding an auctioneer. Because this event is run on traditional lines a professional auctioneer will bring a touch of reality as well moving the bidding along fast and keeping the patter going. If someone local wants to have a go they need to have a 'presence', keep calm and have a few trial runs before the day. I really do recommend the professional as it is stressful work keeping up the pace for the whole show.

At this stage you need to go looking for your donations and promises. Try to get specific commitments from people. It is not enough to get a vague 'Oh, all right then'. Type up the promises and get them signed before the donor can back out. Make it clear that each offer of help is kept open for a year only.

What do we do on the day?

Prepare your room as in the Dutch auction, Event 10. Place the cashier's desk at the back and arrange to have it staffed all the time, not just at the end, to avoid queues. Hand out or sell a catalogue or list of all the lots so that people can study them before the bidding begins. (If you are running the event in its own right, you can sell refreshments for half an hour or so before the start to enable people to buy and study their catalogues.) Set a target at the beginning of the auction and announce that you hope to achieve this by the end of the evening. Every now and then you can interject with the running total to keep the incentive going.

As each lot is sold the clerk should make a note of the name of the winning bidder and a steward should pass them a slip to be exchanged at the cashier's desk.

During the auction you can sell drinks and snacks from a waiter/waitress service. This prevents the disruption of a constant stream of people getting up to visit the bar.

Examples of promises

- 2 hours gardening
- 1 morning child minding

- 1 home-made cake
- Handyman for a day
- Trip in a boat
- Free meal at a pub
- 4 pantomime tickets
- 2 sessions baby-sitting
- Meal cooked in your house
- Football coaching
- Housework
- Cleaning cars
- Decorate a room
- A day's fishing
- A round of golf with a professional
- A week's holiday in a country cottage
- A make-over at the local beautician
- Tour of the local fire station
- One day's produce from allotment

Variations

- **Surprise auction:** To add a bit of spice, keep three popular lots in unmarked envelopes, let it be known that the next lot is one of the three things, but you don't know which! People make blind bids and get a surprise at the end. Don't announce what each lot is until all have been bought.
- **Silent auction:** If there are too many lots to get through you can hold a Silent auction alongside the Promise auction or Dutch auction. Display details of each lot and the reserve on blackboards or on large sheets of card on the tables. Bids are written alongside together with the name and address of each bidder. Leave plenty of space to allow bids to be crossed out and replaced several times. See that new bids are higher than the ones they replace!
- **Sealed-bid auction:** Display the lots as above and make pens, paper and envelopes available. Bidders place bids in sealed envelopes and place them in a box. The winners are announced at the end. Proceeds are usually lower for this method.
- **Slave auction:** All the lots are promises of services. So your 'slave' might offer to cut your lawn every week for a month, or cook a meal every weekend in August or chauffeur you about for a morning.

What happens at the end?

Try to persuade all bidders to pay for and collect their lots, where appropriate, on the spot.

Make sure that you thank your auctioneer; present him or her with a bunch of flowers or a bottle of something.

Ensure that you have arranged for some volunteers to help you clear up.

Afterwards, write thank you letters to commercial donors, your auctioneer and all who acted as stewards or clerks and cashiers on the night. Make sure that you publish how much you raised in the local newspaper or on a local notice board. People like to know that an event they supported was a success and those that couldn't make it might be prepared to come next time.

Possible problems

Occasionally you might have a dispute between bidders; make it clear that the auctioneer has the final discretion.

You may feel it necessary to announce that your group accepts all donations in good faith and does not accept liability for bad workmanship or faulty goods. There is no exchange or refund.

> **Handy hint**
>
> It helps if you publish a reserve price to give people an idea of where to start the bidding.

Plus ... and minus:

- Popular and unusual idea.
- People like to donate services.
- Good PR. The memory of the auction and the cause is kept alive as people redeem their promises throughout the year.
- Needs no special equipment.
- Can piggyback on another event.

- Does rely on the quality of your auctioneer.
- Can be hard work and time-consuming collecting promises.
- Not suitable for children.

EVENT 18 RAFFLES, TOMBOLAS AND SWEEPSTAKES

All you never knew you needed to know!

I have arranged the layout of Event 18's entry a little differently to those of the other fundraising ideas collected in this chapter. Games of chance are governed strictly by law and I feel some general explanation is warranted before the 'recipe' is given.

There cannot be anyone reading this book who has not at some time been a participant in a raffle or tombola, unless they are a member of a particular religious or ethical group that does not agree with the element of gambling involved. Virtually every event uses one of the two to swell funds and encourage the public to stay a little longer and spend a little more money. Many people will be so familiar with the workings of both as to skip this chapter altogether. If you are not inclined to read further, may I please suggest that you turn to Chapter 6 to satisfy yourself that what you plan is legal.

Good fun and lucrative as they are, raffles, tombolas and sweepstakes are all a form of gambling; they are all games of chance and as such come under the Lotteries and Amusements Act 1976 updated by the National Lottery Act 1993.

There are, broadly speaking, three types of lotteries that affect small or medium-scale fundraisers, being those which are small, private or social. Each has different levels of regulation. For our purposes, (i.e. charitable and fundraising organisations) almost all raffles and tombolas will be either private or small if they are to be part of another fundraising event (see Chapter 6).

What's the difference between a raffle and a tombola?

I believe the border line to have become a little fuzzy over the years. But as I see it, a raffle is the opportunity to buy tickets, or chances, to win one of a small selection of prizes. The draw for these prizes is usually held at the end of a specified period of time. A tombola, on the other hand, works by selling tickets as before, but the draw is made from a revolving drum (from the Italian *tombolare* – to somersault, for those who are interested) by the player at the time of purchase. The prizes tend to be more numerous and of a more modest nature.

Both tombolas and raffles have their places. Tombolas are useful at fetes and fairs or other events where the public are passing through. Names and telephone numbers need not be taken and the business is wound up then and there. Raffles are particularly suited to dinner dances or other events where you hang on to your audience for a length of time, at the work place or within a club where the same people meet over a period of days or weeks. Over a longer period of time and for large prizes where you are opening your raffle to the general public you will need a Lottery Licence. But that is a very different kettle of fish and you can read about Social lotteries in Chapter 6 as mentioned above.

HOLDING A RAFFLE

Operating requirements: 2 or 3 (or more) people selling tickets.

Equipment needs: Book of numbered tickets with stubs. For a raffle that runs for longer than one event and takes place within a club i.e. a private lottery, your tickets need to bear the price of each ticket and the name and address of the promoter. Small lotteries can use cloakroom tickets.

Lead time: A week or two to collect the prizes.

Initial cost: A couple of pounds for cloakroom tickets. £60 or more for specially printed tickets.

Suitable for: All charities but check that they are not averse to gambling.

Expected return: If your prizes are donated, all proceeds bar cost of the tickets and perhaps a site fee is yours.

What's in it for contributors: People love a chance to win something for very little. The gambling instinct, if you like.

Special requirements: Study Chapter 6 to ensure that you know your legal position.

Variations on a theme: Numbered programmes – programmes display a 'lucky number' on the front and the draw is made at the end of the event. Programmes can double as entry tickets or be sold separately. Don't forget to sell advertising space to boost funds. 'Guess the birthday of a soft toy.' The toy is the prize. People write a date on a ticket which is then put into a draw. The date and the name of the player is recorded in a diary (thus ensuring that two people cannot choose the same date).

What is the best way to sell tickets?

Make a good display of all your prizes near the entrance so that people can gain enthusiasm, and place one ticket seller beside the display to keep an eye on it. Disperse your other sellers into the crowd to keep walking and asking. The secret of selling raffle tickets is to approach people while they have their purses out. Remember to make a note of people's names, and a contact number if you don't know everyone, on the stub unless you are sure that everyone will be present at the draw. Some raffles operate on a 'strictly present' basis, i.e. if nobody comes forward to claim the ticket another number is drawn.

As soon as one book is empty return it to the coordinator (at the stand) to fold up the stubs and start getting the draw ready. For a big raffle you could be tearing and folding for ages unless you do this as you go.

Announce the draw 15 minutes before it is made to enable last minute sales; use a VIP or a neutral person to draw the first ticket. The winner then draws the next ticket and so on. Prizes can be allocated on a first, second, and third basis or winners can be free to choose whatever they like from the selection.

HOLDING A TOMBOLA

Operating requirements: 2 people selling tickets.

Equipment needs: Book of numbered tickets with stubs. Cloakroom tickets are fine. Spinning drum which you can make or hire from specialist companies. You can, of course, use any container that you can seal and give a good shake.

Lead time: A week or two to collect the prizes.

Initial cost: A couple of pounds for cloakroom tickets.

Suitable for: all charities and most events, but check that the organisation you are supporting is not averse to gambling.

Expected return: If your prizes are donated, all proceeds (bar cost of the tickets and perhaps a site fee) is yours.

What's in it for contributors: Again, people love a chance to win something for very little and in this case they can see immediately if they are a winner.

Special requirements: None as long as you stick to running tombolas at other one-off events and the money spent on the purchase of your prizes at the event is under £250.

Variations on a theme: Alcoholic bottle stall (you do not need a Liquor Licence). Non-alcoholic bottle stall. Groceries stall. Fruit stall.

How does it work?

Each prize has a number taped to it in an obvious place. Usually the numbers used are those that end in a zero or a five to make for easy detection. The companion ticket is folded small, so the number is not visible, and put into a container or drum. Biscuit tins are an ideal alternative as you can put a lid on if the wind threatens to blow a cloud of confetti into the air. Now throw away all the other five or zero numbers to avoid confusion. Fold up the rest of the tickets and place them with the others into the drum. Mix them well.

The player pays a set price for five tickets or gets 11 tickets for the price of ten. If a ticket ending in a five or zero is drawn you know they have won a prize.

If you are including alcohol, children under 16 should not be allowed to buy or sell tickets. You might be able to buy bottles from an off-licence on sale or return which can help your overheads.

The use of attractive fruit as tombola prizes

Several attractively prepared boxes of fruit, ranging in size from, say, a few apples and pears or a large bunch of grapes, a couple of kiwi fruit and a hand of bananas right up to a large presentation pack including melons, a pineapple and a pile of other fruit all make good prizes. Prepare the tickets in just the same way as above.

Ideally the fruit should be covered in some way. If you use clingfilm it can sweat in hot weather unless you punch a few holes in it but in any case you should find a shady spot for your fruit tombola stall.

A fruit stall is often very popular and there are obviously no restrictions on who can buy tickets. You might be able to find a friendly greengrocer to donate the fruit or sell it to you at a discount.

Possible problems

Bottle stalls and fruit stalls are classified as 'small lotteries' and do not need registration. However, money spent on the purchase of prizes, for all the stalls at the event – not just one type of stall – should not exceed £250. There is no restriction on the value of donated prizes.

If you are offering food or drink on a tombola stall check the 'use by' dates carefully and don't offer anything that isn't tinned, boxed, bottled or dry goods in a packet. You are liable under the Food Safety Regulations even though you are not offering goods for sale as such.

Plus ... and minus:

- Very little outlay, organisation or staff.
- Suits every pocket.
- Very good to boost funds at other events.
- Good variations to suit a variety of ages and events.

- Restrictive where the cumulative value of prizes is concerned.
- Be careful that you operate the right kind of 'lottery' at the right event.

SWEEPSTAKES

Sweepstakes consist of a private gamble on the outcome of a public event. In other words a group of people, quite independent from commercial betting shops, decide to bet amongst themselves on the forecast of an event totally out of their control such as the Grand National or the General Election, for instance.

In the main, I feel that sweepstakes are not very useful fundraising tools. They are confined to work within the remit of a private lottery which means that you can only use them within your club or work place, because you are playing for cash. Furthermore, a sweepstake is only a true 'sweep' when all the stakes go to make up the prizes, which doesn't really help your fundraising operation. You could, collectively, make a decision to play for 50 per cent of the stakes but you might just as well make a simple donation, for the few pounds that it will bring in.

EVENT 19 SAFARI DINNER

A meal with courses taken in different venues

Operating requirements: Coordinator, treasurer and 3 hosts.

Equipment needs: Enough chairs, tables, crockery and cutlery. Mode of transport if too far to walk. Suitable means of keeping food hot if necessary.

Lead time: 8 weeks minimum.

Initial cost: Cost of ingredients and invitations only.

Suitable for: Small but continuous fundraising. Good in rural areas where there is not much ready entertainment.

Expected return: Work on a 200 per cent mark up on the cost of ingredients, the same as restaurants. Then subtract the minor costs of invitation cards and postage.

What's in it for guests: An enjoyable evening out, a chance to meet some new friends, and the opportunity for someone who enjoys cooking to take part but without the worry of producing a whole meal.

Frequency: This idea is equally suited to the 'one-off' or as a regular date for the same bunch of friends.

Variations on a theme: Cycle safari – for the environmentally conscious where all the guests have to travel via bicycle. (Safety note – make sure all guests wear safety helmets and reflective bands especially at night.) Picnic safari – you don't have to travel from spot to spot, but everyone brings part of the picnic. Safari luncheon; Safari children's tea-party – choose a park or a field and let the children go to a special tree for the sandwiches, another area for jelly and yet another for cake. This is a good way to raise money for a mums and toddlers group.

How does it work?

Guests arrive at separate houses for different courses of a dinner party. Tickets are sold in advance via invitation only.

How do we get started?

Find two or three people who are happy to host part of your event in their house and discuss timings, menus and a budget.

You are now ready to prepare a guest list. Divide the list between the hosts to make a good mix. Keep places to a maximum of 20 and a minimum of 8.

You will probably need to send out at least a third more invitations than you think you will need. Remember to include the date and time of the first course, the names of the hosts and the addresses for all parts of the dinner, an address or telephone number for the RSVP, the price of the tickets and the name of the charity or group for whom you are fundraising.

After a couple of weeks, if you have not heard from people, make a follow up telephone call. It can help if everyone agrees on certain tasks and the main coordinator prepares a note to confirm who is doing what. This saves arguments, acts as an 'aide memoire' for others who will all be leading busy lives, and makes sure nothing is forgotten.

How much time can we allow between courses?

Assuming you are holding a three-course meal, a good basis to work on is an hour in each place and 15 minutes change over. So, if the first house opens its doors at 7.30pm for drinks and chat, the guests sit down for their starter at 8.00pm and they can move on at 8.30pm. The next host expects his or her guests at 8.45pm, they start their main course straight away and they will probably be ready to push off at 9.45pm. The last host serves the pud at 10.00pm and everyone stays for coffee for as long as they wish. If you decide on just two or four or even five (some meal!) venues you can adjust your times accordingly.

What shall we serve?

Well that is really up to you and perhaps the season in which you hold your party. Remember that your guests will sometimes get behind schedule so forget soufflés or other delicately timed creations or food that looks very tired if it is kept warm for any length of time.

You want to make some money out of this bit of fun so don't price yourselves out of the market by choosing smoked salmon, quails' eggs and strawberries at Christmas. On the other hand some people (by no means all …!) might feel a bit peeved if they were given a fry-up and chips.

If guests are all arriving on foot you can serve as much alcohol as you like (work your budget out at two glasses a head or they could 'bring a bottle' to keep costs down) but it is always sensible to remember to have plenty of juice or squash for drivers or for people who just don't like quantities of wine: it is hard to keep tabs on how much you have had to drink when you go from house to house with a fresh glassful each time.

What if I have more than 20 positive replies?

You could suggest to the latecomers that your party is full up now but you will be happy to put their names down for another party in the future; you can even ask them if they would be happy to be a host at a later date. Don't be tempted to have more than 20 guests unless your hosts own baronial halls deep in the countryside with unlimited parking or, if you are certain of fine weather, everyone can be accommodated outside and have a barbecue.

Can I use the party to raise more funds?

Of course you can. Try a raffle. Or if one or more guests play a musical instrument finish the evening with a concert of paid-for requests. Don't forget to ask people to host another party before they go. Get a signature, so they can't back out!

Possible problems

If you do not restrict ticket sales to private invitation only you will have to apply for a Liquor Licence.

Make sure that each venue has adequate parking and that all the guests know how to get there.

If someone has drunk too much to drive home safely make sure that a lift is available.

> **Handy hint**
>
> Warn your guests when there is 15 minutes before you are due to leave for the next venue. This allows people to finish conversations, dash to the toilet and find coats without feeling too pressurised. If you are getting very behind, telephone the next host to say that you will be late.

Plus ... and minus:

- Provides a really good social event with total control over who attends.
- Can cater for special needs.
- Very flexible.
- Popular.
- Can include the whole family.

- Not a real money-spinner, but it helps if people bring a bottle or even contribute some food.
- Restricted numbers except in special circumstances.
- Can become a little chaotic unless tightly organised.

EVENT 20 SNOWBALL PARTY
A party where the guests hold more parties

Operating requirements: Initial host/hostess, treasurer.

Equipment needs: Nothing other than a persuasive letter writing technique.

Lead time: 2 weeks to prepare the first party. 5 weeks to run the appeal.

Initial cost: Just a few pounds for stationery, postage and refreshments.

Suitable for: Human interest causes.

Expected return: Potentially hundreds of pounds.

What's in it for contributors: Feel-good factor plus an informal get-together with friends. Very good for parents with young children, or retired people.

Frequency: You should only use this idea once. If your area has already had a snowball party going around then leave it for at least a year.

Variations on a theme: Pyramid party. Same idea, just works from back to front. i.e. first host holds a huge party of 50 or more guests. Guests invite half the original amount until it gets down to lots of parties of just two. Some organisations prefer this method as it peters out naturally without having to put a time limit on the whole thing.

How does it work?

The principle is the same as for a chain letter. OK, suppress your prejudices and I will explain!

You hold a tea party or a coffee morning for five friends. They each pay a minimum of £2.00 and agree to hold a party each for at least two friends, who pay £2.00 to come and throw a party each for two of their friends and so on ...

The parties can go on ad nauseam but in general it is best to publish a date, on the accompanying literature, by which all the fees should be in and you call a halt. There does come a point when everyone has been to at least three parties and there is no one left in the area to ask!

How do I get started?

This idea works best where a few heart strings are being tugged. The most successful snowball party I have experienced was launched by a desperate couple who had to raise enough money to send their little boy to America and pay for a life-saving operation within the next six months.

Your initial invitation and accompanying explanatory literature has to be absolutely right. It might even be worth paying for a professional PR person or copywriter to prepare it for you. If there are nationally produced pamphlets available to explain a particular condition or situation, so much the better.

At the first party you will be in a very positive position. Your friends will all know you well and be on your side from the start. You will be there to answer questions and be persuasive. The next and subsequent parties will not be so easy.

You could host two or three 'first' parties with people from different areas. In this way you can run consecutive snowball parties without the danger that you will run out of guests and you will make double or three times the proceeds.

How do I ensure that subsequent parties are a success?

Firstly you must make it easy for people to contribute. It is the responsibility of the hostess to collect the fees and send them on to you. She will hand out literature about the cause and invitations to be used for the next parties. Guests can either write to you for more copies of invitations and leaflets or they can opt to photocopy more for themselves. The latter is really the easier.

Make sure you include: the invitation, with the minimum donation made very clear; a piece about this particular appeal to include the tearjerker; your target figure; how it works; where to send contributions and when it is to stop; a general pamphlet and a thank you note. The thank you note should include a further invitation to send a larger donation and/or a name and address so that they can be informed of the outcome.

How much could I make from this?

Lets do a few sums based on the premise that the appeal is to run for five weeks. Assume that the parties are held weekly and the minimum fee is £2.

Of course, not every guest will hold a party but there will be others that invite more than two and some may donate more than £2, so what you lose on the swings you gain on the roundabouts.

The first party has five guests (= £10). Week 2 and five people invite two more people each (=£20). Week 3 and ten people invite two each (=£40). Week 4 and 20 people invite two each (=£80). Week 5 and 40 people invite two each (=£160). Now add it all up and you have £310. If you have three snowballs growing at once you can make £930. Good money for letting something largely take care of itself!

Plus ... and minus:

- Very good idea for people with little time to spare.
- Good return for initial effort.
- Needs very little outlay.
- Gives retired people or mums with toddlers an excuse to socialise and get involved where other projects might be impossible. Good also for the elderly or out of work as there is little outlay needed all round.

- Quickly goes out of your control.
- Finite number of parties that can happen in one area. By week 6 you will expect 80 people to hold a party, which is unrealistic.

EVENT 21 SPONSORED ACTIVITIES

Individuals pledge to collect money for
activities achieved

The London Marathon is probably the most well known sponsored event in the
UK. It has acquired the kind of reputation and kudos that other race organisers
can only dream of. Where else can you expect national television crews to turn
out in full for hours on end so that continuous progress can be broadcast and the
results reported in all the headline news?

But sponsored events need not be on the grand scale of the London Marathon to
achieve a good result. In this section I will go through three ideas in detail, but
don't stop there. Use the basic outline to work out your own ideas – you are
only restricted by the limits of your own imagination. As well as the more usual
sponsored swims, walks and runs, I have heard of sponsored beard shaves,
bungee jumping, chess marathons, and group silences. The Norfolk churches
hold a very successful sponsored cycle ride around 60 or more churches every
summer. Children attempt hopscotch marathons or carol singing. Knitting clubs
organise sponsored patches; as well as sponsoring each knitter 2p a square you
get the most wonderful patchwork blanket to donate or raffle for further funds.
Sponsored orienteers collect money on the amount of seconds they knock off a
specific time or the number of markers they manage to record. I have even heard
of a sponsored vasectomy! And I know of one brave leukaemia patient who had
a sponsored head shave in public just before he went into hospital to undergo a
gruelling period of chemotherapy when he was told to expect considerable hair
loss anyway. You have to admire someone in such circumstances being able to
look on the positive side of something so uncomfortable.

Whilst you should treat each event and activity separately there are, however,
some general rules of thumb and tips that can be universally applied.

Collections

Collections taking place in a public place are governed by law and a collection
does not have to be money. This means that children, or adults, going from door
to door or standing outside a local shop asking people to sign their sponsorship
forms is illegal without permission. (See Event 22 for information on street
collections, definitions of public places and how to apply for a permit.) Of
course, what you do within a school, office or your own home is your business
but make yourselves and your teams aware what is, and what is not, permissible.

Swelling funds

If you number all your sponsorship forms you will be in a position to offer a lucky draw for all participants or helpers who return them with more than, say, £5 (check Chapter 6 for lotteries registration if necessary). If your event is in the form of a race you will also be able to log each entrant through the finish and tie up the number that they wear on their vests with the number on the form (see below).

Ask a local business to donate a prize for the draw and a prize for the person who raises, and collects, the most sponsorship. These tips help to raise extra funds and give that all important encouragement to people to collect all their pledges.

Suggest that each competing individual gathers a fundraising team of three or four people. S/he can concentrate on the activity, especially if it is something like a marathon which needs training, whilst others concentrate on raising and collecting money.

National or local personalities are very valuable both to start the race or to compete. Let it be known right from the start that your VIP will be racing too and you will gain all sorts of extra entries just so that people can catch a glimpse or the possibility of a chat with the 'star'.

Particularly appropriate entrants often make very successful fundraisers. Think of Keith Castle who ran for charity after his heart transplant. Somebody in their sixties joining a roller marathon in aid of Age Concern would gain a lot of support and possible media coverage for your cause, but do be sensitive when asking people to help. The last thing you want is to be seen as blatantly using people for your own ends, however laudable these might be.

Collecting pledges

The onus is on the competitors to collect their own contributions. When you sign the forms to say that they have completed the race or clocked up so many miles, make a note of the total amount promised. I have heard complaints that people can lose interest in collecting their sponsorship after the event and a significant percentage of promised money is never forthcoming. There are ways to overcome this.

- Make it clear that the total recorded after the race is expected to be paid by the competitor even if s/he does not collect all that is owed. If there is a possibility that money might come out of their own pockets there is a powerful incentive to collect thoroughly.
- Whilst it is unreasonable to expect a cheque on the day of the actual event, do publish a realistic date for all sponsorship monies to be paid in full. Two to

three weeks is reasonable. After this date you can send a reminder letter and possibly make a follow up visit although in the majority of cases this will not be necessary.

- For a small event give three or four alternative contacts to pass funds and sponsorship forms to. For a large event it is worth while opening a special account at a bank or building society so that competitors can pay money in at their local branch. The cashier stamps the form and the competitor then sends the stamped form to the organiser to prove that payment has been made.

Sponsorship forms

Every form should include the name of the benefiting charity, the name and nature of the event, where and when it is to be held, who is organising the event, a contact address and telephone number, space for the name of the competitor and a statement indicating that the competitor is responsible for paying the amount totalled. (This statement should be signed by the competitor: failure to sign the form means that it will not be stamped at the end of the event to prove that the activity was completed.)

Then you need five columns headed 'name of sponsor', 'address', 'amount per ...', 'total', 'signature', and at least 15 blank rows down. At the bottom of the form you need a space to enter the accumulative total, instructions for paying in the money, and the date for the final payment to be made. There should be a space for the official stamp and the final number of laps, or whatever, achieved or completed. If the event has attracted company or Sports Council sponsorship the appropriate declarations and logos should also be included.

PR opportunities

Consider a sponsored race for part of the launch for a new cause. Even if you don't raise thousands of pounds for the appeal it is a very good way of spreading the word and increasing public awareness. You will get ten or a dozen sponsors for each competitor, all learning about your cause and passing the word on, quite apart from the crowds who you hope will attend the actual event.

Types of sponsored events

On the whole you can divide sponsored events into three groups although some can be a mixture of the first and last.

- Major events where individuals take part but acquire sponsorship for their own causes (such as the London Marathon).

- Those where individuals or teams attempt a death defying or extraordinary feat on a unique basis. (A parachute jump or bed push, for instance.)
- A collective event that encourages many people to enter and all raise money for the umbrella cause. (A fun-run is a good example.)

Given some ideas for events along the above three lines, you should be able to adjust and temper the advice given above and below to run almost any type of sponsored event you might care to think of … so on with the details.

BED PUSH MARATHON

Operating requirements: Committee consisting of a coordinator, treasurer, secretary, and several other members to assist on the day according to the size of your event. Stewards for the route. First-aider.

Equipment needs: A wheeled bed for each team or insist they supply their own. Collection tins. Fancy dress. Sponsorship forms. Starting tape. Refreshments. First aid kit.

Lead time: 3–6 months.

Initial cost: Cost of publicity and printing sponsorship forms. Prizes and medals should be sponsored. For a large event you should be able to attract company sponsorship to pay your administration and publicity costs.

Suitable for: Hospitals, GP's surgeries, playgroups, schools, children's- or illness-related charities.

Expected return: This really does depend on how diligent your pushers are at obtaining sponsorship and how much you manage to collect 'en route'.

What's in it for contributors: A thoroughly enjoyable, and competitive, event that is as much fun to watch as to take part In. Sponsors are only relieved that they don't have to join in!

Frequency: Annually in the same area, but you could run more if you change the route, although your sponsors might get a little tired.

Special requirements: A Street Collection Permit from the local authority. Police support.

Variations on a theme: Circular bed push – takes place over a circular route, perhaps around a park or a pedestrianised city centre, for a specified number of circuits or time.

How does it work?

A team, or teams, of people, often in fancy-dress, push an occupied bed along a prearranged route. Money is collected through sponsorship and by collection alongside the bed or in pubs, or similar, afterwards.

In detail, the 'patient' is pushed for 24 hours or as long as the teams can keep going. You need several teams of at least six people (one in the bed, one on each corner and a collector), who each push and collect for an hour at a time. Sometimes you have competing teams, but more often than not it is just the one bed with several teams all working together and taking their turns. The more people you have involved, the more money you will raise. The 'patient' might volunteer to be pushed for the whole 24 hours and attract special sponsorship and media coverage.

Usually a marathon will take place over a circular or roughly a figure of eight course along public roads although you can organise the event like an old-fashioned steeplechase and progress continually along one route. The police may not be too happy about you covering the same route several times, however a Sunday marathon might enable you to use a short city centre route or you could consider a public park as you would a pram race, although this might become rather tedious. The plus point of keeping the whole event fairly compact is that you can make a permanent site for your 'pit stops'.

How do we get started?

Form a committee and contact the police to help work out your route and a date. It may be that they will want to arrange to cone off an area to stop cars parking on the roadside or they might insist that they provide a motorcycle outrider to warn other road users that you are coming. They might say that you can only do it on a Sunday when traffic is at its lightest. Ideally, you will want to use a city centre for at least part of the route on a Saturday afternoon. Some police forces are very anti-bed pushes due to experience of badly organised events in the past, not only because of congestion but also the risk of accidents on major, but narrow, roads.

You will need to work out your stages very carefully and to supply a support crew. The teams may need a couple of mini vans to transport them when they are resting or having refreshments. You will also need an experienced first aid officer, plenty of food and drink and some planned loo stops.

Make sure that you will be granted a Street Collection Permit for that day. Most local authorities will not allow more than one group collecting in the same area on the same day (see Chapter 6 for further details).

At least four weeks – possibly more for a large event – before the event send out an advice sheet and the sponsorship forms.

How do we 'sell' the idea?

Having arranged your route and the date, you are now in a position to start your publicity. You will need to advertise for teams. This might be an in-house 'press gang' operation for a hospital or school or you could advertise through the chamber of commerce, pubs or in the newspaper if you are opening the event to the general public. Advertise your prizes to inject some healthy competition between rival teams.

You should also start planning your publicity to ensure that people come out to see the push, to donate money and to raise the level of awareness for your cause.

Whilst you aim for a minimum of six in each team, ideally there should be as many volunteers, who may not be affiliated to a team, as you or they can muster to carry collecting tins or buckets and run alongside. So make sure the call goes out to collectors in your publicity from the beginning.

What happens on the day?

Make sure your teams are absolutely sure of the route. You may need a navigator on a bicycle to lead the way. Try to arrange your start from a popular pedestrian area or town centre garden. Raise a tape and use a noisy starting pistol. Borrow a 'Personality' or local politician or senior officer of your charity to start the race and suggest that a local radio station might like to broadcast from the route. Use your VIP to reinforce 'rules' of behaviour and remind the teams that collecting money is the name of the game. Keep tabs on how the race is going. For the 'marathon' version telephone your local radio station several times to let them know how it is progressing.

What happens at the end?

Finish in another popular spot, or arrive back at the start. Try finishing near a bandstand which you could use to hold a winners ceremony. Give each member of the teams a ribbon with a little medal. These are fairly inexpensive and are easily available from trophy shops. Your VIP can present the trophy. You can keep up the momentum by providing music and refreshments: keep collectors collecting until the bitter end!

Individual sponsorship forms need to be signed or marked to indicate that the competitor completed the route, or pushed for so many miles; a table set up just after the finishing line is the best place to organise this. Have at least four officials with rubber stamps to prevent queues forming.

If your runners are running over a long period of time arrange for refreshments or at least a cup of hot soup to be available.

Possible problems

You might find that your local police have banned bed pushes. Don't argue with them, just choose another fundraising idea that they are happy with, or try another area.

Street Collection Permits often need to be applied for up to a year in advance. Officially, open collecting buckets, or barrows, are illegal as collecting tins are supposed to be sealed. In some areas open containers are tolerated and it is obviously much quicker and easier for people to throw money into a bucket than have to feed it into a slot.

Make sure someone is specifically responsible for fulfilling the conditions of the permit and don't forget that collectors have to be 16 years old or over (18 in London). You will have to make a full financial return by law by an appointed date. It is easy to forget this after the event is over.

A conventional hospital bed may not stand up to the test of a marathon. Consider getting it specially strengthened or swapping it half way along the route. Rubber tyres make a much more comfortable ride, but include a spare wheel and a puncture repair kit. Remember that people can get injured during this sort of event, so be prepared for all eventualities.

> **Handy hint**
>
> One member of the team can follow behind pushing a wheelbarrow. Buckets get heavy and periodically collectors can empty them into the barrow. Spectators can also throw coins straight into the barrow. This also makes a good 'photo-opportunity' for the press.

Plus... and minus:

- Can be a very exciting and profitable event.
- The event is suitable for families to watch.
- The marathon is unusual enough to attract media coverage

- Probably better not to enter under 12s in the teams.
- Need support of police.
- Need Street Collection Permit.

FUN RUN

Operating requirements: Committee consisting of a coordinator, treasurer, secretary, and several other members to assist on the day according to the size of your event. First-aider.

Equipment needs: Suitable venue – marked out park, field, playing field or recreation ground is ideal. Collection tins. Starting and finishing tapes. Public address system or megaphone. Starting pistol. Refreshments. First aid kit.

Lead time: Four to six months.

Initial cost: Very little outlay. Prizes should be sponsored.

Suitable for: Anything and everything.

Expected return: Work on an average of £15 raised by each entrant. Hopefully you should be able to do much better than this. The collection should bring in another £50–£100 at a small event. If you sell refreshments you can raise more money.

What's in it for contributors: As above, a thoroughly enjoyable, and competitive, event that is as equally fun to watch as to take part. Prizes for different 'classes'.

Frequency: Annually in the same area.

Special requirements: A Street Collection Permit from the local authority. You might need to inform the Police.

Variations on a theme: Pram race. Waiters race – individuals have to race over a given route dressed as waiters carrying a metal tray, bottle and two (unbreakable) glasses, as supplied by the organisers. Pancake race for Shrove Tuesday – the Gas Board can set up mobile stoves to cook pancakes on site – individuals run (in fancy dress) carrying frying pans with pancakes, tossing as they go.

How does it work?

Teams or individuals race against each other (or against their own stamina/determination) over an arranged route. You raise money from entry fees, sponsorship, a public collection and refreshments or side stalls. The idea is make the event as silly as possible to attract a large crowd as well as competitors.

You could charge, say, £10 entrance for each team or £3 for an individual which would pay for a trophy for the winners if you wanted to make this an annual event. Persuading the competitors to enter in fancy-dress all helps the event to be more PR-worthy. It is also more of a laugh for all concerned. Prizes can be awarded to the best (and worst!) dressed teams.

How do we get started?

Form an organising group as above and decide on your venue and a date. Fun runs are best held in the mornings; perhaps the middle of July and August are best avoided so that competitors do not suffer from heat exhaustion. If you are to dress up as Fozzy Bear or a Smurf, much better for it to be less than 20 degrees; on the other hand you are unlikely to get much of a turn out if you choose the Easter holidays when it can still be very chilly. Remember that school half-terms are notoriously bad dates due to people taking long weekends away.

If you are planning a large event on a central site look for company sponsorship early on. Your benefiting charity may be experienced in finding sponsorship and might be able to help you here (see Chapter 5).

Find a bank or building society that will be prepared to open a paying-in account for you and get your sponsorship forms printed. You will need at least 500 for a medium-scale event and if you have them printed on white or a pale colour (not pink or red) you will be able to photocopy more if you run out.

Try not to have too many rules. Almost anything goes. If people want to enter a team of two, three or even six, let them. If children under 10 want to start half way up the field, why not? It's not a sporting event and your main aim is to make money and have fun so let the event grow organically. Just keep a special eye on safety issues.

Remember to request the St John Ambulance or the Red Cross to attend. You will need them for minor sprains if nothing more serious. When you plan your site allow for an emergency vehicle route, just in case you need to get an ambulance through in a hurry.

You will need toilet facilities, somewhere for people to sit and you should organise a tent or building where runners can have blisters dressed or get cups of tea free of charge. Outside you can have refreshment stalls for spectators from which you hope to make a small profit.

You will need to think about car parking and you may need the police to advise you in this area. Whatever you do, make sure that runners and cars are kept well apart.

As in the bed push marathon, make sure that you will be granted a Street Collection Permit for that day.

Four weeks before the event make advice sheets and sponsorship forms available from well publicised sources. If you can involve the local radio or newspaper office, their reception areas and that of your sponsoring company all make good pick-up points. You must also have a telephone contact advertised so that people can ring in and be sent a form.

What about publicity?

If you involve the media as suggested above, you are half way there. They will take on a good deal of your advertising requirements for you, but you will still need some good quality posters and leaflets to pass on to as many public buildings, libraries, sports clubs, schools contacts of your charity, etc. as you can. Look for competitors as above in hospitals, schools, factories, restaurants and pubs or advertise through the chamber of commerce magazine or in-house council workers' newsletters.

What happens on the day?

Arrive in good time. People will want to check in up to an hour before the start of the race. They should hand over their forms and be given a corresponding number to pin on. The forms are kept in numerical order so that they can be found quickly as each runner finishes, marked with the number of laps achieved and rubber stamped.

Use stewards wearing brightly coloured waistcoats to direct runners to the checking in areas. Checking in should stop within 15 minutes of the start time to enable the organisers to arrange the forms into the correct order and divide them into batches ready for the finish. See 'Possible problems' at the end of the this section.

Encourage your VIP competitors to mingle with the crowd and start to build up some excitement. Use a compere to organise the competitors and control the crowd. Music always adds to the attraction of this event.

Measure your track in advance and mark it out in tenths of a mile. The whole circuit needs to be half or one mile so that you can work out how many miles each runner completes. If your track is any shorter than half a mile then you will start to get stragglers caught up by the front runners and you won't be able to work out how many laps they have completed. Make sure that you have a board clearly visible from the track and the checking in tables showing what lap is being run. Some events have several people employed as 'lap recorders'. They must be responsible types, able to keep 'awake' – there is plenty of room for acrimony at the end if runners feel short-changed.

As runners finish, they can peel off to one side to have their forms stamped and medals given out if you are using them.

As soon as the event is over you can present the prizes to the person or team completing the most laps. Other prizes such as the silliest costume or oldest runner can be given out also. Unless you have a computer on site (and you can provide one easily with the advent of the laptop) you will have to delay presenting the prize for the person who raised the most amount of money.

Make sure that everyone involved is thanked profusely and that you clear the area of litter and equipment before you leave.

What happens after the event?

For two or three weeks after the event your main concern is to retrieve all the pledges. If you operate using the guidelines as outlined at the beginning of this chapter you should be able to bank 80 to 90 per cent of promised monies.

When you have completed your accounts, organise a 'grand handing-over'. Invite the press, the company sponsors, donors of prizes, your sponsorship winner and anyone else who helped in a big way as well as a representative of the cause for whom you were all fundraising. Arrange for some photographs of the giant cheque and the prize being presented to your most successful fundraiser to be taken, in case the newspaper photographer is late or doesn't show up.

If you get the feeling that the event would benefit from another airing make some arrangements to meet after a month or two so that you can discuss organising a similar event for next year.

Possible problems

As in the bed push marathon, be aware that you might need to apply for permission to hold a public collection up to a year in advance on popular days.

Unless you organise your checking in tables very carefully you are liable to hold-ups which is very undesirable when you have exhausted and possibly injured people waiting for you to find forms and stamp them. Organise four to eight funnels with ropes or crowd control barriers to direct numbered entrants. Each funnel should be marked clearly 1–30, 31–60 or however you chose to separate your runners.

Handy hint
Hold a children's fun run an hour before the main one gets started and halt it after 45 minutes. This gives the little ones a chance to compete but stops you getting your main event snarled up with very slow runners.

Plus ... and minus:

- Great fun and potentially lucrative event.
- Needs careful but not prolonged organisational skills.
- Shouldn't require large setting up costs.
- Very attractive to potential sponsors.
- Easy to publicise.
- Family event.
- Easy to scale up or down according to circumstances.

- Needs a lot of volunteer helpers.
- Can be chaotic if not organised properly.
- Can involve injury, needs professional medical teams available.
- Not suitable for very young children.

POLE SITTING (AND OTHER ZANY FEATS)

Operating requirements: One individual and perhaps a sponsorship coordinator.

Equipment needs: Custom-built pole or a platform in a suitable tree, ideally in a public place. Public address system or megaphone at the start.

Lead time: A few weeks.

Initial cost: Very little outlay, most of the publicity is done through the media. The cost of sponsorship forms. Try to get the pole donated.

Suitable for: Anything and everything.

Expected return: Almost everything received is profit.

What's in it for contributors: I think this one appeals to people because it is so weird and sponsors are glad that it is someone else attempting the record.

Frequency: One-off.

Special requirements: If you plan to pole-sit in a public space you will probably need permission from the local authority.

Variations on a theme: As an individual you can try a 'sponsored-almost-anything'. You only have to choose something that you want to try yourself and that you think will capture the public imagination.

What on earth is pole sitting?

This is a truly bizarre activity which started in America. A specially constructed pole, the taller the better but at least seven feet high, is set firmly into the ground. On top of this telegraph-pole-like structure is usually a barrel or a small shack.

Sitters sit for days, weeks, even months at a time, apparently without falling off, being fed by volunteers who pass up food and drink at intervals. And ... No, I don't know the answers to your other questions! I guess it is all according to the individual. According to the Guinness Book of Records a woman, Mellissa Sanders, lived in a hut measuring 6ft by 7ft on top of a pole in Indianapolis for a total of 516 days. Whew!

Pole-sitting in this country is not yet a popular occupation. It is certainly not something that I have tried. A man called Rob Colley stayed in a barrel on top of a pole 43ft high at Dartmouth Wildlife Park for over 42 days, completing his 'sit' on 24 August 1992 (source: *Guinness Book of Records*). I think most charities have had parachutists, bungee jumpers and bridge swingers, so I am offering this challenge to a UK pole-sitter: come forward and see if you can capture the nation's heart, and money. I should love to hear how you get on.

How shall I get started?

Well, if it were me (which it won't be!) I should start practising on a small pole first. Try a barrel on a tea chest and see if you can cope with several hours without falling off or becoming so cramped you have to descend.

When you are quite good at your chosen occupation contact the media or the *Guinness Book of Records* and state that you are going to set a UK pole-sitting record.

Having achieved some media interest you could contact BT or a timber company and see if they will supply you with a pole to sit on and erect it for you. BT were extraordinarily helpful with the 'Fire Over England' project in the 1980s. Pole-sitting just might be the sort of crazy idea that interests them. Any number of breweries or cider companies should be happy to supply you with a barrel.

What do I do to get a record into the *Guinness Book of Records?*

You need to put your idea into writing in the form of a brief proposal at least two months before you attempt the record. Fill in the form found in the 'Make a Record Attempt' of the Guinness World Records website *www.guinnessworldrecords.com.*

How do I go about getting the sponsorship?

Some ideas work best run hand in hand with the benefiting charity. I think this could be one of them. Suggest that you do the sitting and finding the volunteers to look after you and they organise a nation-wide sponsorship drive. You could both be on to a very good thing, you for notoriety and the charity for the cash. For a more usual type of individual event you will have to find a sponsorship team yourself.

What about when it is all over?

Well, when you have had enough sitting 'atop your pole (or if you fall off when you go to sleep) announce your national (or regional) record and start to collect your sponsorship money. Give yourself and your sponsors about a month to get your total in and then announce your final figure and arrange a hand-over as outlined above.

Your ace is the uniqueness of your idea, so play on it for all it's worth, as you would do if you had been undertaking a challenge that was spectacularly dangerous or impressive. Use the media as much as you can and then set about breaking your own record.

Plus . . . and minus:

- It is your idea and you can do just what appeals to you.
- You can make the event as high or low-key as you wish.
- If you chose a really zany idea you should find it easy to gain media interest.
- If you aim to beat a record you will gain extra media coverage.
- If you work with a charity you can leave all the actual fundraising to someone else.

- Hard work to find your own sponsorship.
- Often experimental, but that has its compensations.
- Might find local authority resistance.

EVENT 22 STREET COLLECTION OR FLAG DAY

Collecting donations from the public in the street

Operating requirements: Representative of bone fide charitable or benevolent organisation. As many collectors, over 16, as you can muster.

Equipment needs: Collecting boxes or tins. Flags or stickers if required.

Lead time: 3–6 months.

Initial cost: Nothing or very little if you are using stickers. The charity for whom you are collecting may supply their own.

Suitable for: All types of fundraising. City centres, parks, at other events, open air meetings, arcades, stations, cinemas, pubs, theatres or even the frontage of shops and stores.

Expected return: How long is a piece of string? Seriously, the more collectors you use, the more cash they will collect.

What's in it for contributors: Nothing, bar the warm glow of a happy conscience! But people still give.

Frequency: As often as you like on private property. You may be restricted to just a few times a year if you want to hold you collection anywhere deemed to be 'a public place'.

Special requirements: To hold a collection in a public place (not necessarily the same as public property) you will need a Street Collection Permit.

How does it work?

You do nothing other than ask people to give you money for a particular cause. Sometimes they will and sometimes they won't but you can't follow people around or coerce them. You need to display the name of your charity clearly.

There are ways in which you can dress the collection up to entertain, educate or appeal to potential donors.

Will I need to apply for a Street Collection Permit?

The Local Government Act 1972 gives powers to local authorities to regulate collections on public property. The Charities Act 1992 tightened these regulations further (see below) and you will be required to comply with this legislation whenever you hold a collection on any street or public place.

Whilst shopping precincts may be deemed to be a public place, cinemas, theatres, railway stations, steps of churches or within the boundaries of a shop are private, at least for the present. The legislation described above will be replaced shortly by Part III of the Charities Act 1992 (Sections 65–74) regulating what will become known as 'public charitable collections'. As yet the new regulations have still not been published but the definition 'public place' will be extended, definitely to include shopping precincts, shop frontages, highways and railway stations. Offices, hospitals and schools will be exempt as will any place to which a ticket must be purchased to gain access.

Although requirements vary slightly around the country, broadly the basis on which a permit is granted is very much the same and this is unlikely to change.

You are required to apply, in writing, to the administration department of the district council covering the area where you intend to hold the collection, at least one month prior to the event. In practice you may have to apply well before that to ensure you book the date you need. Be warned that there is much competition for Saturdays and the weeks approaching Christmas.

There are rules that apply and you must adhere to them. These are set out below. You will also be required to complete a return slip giving the council information including the total amount collected, who counted it and a list of all the collectors.

Where the new regulations may show significant changes is covering matters relating to the keeping and publishing of accounts, preventing annoyance and carrying certificates, so make yourselves aware of developments by contacting your local authority.

Requirements for the granting of a collection permit

Generally, the basis on which a permit is granted is as follows:

- Only one organisation to collect each day and that group must only collect on the allotted day and between the times as stated on the permit and in the permitted place. (The permitted place may be the whole of the town centre or it could be restricted to just one street.)
- People carrying collecting boxes should remain stationary and must not coerce passers-by or show intimidating behaviour.
- Collections have to be made in sealed boxes – usually available from the benefiting charity – although many authorities are tolerant when it comes to

using buckets, etc. in moving processions or at fun runs, for instance.

- All collectors must be aged 16 (18 in London) or over and be acting voluntarily. They must wear badges and carry authorisation from the promoter.

Where might I collect without a permit?

Assuming that you have requested and obtained permission from the owners, you may collect anywhere on private property as outlined above. However, where, before the new regulations, you were allowed to hold a collection at an open air meeting or an event on public land, you now will have to obtain a permit unless you are selling tickets to that event. In short, most events that charge an entry fee will be exempt. However, areas of private land to which the public have general access will be seen as a 'public place' in the eyes of the law.

Some of the places that successful collections have been held include private houses; pubs; trains; railway, bus and underground stations, inside shops and stores; after the show in a cinema or theatre; as part of an event on a private field or in a garden; and, of course, every Sunday in churches all over the country. Interestingly if someone lives in a pub (and most of them are residentially occupied) a collection, especially a pub-to-pub collection, might be liable for a house-to-house collection permit, although I have not heard of any such enforcement.

How do I obtain the collecting boxes?

If you contact the benefiting charity's headquarters to explain your plans, and you should do so to get their approval for your idea, they will advise you. Stickers or flags may be made available, record sheets and seals will certainly be so.

Officially, the tins or boxes need to be closed and sealed and this is good practice as it assures the donor that the money will go where it is intended. Each box should be numbered. All boxes should be opened in the presence of two people, with the contents of each box counted, checked and recorded as soon after the collection as possible.

Occasionally you might be able to use buckets or other open topped collecting tubs, especially for a fun run, street procession or sponsored walk. In this case all the collection buckets will have to bear an official sticker and collectors must still be over 16. Buckets should be emptied at a supervised central collection point and directly the event has ended monies should be removed to a secure place for counting to take place. Be warned that counting can take hours! At the end of the Lord Mayor's Street Procession in Norwich in excess of several thousand pounds in small change is regularly collected during the space of an evening. Counting the proceeds is a mammoth task and involves experienced volunteers from the council's treasury department using special coin weighing machines; it still takes most of the night.

How can we make our flag day more exciting?

Try putting all the collectors in fancy dress. This is particularly good if you are fundraising for an animal charity. Remember, though, that some people feel intimidated or frightened by people in fancy dress so make it appropriate and leave some collectors in regular clothing.

For a charity that is, perhaps, less popular or well known, ask for permission to mount a small mobile exhibition alongside the collectors explaining your cause and handing out leaflets to those who show an interest or run a collection 50:50 with a more popular organisation.

Try running your collection alongside another event, although you will have to choose carefully as there will be some competition unless the event is for the same cause.

Get permission to play music, borrow a barrel-organ or perform some circus acts to grab the passer-by's attention. (Don't forget that if your flag day turns into a musical event you may have to apply for a Public Entertainments Licence, see Chapter 6.)

Think up some zany ideas. Collect from horseback or use some other old fashioned means of transport.

Use strange collecting boxes, if you are allowed, such as policemen's helmets when collecting at the Police gala day, Wellington boots for the Gardener's Benevolent Fund or bedpans for the hospital.

Handy hint

Invite all your collectors to an official hand-over of the final total. Ask the bank to prepare a giant cheque and take a photograph of everyone holding it. People do like to feel appreciated and it also provides a good PR opportunity for your cause.

Plus... and minus:

- No need to hire a venue.
- Very little organisation required.
- Works well with another event.
- No outlay.

- May need permit.
- May not be able to collect on the day you want.
- Not suitable for children under 16.

EVENT 23 SPINE-CHILLER TRAIL
Guided ghostly walk

Operating requirements: Coordinator/guide, treasurer.

Equipment needs: Strong, clear voice that will stand the course, torch.

Lead time: Two weeks minimum, but allow yourselves enough time to advertise.

Initial cost: Just publicity costs.

Suitable for: Local appeals and charities. Needs to be in a well populated tourist area.

Expected return: £75–£100 maximum, each trail.

What's in it for contributors: An interesting and creepy, guided tour.

Frequency: Every Sunday from March to October providing you are not under threat from commercial or official Tourist Board competition.

Special requirements: Thorough knowledge of your local area and its history. You may need access to buildings and permission to poke about the grounds of others.

Variations on a theme: Apart from a general guided tour, what about an architects trail, or a bridges tour in London, a riverside walk, or an owl trail in the countryside. How about an early morning river trip if you know someone who would lend a cruiser or an electric boat, or a brass-rubbing tour in the city. Heritage tours are often popular as are, unaccountably, guided trips of the sewers!

How does it work?

A group of up to 20 people pay about £5–6 each to be told ghostly tales and led into spooky places for about an hour and a half.

How do I get started?

Perhaps you are interested in this idea because you know some tales about the area in which you live. Gather as much information as you can about a couple of square miles and explore any churches, ruins, graveyards, old houses, woods or cliffs that might have appropriate legends associated with them. Reject the temptation to make things up, but do dress up historical facts by learning to paint verbal pictures and making suggestions as to what may have happened as the background to a particular event. Use the library or local historians to direct you. Aim to be able to talk about everything without having to refer to notes.

Devise a route to cover as many interesting places as you can without covering the same ground twice. You should hope to be back where you started, or at a friendly pub, within about an hour or an hour and a half. This includes stops where you will talk. It might be a good idea to arrange your start and finish by a cathedral or in a hotel where people can congregate without getting too wet or cold before you set off.

Make sure that you get permission from all the appropriate authorities to traipse around their property or through their gardens. Where you can, obtain access to the inside of churches, up towers or sites of grim happenings but don't plan more than three or four of these explorations or you will restrict the time you can spend looking at other things.

Should I arrange more than one trail?

You won't need to devise more than one route, but you do need to run it fairly often if you are going to make any money from the idea.

Your publicity will take up all you make from the first trail, but it won't cost you any more to market 20 trails than if you were just selling a one-off.

So how do I market it?

Decide on all the dates you will run the trail, then advertise the whole list. Print some A5 leaflets to describe the evening. Publish the price, the dates and the time and place you start from. Give a telephone number to ring so walkers can book, but leave payment until the night, in cash.

Let the local tourist information centre know of your plans fairly early on. They will be able to advise if you have competition and may be able to take bookings for you. They will certainly add your trails to their list of events. Send press releases to the local media and an invitation to a couple of journalists and a photographer to join the group for the first one. Consider advertising in the 'what's on' column of the local paper if it is not too expensive. They may do a free entry if they know it is for charity.

How do I organise the trail on the night?

Arrive about ten minutes before the set off time; about 8.30pm is about right. You may need to make it later in the summer as it will still be light until 9.00pm. Try not to have more than 20 people on one trail or it will be difficult to keep everyone together and they may not all be able to hear you, especially if it is windy.

Start on time and always keep to your planned route and talk. You will have to be very experienced before you can extemporise successfully.

You will save yourself a big worry if you ensure that at least one other person knows the spiel and the route as well as you. If you are stuck visiting Great Aunt Nora, or the dog has to be rushed to the vet or you just fancy a Sunday to yourself you will feel happier knowing that there is a stand-in.

Give people an idea of how long the walk will take and let them know where you plan to finish if it is not where you started. Ask for questions and when everyone is happy with what is about to happen, collect the money so that people can drift away later if they are cold or tired (not bored, of course) and you don't lose out.

Arrive at your final destination punctually, spend some time answering any more questions and give people a little one-to-one attention. This helps your customers feel they have had value for money but gives those who want to an opportunity to do so to go home.

Afterwards, put your feet up, get yourself a drink and have a rest. You will have earned it!

Handy hint

Above all, be professional. Go on a few other trails to see how they are done.

Plus ... and minus:

- Very little outlay.
- No venue to hire and no infrastructure.
- Only needs a couple of people to set up and just one guide each evening.
- Good for families though probably best to suggest over 7 years old only.

- Needs careful planning and you might need to obtain several permissions.
- Best in well populated tourist area.
- May have commercial competition. In York, for instance, guides and their audiences are falling over each other at every popular monument.

EVENT 24 STALLS AND SIDESHOWS

Many events rely on stalls and stands to provide interest and colour, and they can be a great source of revenue. The WI have got so good at running stalls that they now have a commercial operation called WI Markets doing nothing else but holding regular sales from stalls of produce and goods. Village 'fayres', church fetes and other fundraising days often consist of little else. And as long as the variety and quality of activities and items offered for sale are well considered, visitors will feel they have had an enjoyable afternoon out. It is, after all, the backbone of English country summer activities.

However, a motley collection of doors on trestles selling junk that is only worth putting in the bin, a stall offering insect covered, tired looking cakes, and a tombola comprising out-of-date cans of beans and tinned tomatoes, all dotted about over a windy field, is not going to inspire anyone to part with their money or come again another time.

In this chapter I hope to encourage you to design and prepare your stalls attractively, we will look at how grouping them correctly can make all the difference to your proceeds and finally I shall give you loads of good, and proven, ideas.

How do I make a stall?

The door over two trestles, as described above, is not such a bad idea in itself. But you do need to pretty it up in some way. Sheets, tablecloths and non-rip crepe paper secured firmly with drawing pins are all ideal. If you are running a stall regularly you might consider dyeing a sheet or two a darker colour to provide an eye-catching backdrop to your wares.

Suit your colours and surfaces to your produce. It is pretty obvious really; green or brown for vegetables, a bright tablecloth for cakes, Hessian or bare wood for plants, pink or powder blue for baby clothes, black or red for shoes, etc. This all helps to give your stall an identity of its own and helps customers subconsciously gravitate towards the kind of products that they are particularly interested in.

You might be able to borrow some trestle tables from the local community centre, school or church hall. These are ideal as a longer than average table length is required for most stalls. Remember, however, that if you damage them you will have to pay and they may not be so helpful next time – use picnic cloth spring clips for holding on cloths instead of pins and nails. In extremis you can hire tables from marquee firms or some tool hire companies.

For a more sophisticated appearance try hanging a banner or flags flying between two seven foot poles nailed or tied firmly onto each end of the table or pushed into the ground. For a bottle stall or a stand selling lots of small items use risers (small blocks or shelves) to display your products to advantage. This can help a small display look more substantial especially as stock gets low towards the end of the day. Make risers from bricks or weighted boxes covered in wallpaper or cloth. Use velcro to stick packaged samples to a back board. Some stalls look better with a background and the sales person selling from the front. Embroidery, jewellery or other delicate items are enhanced by this treatment.

Remember to provide yourself and your helpers (at least two per stall) with something to sit on. Standing for four or more hours is tiring and you will know all about it the next day. You will also need a float of money and something to put it in. A couple of plastic boxes, one inside the other, will do. Put notes in the bottom box and they will not blow away or be obvious prey to the opportunist thief.

Pack an emergency bag the night before your event and include scissors, paper, pens, drawing pins, a staple gun, sticky tape, safety pins and dress-maker's pins (as appropriate) so you can make extra price labels if necessary. A couple of large round stones are often useful as paperweights. You might need a large piece of card to give your stall a title, such as 'Tombola', 'White Elephant', 'Guess the Weight of the Cake', etc. so that customers can see from a distance what you are providing. Include some plasters, sting relief cream or midge repellent if you are outside. A hat or coat can be very welcome if you are stuck behind a stall for hours at a time in hot sun or a keen wind. Remember, also, to make provision for refreshments for the helpers. Usually you will be able to get the odd cup of tea on site but you will be very popular with your neighbours if you pack a flask and a couple of mugs!

Make sure someone will be bringing a basic tool kit and a hammer and nails. Pack these too if not. I have never known an event yet that didn't need some kind of major repair made or some ingenious device erected just before opening time.

Where do I put my stall?

The most well organised fetes plan their site layout well in advance and erect a site plan at the entrance so that stall holders and visitors can see at a glance where everything is.

Sometimes you walk onto a site and know immediately who the coordinator is, and not because s/he is clasping a clip board or sitting behind a desk in the secretary's tent. No, s/he is the person running about all over the area trailing a tail of worried-looking people, all of whom are trying to get their questions answered. This should be avoided at all costs!

At a big show stall holders should be given the number of their pitch in advance and the site laid out carefully to allow vehicles behind each row. They will then be able drive straight onto the site, find their pitch and unload their products all without bothering anyone.

If it is you who is arranging where all the stalls should go there are some basic rules to follow, the most important being to keep your stalls close together and tightly packed. Just because Farmer Jones has lent you a 50 acre meadow doesn't mean that you have to use it all. It is much more attractive to have a busy, exciting corner than a whole field covered in lonely little stands requiring a Sherpa to guide you between them.

Take some tips from the big stores and supermarkets. Put a few bright, popular stands near the entrance to encourage people through the gate. A fruit raffle or preserve stall might be good. Then come the stall store-cupboard basics such as fishing for ducks, steady hand driving or a hoopla. You might see some speciality products next, appealing to a specific market. These could include more vigorous activities which keep the men happy such as a coconut shy, bowling for the pig, catch the rat or Aunt Sally.

You can develop a noisy, fairground area which you can follow on with a different group of stalls appealing to another type of customer, perhaps craft stands and handmade clothes. Do you see the idea? Keep the site in bunches of like with like, similar to a department store. People enjoy one activity and look around to repeat the experience immediately. If they don't like what they see they can move swiftly through that 'department' until they come to an area in which they feel more comfortable.

Save the refreshments to the end of the site. Encourage your visitors to walk past every available activity before you allow them to sit down and enjoy a cup of tea. The cake stalls go here too. Imagine resting your weary feet and tucking into the most delicious chocolate cake with some home-made lemonade. You lean back in your chair to enjoy the sunshine and your eyes rest on a table full of glorious cakes for sale. Would you be able resist buying one or two to take back home? The same goes for strawberry teas. Arrange to sell extra punnets of strawberries and raspberries next to where the teas are served.

If you have a car park, plan an outpost from your fete and sell your garden produce – flowers, vegetables and plants from here. Customers are more likely to buy these bulky and often heavy items if they can put them straight into their cars.

Where stalls are just part of a larger event arrange your selling area around the outside of an arena or at least confined to one area. Keep children's activities near the refreshments so that mums and dads can sit down whilst keeping an eye on little Tommy. You will sell extra cups of tea and especially the odd beer or two if the children are occupied. But remember that children must not be allowed in licensed areas.

It is kinder, but not such good business sense I agree, to keep sweet stands and candy floss away from the children's activities. I get really irritated when I am forced to buy sweets for my children to stop them from ruining a day out because the organisers have stuck temptation right under their noses. My opinion is that parents should be allowed to make their own decisions and I have actually gone home early because an event has been so overbalanced with sweets and junk food. The same goes for too many collectors rattling tins under your nose at every corner, however good the cause. The secret is to keep a good variety and moderation in everything.

And now for the ideas.

Handy hint

To give an incentive to stall holders to make their stalls look good run a competition for the 'best-dressed stall'. Ask a VIP to judge and present some rosettes towards the end of the afternoon.

LUCKY NUMBER

Equipment needs:

- An easel or table secured firmly on a slight slope rather like a designer's drawing board.
- A large sheet of paper or card marked out into numbered squares about 5 x 5cm large. Write the numbers in the upper half of the square only and leave the lower half blank. Or write them large but in a pale crayon so that you can write over.
- Biro and float.
- Prize or prizes.

How it works

This is a game of chance. Agree with a colleague which number is the 'lucky number' and make a note of it. Players pay for each chance. They choose a number and write their name (and telephone number if they are not planning to stay to the end) in the square. The winner is the person who wrote his or her name in the pre-agreed numbered square. Obviously the bigger the card, the more squares you can have available and the larger the proceeds.

GUESS THE NUMBER OF SWEETS

Equipment needs:

- Large clear jar.
- Known amount of sweets.
- Record pad and biro.
- Prize (which may be the sweets themselves) or cash.

How it works

This game is classified as a game of skill. It is very flexible as you can walk around with the jar or have a stall. You can adjust your product to suit the occasion, for instance at a model-makers exhibition you could fill your jar with nuts and bolts.

Your player makes a guess as to the quantity in the jar and you record their name and telephone number on the pad. The winner is the contestant who comes nearest to guessing the correct figure. In the case of more than one correct answer, the first guess is the winner.

GUESS THE WEIGHT OF THE CAKE

Equipment needs:

- Large cake wrapped tightly in greaseproof paper (a fruit cake is best).
- Record pad and biro.

How it works

This is a popular variation of the 'guess the sweets'. Remember to wrap the cake carefully because people will want to handle it. In this case the prize is the cake and the game works as above. Other variations can include guess the weight of the baby or the dog or anything else you care to think of.

DOOR KEYS

Equipment needs:

- A clear fronted box with a Yale lock and two keys.
- A large box filled with as many Yale keys as you can get hold of.
- Prize that fits in the box.

How it works

Charge 10p or 20p for a chance to pick a key and try the lock. The one who opens the box wins the prize. Those who are unlucky replace the key into the box for others to try their luck. The more keys you have the harder it is. Keep a spare key out so that you can open the box!

LUCKY DIP OR BRAN TUB

Equipment needs:

- Tub or barrel half full of bran, sawdust or straw. For a particularly revolting variation of this game you can mix the bran with water, wrap the prizes in plastic bags and have a SLIME DIP! (Don't use wallpaper paste as they frequently have toxic fungicides added.)
- Selection of small prizes.
- Wrapping paper (could be newspaper) and tape.

How it works

Everyone has played this game at some stage or another, but it is often a disappointment, both in terms of how much money is made and the suitability of the prizes. Very simply, you pay your money and have one dip into the bran tub. Whatever is retrieved is kept.

A slightly mean, but more profitable, variation on the original – remember everyone wins a prize – is as follows.

First, to ensure that prizes are suitable, arrange two tubs. These are separated into 'three years and under', and 'four years and over' or 'boys' and 'girls' (with a proviso that under 36 months is not recommended – you have to be very careful about toys for small children). Now comes the mean bit: put presents in two thirds of the boxes but leave one third empty, wrap them all up and bury them as usual. Make sure that your display indicates that you might not win anything such as 'Try your luck at winning a prize'.

Fix your charge carefully. Add together the value of all the prizes including wrapping, bran and tubs if you hired them, double it, then divide by the number of prizes. You will make double your money on each prize plus what you make on the empty prizes.

There are commercial companies who provide egg-shaped capsules containing prizes.

CATCH THE RAT

Equipment needs:

- Long, substantial tube. A 5ft length of guttering downpipe would do well.
- Wood and gutter brackets.
- Long handled mallet or croquet mallet (but it must be pretty beefy as it will come in for some punishment).
- Wooden ball or supply of plastic balls of a diameter to roll down the tube easily.
- Grass paint (whitewash) such as is used on sports pitches.

How to make your rat launcher

Fix the tube to a framework of wood using the gutter brackets allowing a 60 degree angle to the ground. The tube should leave a space between the end and the ground twice the diameter of the ball. The tube should be open at both ends. Paint an 18 inch diameter circle on the ground in front of the end of the tube. You can experiment to find the optimum place, depending on the degree of difficulty. Paint a rat's face on your ball, for added authenticity.

How it works

There is one attempt per charge or three for a discount. The 'catcher' grasps the mallet, looks at the circle and says go (or not if you wish to make it harder!). The operator releases the 'rat' at the top of the tube and the punter has to try to smash it before it leaves the circle when it appears at the bottom.

This looks so easy but it is really difficult to hit the rat in the circle. You need superhuman powers of concentration and reflexes. Those of us, and we all know someone, who will not be beaten try again and again and still come back for more serious humiliation!

Variation

Instead of using a ball you can use a bean bag with a painted face, string tail and ears to look like a rat. Fix your downpipe to the base board but leave 18 inches of wood below the opening. The 'catcher' has to thwack the rat against the board, using a baseball bat or similar, before it hits the ground.

FISHING FOR DUCKS

Equipment needs:

- 10 ducks carved from balsa wood, the bill is given a slight hook downwards, and painted.

- 20 × 6 inch nails.
- 2 × 'Fishing lines' made from bamboo, light string with a small brass ring instead of a hook. This must be able to fit over the duck's bills. One is a spare.
- Large tin bath, half filled with water.
- Waterproof felt pen.
- Stop watch.
- Prize or cash prize. (As this is a game of skill you are not restricted to non-cash prizes.)

How to make your ducks

Hammer two nails into the bottom of each duck to resemble legs. This will keep them upright in the water and provide some stability when being hooked. Write numbers, one to ten on the base of each duck.

How it works

Each 'fisherman' pays a fee for a designated length of time fishing. You will have to adjust the time according to how easy your ducks are to hook. Usually it is between 30 and 60 seconds.

Using tremendous skill, your customer must stand upright and holding the bottom end of the rod try to place the ring over the duck's bill. Having done this they then have to lift the duck completely out of the bath. They then try for another duck again and again until the time runs out.

The operator counts up the numbers displayed on each duck caught. Anyone reaching a score of 35 or more wins their money back or has a free go. These contestants have their names recorded and the highest score of the day wins a prize.

There are commercial hook-a-duck games that you can hire. Look in *The White Book* (see Publications at the back of the book) under 'fairground suppliers'.

TREASURE ISLAND

Equipment needs:

- Map of the treasure island. This can be as elaborate as you like. If you plan to use this idea regularly you could try making a relief map from oasis covered with fabric and painted. Otherwise a creative piece of art work attached to a pin-board is all that is needed. The easiest map of all is a map of your area and the treasure is positioned by coordinates. The nearest wins.
- A supply of 'flags' made from paper glued around long dressmakers' pins.
- Prize or cash.

How it works

This is a game of skill particularly if you include some very subtle clues. The contestant selects a spot on the map where she thinks the treasure might be buried (or sunk) and plants a flag marked with her name and telephone number. The winner is the flag coming closest to the prearranged 'x marks the spot'.

In the case of a flat map you could actually mark the X on the reverse of the map. For a more dramatic effect (especially if your event is indoors) you could write it on the map in security ink and borrow an ultra violet light to make it visible at the end of the day. Usually the correct answer is placed in a sealed envelope and pinned to the board to be opened at the end of the day in front of everyone.

FACE PAINTING

Equipment needs:

- Good quality face paints.
- Chairs for painter, subject and queue.

How it works

Every fete and fayre these days has a children's face painter, so little explanation is really needed. Usually the local community can direct you to the most creative person to run this activity and they will almost certainly own their own set of face paints.

BALL-IN-A-BUCKET

Equipment needs:

- Plywood sheet at least 18 inches tall by 3 feet wide.
- A length of 4 × 2 wood.
- Hammer and nails.
- Paint.
- Two plastic buckets, or large flower pots.
- 8 tennis balls.
- Grass paint or tape and pegs.
- Prizes.

How to make your bucket catcher

Cut two holes in the plywood so that the buckets fall through and rest tightly on their rims without going right through. Make struts to support the frame at a slight angle to the ground without pushing the buckets back through their holes.

Paint them a bright colour and display the instructions.

Peg the tape or paint a throwing line on the ground 10 or 12 feet from the buckets. You could have a children's line three feet from the buckets.

How it works

For one charge, the player receives four tennis balls which he tries to throw into one of the buckets whilst standing behind the line; if two stay in s/he wins a prize. You can expect two players about every two or three minutes with this popular game but you need to have prizes that are under a pound each to make it pay. Some people become quite skilled.

COCONUT SHY

Equipment needs:

- Traditionally seven coconut rings or pegs are used.
- 30 wooden balls.
- Strong netting and poles to make a safety net.
- A supply of coconuts.

How it works

Set your metal pegs firmly into the ground about two feet apart. Erect a safety net behind and to the sides of the throwing area. It will need to be at least seven or eight feet high to be safe. Arrange your coconuts on the top of the pegs.

Players are given four balls each to throw. The object is to dislodge a coconut off its peg onto the ground, thereby winning the coconut.

It is very hard to knock a coconut off so make sure that you don't buy too many coconuts. Reckon on losing one coconut about every ten minutes, less if you are not busy.

There are companies that rent or sell coconut shies; look in *The White Book* (see Publications at the back of the book) under 'fairground suppliers'.

KNOCK 'EM OFF

Equipment needs:

- Self-supporting shelf or table about ten feet long and five foot off the ground.
- 30 empty tins, painted in bright colours.
- 20 bean bags.
- Throwing line or tape.
- Backing board or catch net.

How it works

Set your shelf up and arrange the backdrop. Stand the cans in pyramids of six cans each. The player has four bean bags with which he tries to knock a complete pyramid off the shelf whilst standing behind a throwing line. Prizes should be kept to under a pound.

AUNT SALLY

Equipment needs:

- A wooden board painted and cut to resemble a face with a hole for an open mouth, just a squeak larger than the ball or bean bag.
- 4 tennis balls or bean bags or if you want to appeal to the dubious end of the market try wet sponges.
- Throwing tape or grass paint.

How it works

This game is very like ball-in-a-bucket. It was my favourite game at school fetes as we had an Aunt Sally painted to look like the headmistress. If you do the same for your school events I can guarantee your sideshow's queues will be the longest. The object of the game is to get two balls or bean bags through the mouth. Keep your prizes under a pound each.

BOTTLE FISHING

Equipment needs:

- 6 fishing rods as in Fishing for Ducks. The curtain rings must be about one inch in diameter.
- A supply of bottles of soft drinks.
- Round table.
- Whistle or bell.

How it works

This game is a race and there is a prize for every winner. Use about 20 bottles at a time and space them out all over the table. Six players circle the table and at the sound of the whistle or bell they start to 'fish' for a bottle. The object is to drop the curtain ring over the top of the bottle so that it rests flat on the neck. It is surprisingly difficult to achieve.

As soon as a contestant rings a bottle the operator sounds the bell and stops the game. The winner keeps the bottle.

Some bottle tops are just too big to accept the ring and the skill lies in judging which is suitable.

HOOPLA

Equipment needs:

- Round table.
- 20 × 6 inch wooden or plastic rings.
- 20 wooden blocks (the size depends if you want players to ring the block as well as the prize.)
- Supply of prizes. Bags of home-made sweets are often popular, soft drinks, toys, coins, etc.
- Tape or grass paint for a throwing line.

How it works

Arrange your prizes on top of each block and space the blocks carefully all over the table.

Players are given three rings with which to try to ring a prize whilst standing behind a throwing line. Some operators insist that the block is ringed also, but most people feel that to ring the prize conclusively is enough. You might want to have a supply of larger rings for small children to use.

WELLY THROWING

Equipment needs:

- A line painted on the grass and a clear space.
- Some Wellington boots.
- Some flags or markers.
- A very long tape measure.
- Something to record the names and throws.
- 2 or 3 prizes.

How it works

Just invite people to pay for the chance to throw a welly as far as they can. This is not as easy as it sounds! Watch out for those who throw backwards instead of forwards! Record how far people throw and give a prize to the furthest throws at the end of the day.

BOWLING FOR THE PIG

Equipment needs:

- Enough stop netting or canvas to line the bowling lane.
- 9 wooden skittles.
- 3 wooden bowling balls.
- A prize. Traditionally a live pig. But you could get a side of ready butchered, frozen pork donated or supply another substantial prize.

How it works

This is a game of challenge. There is only one winner at the end of the day but because the recently vanquished always want a turn to win again, the game is self-perpetuating and you take money on every turn.

A player has three balls with which to knock down all nine skittles. If he achieves a strike he may be challenged and if the new player has a strike he in turn may be challenged. If the new player doesn't manage to knock all the skittles over the original player remains the winner until he is challenged and vanquished.

The winner is the latest person to knock all nine skittles down at the end of the day. Play tends to pick up well at the end so you may have to display a finishing time.

PICK A STRAW

Equipment needs:

- 100 wide drinking straws.
- Large tray of sand.
- Raffle tickets.
- Selection of small prizes.

How it works

This idea works on the same principle as the bottle stall; you pay for a chance to win.

Roll up the raffle tickets and poke them into the straws. Stand the straws in the tray of sand. As with the bottle stall, if you reserve tickets that end in 5 or 0 for the prizes it makes finding them a great deal easier. You could add another variation by including a free turn for any ticket ending in a 3.

MATCHBOX HOUSE

Equipment needs:

- As many empty matchboxes as you can collect.
- Small brass paperclips – the old fashioned sort with two legs that poke through a hole in the paper and open out at the back.
- Glue and sticky-backed plastic (this always reminds me of *Blue Peter*!)
- Coloured paper or Fablon.
- A sheet of plywood.

How to make your house

Glue all the matchboxes together to form a large 'chest of drawers'. This is best made with large-size matchboxes. Get all your friends to buy and collect boxes of the same make. You will need at least a hundred boxes, more if you can manage it. You should have a single thickness of boxes, several high and several wide, where all the trays can slide back and forth.

Take all the trays out and poke an old fashioned paperclip through one end of each tray to make a handle. If you cannot buy the clips, a little knot of ribbon will do just as well.

Cover the edges, back and top of the 'chest' with coloured paper, glue it firmly in place and cover with the sticky-backed plastic (or you could use Fablon), then stick the plywood onto the back. The wood is not strictly necessary but makes for a much firmer structure and, if you allow it to stand proud of the top, gives you a neat area to paint a roof and display any message you might want such as the price or how much you can win.

Now replace all the trays and you should have a pile of boxes with sliders that can be pulled out forwards by the handles but cannot be pushed through to the back.

WARNING! This game is not strictly legal because this is a game of chance and you are playing for cash (see Chapter 6). However, as long as you keep the cash prizes small you should have no problems. You might like to adapt it so that you feel happy using it: there is something very appealing about matchboxes and children like playing the game for small items instead of cash.

How it works

Put coins into some of the boxes and leave at least half empty. Use about 5 one pound coins and increasing numbers of smaller denomination coins.

Customers pay for each turn (or you could have five for a pound or whatever). They are then allowed to pull out a tray and keep the coin that they may or may not find inside.

This game is particularly good as, if you budget properly, you can never make a loss and you can continuously replenish your boxes, though not too often and in strict secrecy, so that your game never runs out.

SCRATCH CARDS

Equipment needs:

- Collection of scratch cards.
- Cash prizes.

How it works

Customers buy a card and follow instructions printed on the cards by scratching off a variety of silver panels. If the customer reveals a particular combination or specific figure, symbol, etc. they win a prize.

Prizes are either given out on the spot or they have to write to the game company for them, depending on the type of card.

Where to get the cards

There are a variety of companies that devise the games and print the cards. You know in advance how much money you will make for your charity, providing you sell all your cards.

Some games arrive with the prize cards separated from the dud cards. It is intended that the operator feeds them into the game at intervals to make the game more attractive. In my opinion this is wide open to abuse and accusation. Unscrupulous operators have been known to withhold all the big prize cards so that they do not have to pay out at all. One very unfortunate fundraiser reported to me that she knew of an even crueller trick. At large events it is not unusual to find that more than one of these scratch card games are in action. Allegedly the operator of one game bought a ticket for another on the same site and as he did so, using sleight of hand, he slipped all his prize cards into the rival box. So be warned.

Other games arrive with all the cards ready shuffled; this seems to me to be a much fairer way of running the game, although there are those who wish that they knew which box held the big prize cards. It would help not to have the main prizes won in the first ten minutes of any event, which can, and does, happen.

Finally, you must remember that you will have to go to every event with a large amount of cash ready to pay out in prizes if necessary. You might choose to use cheques for better security but you need to know that your bank balance is healthy. If you do not manage to sell all your cards you could be quite seriously out of pocket, what with the cost of the game in the first place (anything between £40 and £100) and the prizes.

However, for all these warnings, the games do work, are popular and I know several experienced fundraisers who use them regularly because they get results.

PRODUCE AND FOOD STALLS

You need to read up on the information given in Chapter 11 on the legislation surrounding the sale of food. An overview of your responsibilities is given below.

Over the last few years legislation over what may or may not be sold in the way of foodstuffs has been tightened considerably. Many people think that because their event is very small, not for profit or 'only' for charity or that because food is given away and not sold that the law does not apply to them. If only that were true. But unfortunately the bacteria that cause food poisoning are no judge of charity and salmonella contracted at a community barbecue can be just as fatal as when contracted in a large restaurant.

However, since the Food Safety Act 1990 was published there have been a few changes and these will affect charitable organisations. In the main, legislation is now less prescriptive and the emphasis has been shifted to identify potential risks as a matter of priority and to look at specific contravention as a secondary and less important role.

Inspection 'ratings' have also been changed and village halls, community centres and the like have a lower priority for inspection under the new code, which should make running occasional events a little less worrying. There is also the 'due diligence' defence which has had an important precedent set. Briefly if you are found to contravene the law but that you can show that you acted in a sensible and responsible way and that all reasonable precautions were taken the Courts are likely to take a realistic approach.

It is probably true to say that the local authority is less likely to prosecute, in the event of a serious contravention, quite so severely at a charity event than if you were a multi-million pound burger conglomerate, especially if it can see that you have tried to behave in a responsible manner. But you must make yourselves aware of the Food Safety Act and the Food safety Regulations (General Food Hygiene) 1995 and check where they apply to you and your event. If you use your own kitchen regularly to cook produce for stalls you may have to have your premises registered and inspected. Your district environmental health officer should be able to advise you on specific details for your event.

In general, tea, coffee, squash or drinks sold in bottles or cans, jams, pickles and uncooked fruit are all exempt, as are wrapped biscuits, crisps and sweets, bread and cakes that do not contain fresh cream. Areas where you must be especially careful are products containing the following:

- ice cream
- dairy products
- meat and cooked meat
- fish and shell fish
- pastries or cakes containing fresh cream
- egg dishes
- cooked rice or other pulses.

These are classified as high risk foods and anybody handling these or other unwrapped foods is advised to obtain at least six weeks training though the local authority for which a Food Hygiene Certificate will be awarded.

If you have set your heart on having food or home-made produce available (and it is a poor event that is all food for the soul and none for the stomach) then adapt the advice given on Event 2: Barbecue party and Event 8: Cream teas to fit the size and style of your own event.

Consider theming your stall, either to suit the event, or to suit yourselves. A Victorian cake stall, with everyone dressed in Victorian clothes makes a very pretty scene, or medieval costumes for helpers at a hog-roast.

OTHER SALES STALLS

Whether your stall is selling books, records, Christmas goods, pottery, cards and stationery, dried flowers or handmade quilts you still need to have some sort of pricing system and probably a record of what you have sold during the event. And you need to have thought it through before you arrive at the fete.

As with the supermarket analogy at the beginning of this chapter, spend some time looking at professional retail shops to discover which lines sell well, make a note of display ideas or whether you should be introducing special offers.

What do people like to buy?

With all produce and goods stalls you will soon discover that some goods do better in some areas than others. It is only with experience that you will begin to get a feel for the popular items.

In Norfolk, I know that in coastal areas people are looking for little presents, toys and sweets. Move inland into the countryside and children's clothes, plants and home-made produce go down well.

In the cities and towns, you can be onto a winner with jumble or a craft and handiwork stall . Your area might well be different so learn as you go, but don't be disappointed if your first event doesn't go quite the way you hoped.

Books and records

Books and records are best sold from cardboard boxes or bread crates. Keep them loosely packed so that customers can flick through without muddling everything up. It is often a good idea to divide your boxes according to price rather than subject or genre unless you are a specialist, the exception being children's books which should be kept separate. Don't forget to have a couple of boxes with books at 10p–20p each. Place one at either end of your stall to encourage people to move nearer and browse. These are equivalent to the dump bins that you see placed near entrances of big stores in the high street.

Quilts, lace and dried flowers

Delicate fabrics or dried flowers are best kept indoors as wind can do a lot of damage in a very short time. Use the display techniques as described at the beginning of Event 24 and consider pinning down samples so that you keep the rest of your stock clean.

If you have a local lace-making club, suggest that they bring some unfinished work and provide a demonstration in front of a handicraft stall. You don't have to restrict your sales to lace but it makes a good focal point for the customers. You might be able to buy some basic kits from a wholesaler, which will be very popular given a little encouragement from your demonstrator.

Off-cuts

If you anticipate a good crowd including dads and DIY enthusiasts (school fetes are good for this stall) have a timber sale. Gather all the off-cuts that you can from friends and neighbours. Ask local builders or wood merchants to make donations. Put your stall near the car park so that people can get their purchases home easily or you could offer a delivery service.

Rings and things

Jewellery works well, but you will never be able to compete with the high street so keep your stall either very cheap and cheerful or unique craft work.

Paper goods

Cards and stationery goods are the one category where you should not restrict the price. For some reason, the bigger and more special the cards, the more popular they are, despite a high price tag. Local scenes, paintings on silk, pressed flowers or hand-printed cards will all swell your funds. Look in the *Yellow Pages* for wholesalers or craft workers who will be delighted to sell you cards in large quantities.

If you are very ambitious or know a good artist, you could commission three or four exclusive designs and get them printed. But you will be liable for a quite considerable outlay before you see your money back. So make very sure of your market first.

Clothes

Knitwear and handmade clothes can both be money spinners, but aim for the youngster's market first. Adults are more fussy about a good fit. Children's clothes are cheaper and quicker to make too.

Possible problems

Strictly speaking those stalls or games that are games of chance are governed by the rules of the Lotteries and Amusements Act 1976 and the National Lottery Act 1993. Under these Acts you must not offer cash prizes. Of course the matchbox house does just this. But is it a game of chance or skill? Perhaps you could get round this one by having the matchboxes unattached. Players could then pick them up and attempt to guess, by weighing them, how much the contain. If they are correct they keep the contents. Instead of cash fill them with sweets or pocket money presents.

> **Handy hint**
> Look for items that can be sold for pocket money prices − all under a pound − these are often available already attractively packaged in display trays from a wholesaler.

Plus . . . and minus:

- Great way to use up jumble, extra produce and unwanted presents.
- Easy to keep adding on to an existing event.
- Often needs very little start-up costs.
- Not difficult to organise.
- Lots of attractive stalls can make an event in itself.
- Rarely need more than two people to run each stall.

- Might need to hire special equipment to run a side show, but usually it can be made at home.
- Food stalls are subject to Food Safety regulations.
- Bottle stalls and other games of chance are restricted by the terms of lotteries legislation

EVENT 25 TROLLEY DASH

Winning raffle prize is free groceries

Operating requirements: Coordinator and treasurer. Volunteers to sell tickets.

Equipment needs: 500 tickets with stubs.

Lead time: 8 weeks.

Initial cost: £35 for registration under the Lotteries Act. Printing perforated draw tickets should cost about £40 and you will have advertising costs, allow another £50–£100, depending on how large you expect your draw to be. You may have to pay for the food which will come out of the proceeds.

Suitable for: Almost anything.

Expected return: A typical example might be 500 tickets for £1.00 each = £500, less about £130 worth of goods and £40 for tickets gives you a balance of £330. This is just a small draw but if you set your sights high and you allow enough time to sell tickets your only restriction is the £10,000 limit set by law. Sometimes the store donates the food, but you can't bank on it.

What's in it for contributors: The chance of a big value prize that they have control over. i.e. it is their skill and speed that dictates the value of the prize.

Frequency: You are limited by the policy of your local superstores and by the terms of the Lotteries Act, see below.

Special requirements: This is a game of chance open to the public and as such is covered by the Lotteries and Amusements Act 1976/National Lottery Act 1993. The event is likely to be classified as a 'society or social' lottery (see Chapter 6) and registration is compulsory.

How does it work?

Tickets are sold as in a raffle. The prize is a one-minute dash around a consenting superstore piling as much into your trolley as you can. It really plays on people's greed, this one!

How do we get started?

First, you need to find a willing supermarket manager. Usually the dash takes place just after closing time so that the store is empty of customers. Make sure that he is happy for you to advertise the dash and your charity around the store. Decide on a date for the draw and work backwards to establish your timescale.

You will need to apply for registration with your local authority at least four weeks before you put your tickets on sale. This will cost you £35 for the first year and £17.50 annual renewal (correct for 2003).

If your group plan to hold several lotteries you will still only have to register once but you must hold no more than 52 in any year with a week between each one. Total proceeds must not exceed £20,000, before registering with the Gaming Board, and the largest prize until recently could not have a value in excess of £2,000; however the new National Lottery Act 1993 has now raised this to £25,000 or 10 per cent of the proceeds, whichever is the higher.

Limits on the administration expenses are provided by statute and you need to check this against your budget. The promoter of the lottery must be a member of the society (charity) and every ticket should detail the name of the society and the name and address of the promoter. Tickets must also show the price of the ticket which must not exceed £2.00. Your local authority licensing department will be able to advise and help you with any problems (see Chapter 6 for more details).

Are there any exemptions?

Yes. Competitions are exempt from registration. Amazingly enough, even when there is a combination of luck and skill it is still classified as a competition.

So, hold your draw; but include a question of skill on the draw tickets. Something like 'Where was the first supermarket store opened?' or a multiple choice question such as 'How many tins of beans are sold in the UK every day? a, 10,000; b, 100,000 or c, 1 million'. The first correct entry drawn is the winner.

This is my and my friendly solicitor's interpretation of the law; but as with all legal matters, if in doubt, check it out. On the other hand £35 and a few weeks wait while the licence is sorted is no great hardship so you might prefer to run your dash in the conventional manner and get registered.

How do we sell tickets?

Have your tickets made up in books of 20 and give books to volunteers to sell tickets for you at least four weeks before the dash. There should also be a permanent place to buy tickets from within the store itself.

Log the ticket numbers against each sales person and collect the money regularly to deposit in a separate bank or building society account. Make sure all stubs carry the name and address of the person who bought each individual number. This is most important as it would be impossible for everyone who bought a ticket to be present at the draw.

Start advertising a week or two before the tickets go on sale, to build up interest, using posters in and around the store. Give leaflets to the check-out staff to hand to each customer and send a press release to the local media and to the charity's local newsletter, if they have one. The store itself will often include the dash in its own advertising, as it will encourage people to come to the store to buy a ticket and hopefully stock up on a few items as well.

How do we organise the draw?

Arrange for the draw to be made by a VIP, either someone from the store itself or the benefiting charity. If you set up some sort of platform with bunting or have a band playing outside the store for half an hour or so before the draw you may well make a fair quantity of last minute sales.

Don't forget to inform the Police beforehand. They may have traffic reasons or know of conflicting events that might persuade you to be indoors or plan the draw for another day.

Use a 'roll-up man' with a megaphone to generate a feeling of urgency and a good audience. He can shout something like 'Only 15 minutes left to buy your tickets for the fabulous, one minute, trolley dash to be held here, at (name of store) at precisely 5.00pm next Monday' or 'Just one pound, yes, one pound, for your chance to collect over a hundred pounds worth of groceries in one minute'.

Make an occasion of the draw and give the press (which you will have invited, of course) some good 'photo-opportunities' for the local paper so that they have an interesting trailer for the dash.

Borrow or hire or make a spinning barrel or tombola drum. Place the ticket stubs in it in advance so that all the VIP has to do is spin the drum and draw the winning ticket.

How do we organise the actual dash?

You can set a date for the dash beforehand or you can wait until the draw to set the date. If your draw is a small one it would be kinder to leave setting a date until you are sure that your winner will be able to attend. If you need to fix a date you will need to work out whether you will accept a substitute 'dasher' if the winner cannot be present or if you will draw a second winner.

Send invitations to all you think might be interested. Local journalists, local radio, representatives of the benefiting charity or group will all want to know in advance who is the winner. Don't forget a senior manager from the superstore's headquarters as well as the winner's family and friends.

Allow the winner to choose the trolley that s/he wants to use and let them decide where they want to start in the store. Wines, spirits and cigarettes are usually not included in the dash. Set the clock and ask someone special to start the run.

Arrange a photograph for the local newspaper of the exhausted winner with the pile of goods and run them through the check-out immediately to announce how much was won.

You might want to provide a glass of wine and some nibbles or perhaps the store might provide some refreshment if they are not contributing the goods.

The store may donate all the items in the trolley, they may donate the first £100 worth of goods out of their community budget or they may prefer to accept payment, but then donate the full amount to another charity of their choice. Make sure that they get some publicity out of their generosity also.

What happens afterwards?

Make sure that the store is sent a thank you letter along with anyone special that might have been involved.

Plus ... and minus:

- Exciting event that doesn't take much organisation.
- No venue hire.
- Does not need many helpers other than volunteers to sell tickets.
- Several media angles.
- The supermarket will often donate the prize.

- Might have trouble persuading managers to allow use of their store. Point out that they will take over £100 on the dash and there are many advertising opportunities.
- Not suitable for young children, the elderly, or disabled people.
- Have to be prepared to spend over £100 for the dash whether or not you sell the tickets.

EVENT 26 WISHING WELL
Exploitation of a desire to throw money into water

Operating requirements: Coordinator, treasurer. Three or four helpers.

Equipment needs: Water feature (see below for how to obtain).

Lead time: 1 month.

Initial cost: Very little although you may have to pay for electricity.

Suitable for: All charities. Needs to be situated in secure arcade, public building, large store or shopping mall.

Expected return: Entirely depends on quantity or generosity of passers-by.

What's in it for contributors: Satisfaction of a strange English desire to drop money into water. And, less cynically, something attractive and unusual to look at.

Frequency: Not worth doing for less than two weeks or so. A month would be ideal.

Special requirements: Power supply and secure venue.

How does it work?

This is not strictly a wishing well but I think the principle works just as effectively using a fountain or pool.

How many times have you walked past a fountain in a city square or a well at a heritage centre and seen people throwing money into it? I don't know why they do it, but they do. In droves. And that's without any invitation or sign. During 1992 the Friends of Norwich Castle Museum recovered £1,705 in small change from the well in the keep, so it is a popular occupation! How much more is to be made if you consciously encourage people to part with their spare cash?

This idea brings the well, or the fountain, to the people. They drop their money in, you clear it out regularly and distribute it to your charity causes. Simple isn't it?

How do we get started?

First decide on your venue. Try to find a convenient existing fountain or pool if you possibly can. Milton Keynes already has its own fountains and pools as do many other modern shopping centres, so perhaps you might obtain the use of something along these lines.

However, if you have a great venue but no 'wishing well' it is not impossible to provide your own. Beg or borrow a self-contained water feature (the bigger the better) from a garden centre or garden furniture manufacturer. They get a month's worth of free advertising from this idea so they don't have to be totally altruistic and if you can offer a really spectacular venue you should have no problems borrowing something suitably eye catching.

You won't need a water supply as most water features are self sufficient: the water is pumped round and round and once you have filled it you need only the occasional top-up. However, you will need an electrical supply if you include a fountain, to power the pump. Make sure that your supply is brought in safely. If you are indoors you should be able to position your fountain so as to prevent people tripping over the cable. An arcade might present more of a problem and you may have to consider 'flying' the cable across the rafters and dropping it down beside the feature. Other malls may have power points strategically placed at floor level perhaps to run temporary lights at Christmas.

Ideally your water area should be wide enough to see lots of coins but deep enough to discourage theft unless thieves are determined enough to actually climb in and get their trousers wet. By that time you are in a position of superiority and you can hold their heads under long enough to get your money back! I think that might be classified as assault ... but you get the gist.

What if you don't have a convenient, secure shopping mall available? A large museum might be helpful or perhaps you could persuade the owners of a theme park to let you use their entrance. I've also seen this idea work very successfully in the main entrance to a large department store or maybe a busy train station might be the answer. Think big, and use an area that expects hundreds of visitors a day.

Do we need to advertise?

You are relying on passing trade to contribute to your cause. People are not going to go more than a few yards out of their way to throw money away. You have about five seconds to make an impact, which is about what it takes for someone to walk past and glance in your direction. You need to have immediate appeal and get your message across in just a few words.

Have a couple of signs professionally sign-painted displaying something like 'Help Sick Children (name of charity) Wishing Well – Make a Wish!' Include any sponsors' names prominently.

You can use a couple of easels to show your signs off to good advantage and allow the sponsorship companies (the supplier of the water feature, the owners of the arcade, and the shop supplying the electricity, for instance) a leaflet stand to advertise goods and services.

You don't need to print posters or pay for advertisements. As with almost any fundraising idea, you do need to exploit any public relations potential and send properly prepared press releases out. Follow up all releases with a telephone call to invite photographs or suggest an interview and let the journalists know that you will come back to them at the end of the appeal with the amount raised.

Do we need to provide supervision?

My feeling is not, or at least not all the time. If your venue is fairly well supervised by staff members in nearby shops or has security cameras you may be able to visit only occasionally, perhaps at lunch time when the area is most popular or later in the afternoon when your haul is at its most vulnerable. You will be the best judge of safety at your venue, but in any case you can change your plans as the days go on. There is bound to be the odd person who thinks they will just help themselves to some cash, but in my experience most potential thieves don't think it is worth getting wet for some loose change.

Make sure that the appropriate people know who will be collecting the money at the end of each day. You don't want to have to bail a bona fide charity helper out of prison.

Whilst you won't need a patrol, if you have borrowed your water feature you will have to make sure that it is secure each evening. All electricity should be switched off and you must be able to assure the owners that their precious fountain won't go walkabout. There are serious-minded criminals about who are prepared to drive trucks into town centres at night for the sole purpose of removing concrete planters, cast iron litter bins and benches. It is important, for this reason, that you choose a venue that is locked up at night. Check that any insurance isn't invalidated by your presence and that you have any necessary cover for yourselves.

What happens at the end?

You must thank every one involved, of course. Write letters and let them know how much was raised. If you sense that they were pleased with their involvement, make a tentative suggestion that you might work together again in the future, but avoid the temptation to pin them down at this stage.

Ensure that all equipment goes back clean and in good condition and be there personally when they come to collect it.

Handy hint

You could use the opportunity to mount a small exhibition for a few days to show how previous funds have been used. Specify a particular project and a target figure to be raised at this appeal. People are more prepared to give to something particular rather than to a general charitable cause.

Plus... and minus:

- No committee or lengthy organisation needed.
- Very little outlay or advertising needed.
- Can run for several weeks with little supervision.

- Relies on finding just the right venue and perhaps persuading someone to lend you a valuable piece of equipment.
- Relies on a regular commitment from someone to empty, count and bank money collected.
- Not suitable for children's involvement, although children may number amongst your most generous contributors.

TWENTY-SIX QUICK AND EASY IDEAS

Organising full-scale fundraising events can be very hard work and time consuming. Such commitment is not for everyone.

Maybe you have had a hand in several large scale events and you feel it is time you took a back seat, or perhaps your family has got to 'that stage' – all under five – and is draining you of the last dregs of energy and opportunity. Sometimes we still feel we would like to be involved and are committed to a particular cause but need to take a more low key approach. The following ideas are for you.

You are never going to make thousands of pounds in a couple of weeks but you will be able to provide a small but valuable and steady flow of funds to your cause and perhaps gain a little public awareness each time someone cares to ask what it is all about. Don't feel guilty about not always volunteering for the major role on a committee or taking on the same event, just because it is expected. You can pick one or two of the ideas below and explain that you will still be contributing.

Appeals

Your contribution can be by using a letter, a press advertisement or a leaflet. Do as much or as little as you can manage but do work out a strategy first; you need every message to leave its mark.

Babysitting

Perhaps you could let it be known that you are available to babysit every Friday or every second Tuesday of the month, or whatever. Charge a realistic fee and donate the proceeds.

Bulb growing

Good to run this idea through a club, society or school. Charge to enter, perhaps a garden centre would donate the bulbs, if not they are supplied by the competitors. The tallest plant by a certain day wins a prize. Swell funds by sponsoring the plants by the centimetre.

Coffee morning

Hold an 'open-house' for members of your community. Charge for coffee and biscuits or cake. Ask people to donate cakes or if you have a large party you might need to take expenditure from the proceeds.

Collection box

Keep a collection box in your house by the front door.

Double or nothing

Give a sum of money to members of a club to double (or more) within a certain time. £1 to buy a packet of seeds to grow £5 worth of vegetables. £3 to buy wool for a child's jumper to sell at £5 and so on.

Dressing-up for sale

Children love dressing-up in Mum's old clothes. Ask a group of Mums to a bring and buy party to fill the dressing-up boxes with loopy clothes and hats.

Empties

There are not so many bottles with 'money-back' on them any more but pubs are often glad to have bottles back. Recycling cans and aluminium bottletops can bring in money and there are companies that still collect postage stamps.

Foreign stamps

Have a sale of duplicates in your house or at a club.

Friends club

People pay a subscription to belong to an official group associated with your organisation. They also pledge to fundraise in turn.

Gardening

Make it known that you are available to help in the garden for a couple of hours each week for two months. Charge a reasonable rate and donate all or part of the proceeds.

Go-karting

Take a minibus full of keen karters to one of the local centres that you will find in your *Yellow Pages*. Ask if you can qualify for a group discount and explain that

TRIED AND TESTED IDEAS

you are a charitable organisation. You might get some coverage in the local newspaper for the Kart company, especially if you take a 'personality'. Charge individuals the full price and use the profit. This idea can be used for all sorts of activities: sailing, riding, roller skating, etc.

Hitchin' box

Put a collection box in the car for passengers to make their contributions. Make sure that you don't leave it in view when you park your car.

Homemade goods

Organise a bring and buy sale in your front room or garden of cakes, jams, sweets, vegetables, etc.

Lawn mowing race

Great idea if you need a community area's grass cut. You save money in not paying a contractor and you can either sponsor mowers or charge an entry to compete.

Lecture service

If you are an expert in your field or have something interesting to talk about, offer your services for charity as a speaker.

Newspaper collection

Not confined to newspapers. Offer to collect people's recyclables for a small fee. Make it known that you will be calling in a particular area on a certain day.

Office appeal

It is surprising how much can be raised in just one day if you walk a collecting box around a large office or factory. Make sure you obtain permission to do so. Don't forget the canteens.

Organise an outing

Take a group on a nature walk or a picnic, they pay to take part of course.

Photo flash

If you are a dab hand with a camera, offer to take pictures at a the school fete or local street procession. Take orders for pictures at a coffee morning and profits after your expenses can go to your charity. Digital cameras are perfect for this.

Plant sale

Offer plants or cuttings for sale in your garden to any visitors or hold a bring and buy plant party.

Roadside sale

If you have a productive garden you might be prepared to run a stall for excess produce. Leave the goods bundled or bagged into small amounts and provide an honesty box. You might need a street trading permission if your stall is on the pavement, though not if it is within your garden.

Universal helping hands

A group of people who are willing to help anybody out in the locality for money. You need to have a central number to ring and someone to coordinate the helpers.

Visit a month

A regular collection from the homes of people who have pledged to give so much over a specified period of time.

Window cleaning

People usually have a regular external window cleaner but often don't get around to doing the insides. A dependable and trusted local person to see to the interiors would be a great help to many folks.

Xmas draw

Organise a special Christmas raffle to be drawn at a local shop on Christmas Eve. You will need to register with the local authority (see Chapter 6, under lottery registration).

PART TWO

PLANNING

4

Getting started

This chapter will cover the following topics:
- ▸ The role of a committee
- ▸ Committee meetings
- ▸ The role of a constitution
- ▸ Talking to your local authorities
- ▸ The role of the police
- ▸ Events requiring police permission
- ▸ Booking professional acts.

The role of a committee

I am often tempted to operate as a 'one man band', but even if you have unlimited experience, spare time and resources to set the event up, it is almost impossible to organise the day itself with only one person. You cannot be in two or more places at once or carry the equipment by yourself. You need helpers, and thus in practice you do need a committee, whether it be an informal meeting of two or a formal meeting of ten people.

Committees can prove unwieldy, particularly where members are more interested in an alternative social occasion than getting things done. However, if you have a committee that operates efficiently and is made up of people with different but complementary skills you will be relieved of much of the time-consuming but necessary background work. You will then have the time to get to grips with the real nitty-gritty such as how you are going to make your site secure if you are selling tickets, or how many times mobile WCs will need emptying. Keep a good overview of the progress of the project without getting bogged down by details.

Make the size of the committee appropriate to the event planned or, if you already have a charitable or group committee, elect a few people onto a working committee so that you have a more streamlined group focused on one event. If your event is very small or you really can't get to grips with the idea of working with a group of other people do, at the very least, consider appointing a cashier or treasurer as a second person to check your float, balance or banking. You never want to be put in the position of having the finger of doubt pointed at you even if you know you are absolutely meticulous and entirely innocent.

For larger programmes or neighbourhood events involving several strata of the community, it is probably to your advantage to form a committee and possibly even agree on a constitution, especially if the event is to become an annual tradition.

Committee members

Committees that I have worked with have included people from all walks of life and profession but each with a separate skill or interest in a unique area: business people, school teachers, local politicians, artists or people with a burning interest in the main theme of the event.

If you are working within an organisation such as the WI or a hobbies club you will be able to draw on an established committee structure with members already in place. If you have an existing committee with a lot of 'dead wood' use this as an opportunity to form an executive committee and make sure that you are not carrying members who like to argue and debate but who are not prepared to get their hands dirty. Committees must be run efficiently and professionally and have members who are wholeheartedly committed to the event.

Even if one person does more than one job, on every committee you will need:

- a chairperson;
- a secretary;
- a treasurer.

Don't assume that the chief organiser has to be the person chairing the meetings. Often it is an advantage to take a democratic decision within the meeting because then nobody can feel railroaded. Whoever is chosen as chairperson (and it is probably you since you are reading this book!) make sure they get copies of every communication – even notes of telephone conversations can be important.

The chairperson must have an overview of the whole operation if it is not to become chaotic – they might need to take over in an emergency. Good communications are vital for the smooth running of any event but equally it should be made clear that the chairperson is only keeping a watching brief over other people's patches and that they will only interfere if invited or if the rest of the event may be jeopardised.

In addition to these permanent roles you will need people to take on special responsibilities which will change for every event. These might include:

154

- advertising and marketing;
- sponsorship and prizes;
- programmes;
- volunteers;
- equipment;
- health and safety;
- music and bands;
- catering;
- box office, etc.;
- security.

You may also need professional help in the way of specially invited members who may or may not be co-opted onto the core committee. These could be:

- a police representative;
- a local politician;
- a member of the chamber of commerce, etc.

Such people are there to advise; they should not be expected to make fundamental decisions, nor do they have the right to vote.

Presidents, or even a series of vice presidents, are sometimes appointed before very large or important events. These usually take the form of a 'figurehead' post filled by a well-known local or national 'name' to add credibility to the event and weight to its stationery and advertisements.

Sponsorship members

Many events, especially those at the larger end of the scale are sponsored by one organisation or company. It is politic to invite a representative (if they haven't already insisted on one) to be on the committee or at least act as an observer to ensure that their generous donation is not spent on any nasty surprises. Often they may only want to see the minutes of each meeting but even if they are not interested in being active members they may welcome an invitation for a senior member of the sponsoring organisation to be a vice president on the event committee.

Committee meetings

How often?

How often do all these people have to meet? And how will you find a date to suit all of them every time?

In my experience meetings need not be held more frequently than once a month and this gives you the obvious chance to select say, every last Tuesday or the 21st of each month. This way members can mark their diaries well in advance and try to avoid other engagements. This is pretty elementary stuff, I know, but I am amazed at the number of committees who arrange the next meeting at the one just prior.

The date of the final meeting that you will need just before the Big Day will obviously not follow the monthly pattern and all committee members must be aware of it. This meeting should take place no more than a week before the event and at it you should run through everyone's duties on site, hand out radios and chargers (if you have decided on them over mobile telephones) and iron out any last minute problems that may present themselves. Make sure that everyone is aware of alternative arrangements if circumstances change and who to call on if things start to go pear shaped.

How long?

I can't stand long meetings and usually manage to keep the agenda to within an hour – but do be prepared to sit through a lot of discussion and hear many different points of view if it is a new event. The democratic process is seldom swift and is as good a reason as any for keeping your committee as compact as possible.

The role of a constitution

Do you need a constitution? A constitution is simply an agreement documenting the aims, policies and focus of the group forming the committee. It does not have to be complicated or lengthy. One side of A4 can encompass your agreement and makes it a legal requirement. Your constitution may, for instance, state that you should not be able to make any decisions as any meeting at which there are fewer than three members.

A constitution is a valuable way of informing new members of the aims of the committee. It is obligatory to have one if you wish to a apply for charity registration.

In general the simpler you make your constitution the better. If you are interested in writing a constitution there are publications which can assist you in more detail listed (under Publications) at the back of this book.

> **Key points:**
>
> - Decide if your event warrants a full committee or if you can manage with two or three central organisers.
> - Choose a core committee and vote for a chairperson.
> - Decide if you need more people to make up a non-executive committee but try to keep your group compact.
> - Agree on the dates for regular meetings.
> - Discuss the need for a constitution.

Talking to local authorities

It is always a good idea to inform your local authority of public events, however small they are, and even if you are to use a private building or land. You can get access to the listings and entries in the tourist guides and you might well feel you are eligible for a small community grant if you fulfil the council's criteria (see Chapter 5).

Your local authority may also have equipment available for hire or even for free. Actually I say 'free', but as you no doubt have been told before, 'There is no such thing as a free lunch'. However you might find that the services demanded in return aren't too onerous: a mention on the publicity here, a word in the programme there or a space to put an information stand.

The most useful person to contact if you are doing anything other than the strictly keep-it-in-the-back-garden type of event, is the council promotions officer (given a variety of titles from events promoter, leisure officer, recreation manager, community affairs officer etc.). To find the right person, ring the central administration office of your local council. Ask for the public events organiser and if asked 'which department?' suggest leisure, recreation, tourism or amenities. They will find the right person from that description.

Once again, I apologise if I appear to be starting at absolute basics here, but local government departments can be the stuff of nightmares if you don't know exactly what you want. It is bound to be on the day that you telephone that the person on the information desk is half way through their first day.

Having got hold of the right officer, suggest a meeting and allow an hour to visit the department to explain what it is that you want to do, let the officer make suggestions and advise how they can assist.

> **Checkpoint**
>
> Try not to go armed with a list of demands – remember that with hundreds of organisations all wanting help it is tempting for the local authority office to pick the easy options.

Using council land

If you plan to use council land then this must be booked in advance, even up to a year in advance for popular days, and all sorts of constraints may be placed on you. Bye-laws may exist to keep footpaths open, or there may be limitations imposed on selling food, for instance you may only be able to sell tea in plastic cups and wrapped foods such as sweets and biscuits. The hire fee may be waived for a charitable event, but you could just as easily find yourself being required to pay many hundreds of pounds for a central site.

Read your contract carefully before you sign it. You may be planning a circus event but your local council may have a policy of no performing animals; or a dinner dance to see in the New Year, and the venue's licence runs out at 11.30pm due to noise to surrounding buildings. Make sure it is the right venue for your event (see Chapter 2.)

If you are happy with the contract keep a copy and return one, signed and dated. If you have a committee it might be an idea to let the other members take a look at the contract at the next meeting before signing; someone else might see a problem that you have overlooked. Once the contract is signed there is no going back and usually there will be a fairly hefty non-returnable deposit also. And you must adhere to the rules. If you need to submit the names of traders 28 days in advance or produce a copy of your insurance certificate two months in advance, you really have to do it. Try not to let them have to chase you, however busy you are; it makes for a strained relationship and may jeopardise future plans. If you really can't do something by the time stated, let your contact know as soon as possible and ask for an extended date.

The officer responsible for arrangements concerning council land may wish to be sent minutes, or sit on the committee. It is therefore a good idea to make the offer. As the time of the show approaches, send a letter to the head of department thanking him/her for the officer's time and enclosing a few tickets or a car park pass as a token of appreciation. You will obviously be doing the same for all those offering help such as sponsors or donators of prizes, and so on. You will appreciate that this thoughtfulness can help oil the bureaucratic cogs and may work wonders when you want to repeat the event next year! On the other hand, don't put council officers in the embarrassing situation of having to refuse a gift because it is too generous and might be construed as a bribe, however well meant.

National Trust, heritage land and reserves

Not all land is private or government owned, of course. Large areas of land to which the public has access are administered by charities and trusts. Permission to hold events on these pieces of land is sometimes granted by the controlling bodies but due deference must be given to their requests. Applications should be made well in advance to the local relevant organisation; they will, almost certainly, take it to their headquarters for a decision so don't expect to hear whether you have been successful for several weeks.

The role of the police

I have always had a good working relationship with the police and I consider it a courtesy to inform them of any event where over 75 to 100 visitors are expected. You should note that if there is any possibility of over a hundred people arriving by car the police will certainly need to know. Four weeks warning is usually enough notice for all events other than those listed below where police permission is required.

Find the local police station covering the area where the event is to be held by looking in the telephone directory. All police forces insist that the first approach is made in writing to the divisional commander. S/he will pass the letter on to the appropriate officer who will reply and become your contact. Nine times out of ten, and always if there are traffic implications, s/he will want a brief meeting with you as an individual or ideally an invitation to attend a preliminary meeting with your committee.

Remember, despite the impression you occasionally get from some individual officers, you are only informing the police out of courtesy to gain their cooperation and help. You do not actually have to ask their permission except in the case of those events listed below. However, you are always well advised to go along with police suggestions as they can seek an injunction to prevent an activity from taking place at all, or stop it as soon as it has started on the grounds that you are causing an obstruction.

Access issues

If the access is restricted, be prepared for the police to put up 'no parking' cones along the side of the road so that people cannot block the public highway. Make sure that you have enough spaces within your planned parking area. (See Chapter 9 on dimensions for car parks.)

Sometimes the police will anticipate times of congestion, especially at the end of a timed event, such as a concert. They will insist on operating a one-way system on and off the site, and be responsible for the parts of this system that involve public highways. You must be aware that they have the right to invoice you for expenses incurred.

Contacting the police during the event

Even during a quiet, daytime activity the police may need to be called. Accidents do happen, stock can escape or unleashed dogs cause havoc, fights break out or someone crashes a car. Ask your contact officer for an emergency number and, if possible, the name of the duty officer for that day. Ensure that the number is given to your key personnel on the day and that you all know who has a telephone. You will probably never need to use it, but better to be safe than sorry.

Events requiring police permission

If you intend:

- selling alcohol;
- closing roads;
- running an event with public order issues such as a campaigning event or a circus attracting animal rights activists;
- overnight stays;

you may need police permission and be required to give, at the very least, three months warning.

Alcohol

If you suspect that your event might attract an unruly mob that intend to make full use of available alcohol or even bring their own, it may be sensible to air your concerns with the police informally rather than try to deny potential problems. Far better to arrange for areas to be contained or emergency procedures to be pre-planned than for it all to go horribly wrong and even for accidents or injuries to occur that might have been preventable. In my experience the police are not going to be satisfied with belittling a problem and they will be less likely to assist or be lenient if they suspect that the organiser is irresponsible. Show them that you are prepared to listen and take advice.

They will also wish to know if you intend selling liquor on a temporary licence, unless this will be from a bar of a building that is already licensed (see Chapter 6).

Closing roads

I love closing off roads! What a sense of power! But it can cause a great deal of frustration and upset to local residents and motorists if it is not approached with sensitivity.

Processions, carnivals or fiestas tend to take place in town or city centres and, by the nature of the beast, they are on the move. In some instances this means closing the highways to traffic. This sort of provision needs many months of preparation as police, local authority traffic planners and the residents or local shop owners along the roadside all need to be consulted.

Having agreed that the road could be closed in principle – and you will never get everyone to say 'yes' – a report has to be submitted for agreement in committee by local councillors and procedures laid down. Due warning has to be published and the times of closure kept to a minimum. Occasionally a short, fairly fast-moving procession can be integrated with the traffic thereby causing little disruption and this is clearly easier to arrange.

A city centre event will attract a large crowd and is an exciting event to organise; it is also one of the few times that you can take your event to the audience rather than wait for them to come to you. You will, however, need a good many reliable stewards and helpers and you have to work closely with the police at all times – they really have to coordinate this bit for you and there will be a charge for their time at the event. However the price can be negotiable, especially for charity events. It is always worth asking.

Booking professional acts

When you are getting started on organising your show, it is well worth while considering a professional act. It will offer your show instant glamour and eye-catching billing.

The easiest way to fill your show if you need a few professional acts is to buy the current copy of the *Showman's Directory*. This lists all sorts of entertainment and also any contractors or services and equipment that you might need, and is available mail order from the publisher (see Publications at the back of the book).

Another source of entertainers or expertise is the weekly theatrical newspaper *The Stage* and you can buy a copy off the shelf at any large newsagents or they should be able to order it for you. *Showcall* is another publication that you might find useful, also from the publishers of *The Stage* – it deals entirely with entertainers and again is available mail order. This large directory is published annually and lists acts and entertainers at the front, then agents and managements and finally equipment, etc. at the end. In short if you have the money and copies of *Showcall* and the *Showman's Directory* you can put together a very promising show.

> **Checkpoint**
>
> One word of warning when booking professionals: read the contracts very carefully and particularly check whether you still have to pay the agent if the artiste fails to arrive due to accident, bad weather, poor directions etc. Also check your insurance in case you have to cancel the show for any reason: you will probably still have to pay for the act if they have turned up in good faith.

Key points:

- Develop a good contact at your local authority well in advance and keep the information flowing.
- Explore ready-made channels for obtaining equipment and funds.
- If you think you may need to hire council-owned property – book it up to a year in advance, especially for popular dates such as bank holidays. You can always cancel if reasonable notice is given.
- Check and double check your contracts.
- Tell the truth, the whole truth and nothing but the truth to the police; they are frequently extremely helpful and will be your best friends in a crisis.
- Consider professional acts for part of your show. They add some glamour and give you something special for the billing. But read the contracts carefully, as above.
- Remember, red tape is there to be cut and it is easy if you know the person with the scissors!

5

Finances

This chapter will cover the following topics:

▶ Drawing up a simple budget sheet
▶ The importance of quotations and estimates
▶ Opening and using a bank account
▶ Sources of sponsorship and grants
▶ What you can offer in return for support
▶ Registering as a charity
▶ The financial privileges extended to charities
▶ Paying for professional fundraisers.

Drawing up a simple budget sheet

Some people are drawn to figure work, budgeting or indeed anything to do with money as cats are to cream. They lap it up and thrive on every chink of coin or crumple of note. I am not one! This area is my bête noir, and because I do not enjoy mathematics my budget sheets are as simple as possible. In my opinion, even for the most grand of events, nothing more is needed than two columns for estimated income and expenditure and two for actual income and expenditure with room to balance it at the bottom. All this can be written up simply on balance sheet paper or, better still, you can use a template spreadsheet programme on your computer and it will even work out the sums for you. What could be easier? Nothing … and I still hate it!

The most difficult part of any budget is estimating your income. As with a new product or a young company it is tempting to overestimate wildly due to beginner's enthusiasm. I always work to a ceiling of 50 per cent capacity attendance for any inside event or 40 per cent for an outdoor show. This means that you have built in potentially damaging factors that are out of your control such as weather, competition or just plain apathy. These figures are not written in stone, and as the date approaches and it becomes clear that you are going to do better – by looking at advance ticket sales or extra interest from the media – then you can adjust your estimated balance continuously.

If a large part of your income is going to be from sponsorship or donations then you will have to ensure that they will be forthcoming before you get very far down the line. At least basic expenditure must be met otherwise you will find that you are paying for a costly mistake out of club funds or even worse, out of your own pocket.

The importance of quotations and estimates

Try to obtain a quotation for every area of expenditure or, failing that, at least an estimate.

> ### Checkpoint
> A quotation is a legally binding document and it 'quotes' the exact figure that you will be charged.
>
> An estimate is only an informed guess and if the estimator makes a mistake in judging the job accurately you could find yourself with a larger bill than you expected.

Controlling expenditure

If you have enough time, and a little experience of running the finances of events, your committee should set a budget including any large individual expenses.

However, if this is your first event you would do better to obtain as many estimates for all your expenses as you can and then hold a special committee meeting to talk about how you are going to spend your precious cash. If you have a very large item to be hired or bought you might want to look at some comparative costs or ask for tenders from two or three different suppliers. There might be some arguments but at least you can thrash out some sort of consensus and you, the organiser, will not be accused of being profligate if the profits are not as high as planned.

Negotiating favourable rates

All things are worth negotiating for; times are hard, competition is tough and it is a seller's market. Printers are a good example of companies that are worth negotiating with. Having said all that, companies are pretty canny to the efforts of charities and you will have to compete with other opportunists out there. Get your request in first and shout loudest, this is not the time to be subtle.

Remember that you expect a captive audience and so have a good bargaining hand. Most companies need to advertise themselves and you may be able to obtain services or equipment free of charge in return for flying a company banner around the show ring or giving credit in the programme. If you are looking for a media launch of a 'season' or 'festival' it is worth searching for a sponsor to provide the refreshments and even the venue (more about serious sponsorship later in this chapter).

Scrounging

Some small privately-owned companies may have a director who is interested in your particular cause and is prepared to help purely out of sympathy – but these are few and far between.

If you are looking for equipment or facilities to be lent free of charge you might well find them offered, once. I feel that it is not politic to keep going back to the same people year after year unless they make it very plain that they want to assist annually. However for those who really do want to be associated with the event and enjoy the whole razzmatazz, it can help cement a good relationship to stick with the same donor every year. A small thank-you present to show your appreciation goes down well: a bunch of flowers or a free ticket. People can be very generous where small events are concerned, especially in the more rural parts of the country; you may have to work a little harder in urban areas but you very often will have a more responsive council to work with.

If you are desperate for an expensive or unusual item that you cannot find through the usual channels, your local radio station may come up trumps. They are often happy to give out any request on air provided the event is not for personal gain and of course the person or company able to help gets a good plug too.

Church or parochial magazines are a good market place for requests for volunteers and equipment as well as for advertising the actual show. Remember, though, that they are often quarterly and will need copy well in advance.

Opening and using a bank account

If you are holding a small event in connection with an established club then you will be able to use the club's bank account and chequebooks (signed by the appropriate person, of course). But maybe your show is a one-off. You will need to operate a separate bank account with one of the main clearing banks. These banks are, in the main, sympathetic towards charity events and could well grant you free banking for the first 3 to 12 months. Alternatively the correct building society account can be a good option as these do not incur costs. Check with your umbrella charity (if you have one) that you do not need to go through their trading arm for tax purposes.

In theory you can walk into any bank or building society and open an account in about 20 minutes; in practice you will need to allow about two weeks before you can start using the account. Chequebooks have to be printed and sent out to you, and you need to be sure that the new account is fully up and running.

If you think your event will become an annual show, ask your bank manager if you can leave the present account dormant and then revive it for the three or four months of each year that you need to use it. This decision will be at his/her discretion.

If your event is very low key and all you need is a facility to bank the income then the bank will be happy to use one of its sundry accounts and issue a cheque to the charity or organisation. Clearly this could be used as a way to 'launder' ill-gotten gains so the bank will insist that a person, preferably an account holder, who is known to them personally, presents the money. Generally a small charge is made for this service but most banks are prepared to waive the fee if they know that the money represents funds raised for charity.

Key points:

- Use a simple accounting system.
- Estimate your expenses carefully, allowing a wide margin for problems.
- Make sure that basic expenditure can be met.
- Obtain sponsorship and donations early on.
- Ask for 'quotes' as far as possible.
- Discuss major expenditure with your committee.
- Negotiate over everything.
- Remember to send a 'thank you' for help.
- Use your local radio station for difficult items.
- Use local magazines.
- Open a bank account at least two weeks before you need it or warn a local bank that you would like to bank all the takings on a particular date.

Sources of sponsorship and grants

The way money is distributed between charitable organisations has made a polar shift in the last 10 or 15 years. When I first started looking for funding for community events in the mid-1980s I steered organisers towards public funds, local authority grants, Arts and Sports Council project funding and specialist trusts. Only if there was an obvious connection, or if I knew that annual allocations were exhausted, did I suggest corporate sponsorship. Such sponsorship was usually more trouble than it was worth and companies frequently had little or no experience of partnering the voluntary sector – each regarded the other with a certain amount of suspicion.

Today the situation is reversed. With the ever-shrinking pot of public funds (apart from large-scale lottery projects) charitable organisations have increasingly had to search elsewhere for money. As a result they have become far more businesslike in their approach, whilst provision for corporate sponsorship is included in every company's marketing strategy. At community events today the chances are that you will be plied with professionally-produced programmes advertising the sponsoring company's services. Unfortunately the clash of cultures still raises the spectre of suspicion and each side still has lessons to learn from the other.

Presenting your case to potential sponsors

The difficulties of obtaining sponsorship have increased over the last few years and you will need to be totally professional in the presentation of your case. If sponsorship is crucial to you getting your event off the ground you would be well advised to start early and take very good direction. Whole books have been written on the subject of preparing sponsorship applications. One such is suggested under Publications at the back of this book.

The advice in this book assumes that although corporate sponsorship may be part of your fundraising strategy, it is not the primary one: you have decided that you want to organise an event for reasons other than primarily to raise money. (If it is only money you want, you may need to go back to the chapter on aims and objectives to reassess your decision for an event.)

Contributions in kind

You need some money to kick-start your planning or to help pay for some expensive aspect of the show. Or do you? Perhaps sponsorship, or a donation, in kind would be just as useful, such as the loan of an unused car park on a Sunday to site your event or 100 chairs or the use of a PA system. Some companies like the tax benefits that writing a cheque can bring them, others may not be large enough to have a donations budget and prefer to make their presence felt in other ways. It is crucial that you find out what the company's preferred option is and have some suggestions to satisfy each preference.

Identifying potential sponsors

So, who are these mythical people who might drop money in your outstretched hand? Sadly not as many as you might have hoped. Local companies used to be a good bet but many of them have been gobbled up by larger organisations and their focus is frequently global. Some of the supermarkets have community grants available but they are often targeted at specific areas of the population such as children or whatever is the flavour of the month.

Keep your ear to the ground to inform yourself of personal interests in the business world. If a company director's passion is for steam engines he might be prepared to get involved in a By Steam Rally. It really can be as simple as who you know, so be prepared to pull strings. Get your head around what motivates people and interests individuals. Of course, your event may be so relevant to a specific organisation that they can't say no. Tom Smith's cracker company in Norwich might find it hard to resist a giant tug-o-war involving pulling a world record-breaking giant cracker outside the local TV studios, for instance.

For small to smaller-medium scale events it is unlikely that you will want to apply for a grant of more than a few hundred or, at the absolute outside, a couple of thousand pounds. Some local authorities are still keeping a small budget for community or arts events that they think will attract their targeted audiences or which meet a pre-determined community need. It is worth applying well in advance or seeing the council's promotions officer to find out what is available but you will need to make a professional application.

If you are not successful then you are perfectly justified in wanting to know why, so ask what it was that they didn't like about your application. It may be that their budget was just so small and the demand so high that the line had to be drawn somewhere.

Funding for voluntary and community groups is also available from grant-making trusts and the National Lottery. Small lottery grants are distributed through the Awards for All scheme (see Resources). To search for trusts that have a special interest in your type of activity or your local area, you can use the DSC publications listed under Resources, or the software programme FunderFinder. These can often be consulted through your local Council for Voluntary Service; details of the national umbrella body NACVS are given in the Resources section.

What you can offer in return for support

Where sponsorship is sought from companies, industry or organisations you are usually expected to be able to offer something in return. Once upon a time the feel-good factor was often all that was necessary. Today much more is required and this has, paradoxically, also made accepting sponsorship more difficult.

Whilst the funding organisation is anxious that its name is not associated with any group that is going to bring it unwelcome publicity, neither do you want your organisation to accept funding at any cost. Appropriateness is everything; even as I write, a debate is developing between a breast cancer charity, which has chosen to accept sponsorship from a wine producer, and other cancer organisations who claim that alcohol consumption can lead to increased cases of breast cancer.

An event needs to offer something that companies want and it helps if you use the language that they are familiar with. 'Image' and 'prestige' are two words that crop up time and again. Do they want a caring image or an exciting image? Are they interested in being associated with the youth culture or are they middle-aged and highbrow?

If your charity has a royal patron and your event is of such importance that you will be expecting a special guest you can offer prestige by association. You may well be able to sell several corporate hospitality tents. Or an event might be thought to be prestigious if it is cultural or set in a heritage site.

You might be targeting an audience of particular interest to sponsors. Animal feed suppliers will be interested in a fat stock show, a photographic shop might see potential customers in those coming to a hot air balloon rally or an insurance company might want to have a presence at a quad bike race.

What every company wants is media exposure. If you can offer great photo opportunities or guarantee an event so wacky or 'in-yer-face' that the place will be teeming with journalists and features writers you will stand a good chance of sponsorship.

The most obvious thing you can do to promote image, prestige and media exposure for your sponsor is to support their public 'corporate identity' or awareness. By allowing all your publicity to bear the name, logo or 'house colours' of your sponsors you are helping the company to become a recognised, household name.

You could, for example:

- Allow the sponsor's banners around show rings or around entrances.
- Put the sponsor's logo on both programmes and prizes.
- Give every member of the audience of staged events a pack about a particular service that is offered by the sponsors. (It is a good idea to offer this as a going home present to avoid extra clearing up at the end after people have put their packs under their chairs at the beginning and left having forgotten them.)
- Hold a reception for specially invited guests prior to the event for company VIPs or prestige customers.

- Arrange a special showing of the performance, all to be paid for, naturally, by the sponsors.

Be aware that your sponsors might wish to flood the event with company publicity and that you may wish to limit this. Make sure you know what the event is worth to them in terms of advertising and make sure that the proffered sponsorship deal is equal to this.

Checkpoint

Ask your sponsor what they would like, what they expect and other extras they are prepared to pay for or supply, and make sure that you are all in agreement, putting what you decide in writing if necessary.

But why not cut to the chase. If you don't want to start approaching organisations you have very little knowledge of you can always aim to get help with publicity and marketing by contacting your local radio stations and newspaper office. They will often support you by giving you pre-publicity, free or discounted advertising and then guarantee to cover the event on the day, providing valuable post-event articles that may well set you up for your next event.

Registering as a charity

If you are carrying out very small-scale voluntary fundraising work for 'charitable purposes' that is good enough for the law; you do not have to be a registered charity. And even if you are not an officially registered charity, your event is still entitled to the tax benefits due to formally recognised organisations (see below). It might however be easier to prove your charitable status if you are registered with, and therefore seen to be monitored by, the Charity Commission.

Some charitable organisations are required by law to register (see below). Very small charities will all have unique and possibly changing cirumstances. An hour spent with a specialist charity lawyer to help you decide whether you need to register your charity or not will be money well spent. But you will have to be really very small (having an income of under £1,000 a year) to be exempt.

Registering as a charity is now compulsory for any charitable organisation which has:

- a permanent endowment;
- or uses and occupies land;
- or whose annual income from all sources is £1,000 or more (likely to be £5,000 from 2004).

Registration is fairly straightforward and the Charity Commission (see Resources at the back of this book) will advise you on the procedure. For more information look at *Charitable Status*, published by the Directory of Social Change (see Publications).

The obligations of a registered charity

All registered charities must state the fact that they are registered on all official papers including cheques, stationery, advertising and material placed on websites if they gross more than £10,000 a year: Indeed it is a criminal offence not to do so.

They should also state what they are fundraising for. And this is where legal advice is most important. Should you need £2,000 for a particular project and raise more than that, what do you do with the surplus? You need the wording on all your accompanying stationery, advertisements and letters to be flexible enough to allow you to roll it over into another project, put it on deposit, pay for a survey or whatever you need. If not, you will have to repay any surpluses.

All your activities must be for charitable purposes within the four categories as outlined by Lord McNaughten in the Pemsel case, and these activities must be within your stated objects: you can check the Charity Commission guidelines on their website (see Resources at the back of this book). At the time of writing, these four categories are:

- The relief of poverty.
- The advancement of education.
- The advancement of religion.
- Certain other purposes for the benefit of the community.

Exemptions to registration

There are a number of exemptions to the requirements regarding registration relating to:

- churches;
- certain museums;
- universities;
- schools.

However, even if you are fundraising for an exempt body it might be preferable to set your fundraising up as a charitable body, or under an umbrella organisation, rather than running each event as completely separate fundraising operations.

The reason for this is as follows. If you run two events, and event A makes a profit and event B makes a loss, you cannot recover your losses on the second event, or even the third (to be held in the future), unless the money is being raised for the organisation that is running the event, and that organisation subsequently donates the money to the eventual beneficiary.

Using an umbrella organisation

You may feel that official recognition might be better achieved under the umbrella of an existing charity and this can often save 'reinventing the wheel'. After all if you are trying to raise money for retired hairpin makers and you discover a Hairpin Manufacturers Fundraising Association already in existence, complete with constitution, a trading arm and a charity registration number you might be better off joining forces rather than starting a new group in competition. The Charity Commission states that it is 'usually less effective to have several organisations trying to carry out the same work in the same place, and it duplicates running costs'. I would add that volunteers are often difficult to come by and the ability to pool enthusiastic helpers is frequently more useful to the organisers of potential events.

The overall obligation to observe charity law

A charity can exist without necessarily applying for registration: indeed you might be operating with 'charitable purposes' as defined in law without even knowing it. However, even in ignorance you are still required to observe charity law and are able to receive the tax benefits that are due to registered charities (see below). Clearly, then, it is in your interest to obtain official recognition and have a flexible constitution (see Chapter 4) or other documents drawn up professionally which allows you the options to fundraise how you wish.

The obligation to keep financial records

Whether you are registered or not you must keep proper financial records. Any member of the public has a right to see your formal accounts within two months of a written request. You can charge a small fee for postage and photocopying.

Trading

Charities can only trade for their own charitable purposes and must be authorised so to do by the constitution documents. To trade you do not necessarily have to be a registered charity but in practice nearly all are.

If there are doubts, trading should be conducted through a subsidiary trading company. This is an exceedingly complex area and you need Charity Commission advice if you are going down this route.

Political activities

Political activities are restricted and must be directly relevant to your objectives. Again, consult the Charity Commission for advice.

The financial privileges extended to charities

So what are the special privileges that you, as you are running an event for a charitable purpose, are entitled to? There are a number of benefits but the main three are as follows.

- Exemptions from paying income tax (say, on the income raised by running your event), corporation tax, capital gains tax, stamp duty and inheritance tax on gifts. There are a few exceptions but this is the usual situation.
- Local rates on buildings used by the charity is kept to 20 per cent of usual business rates. Village halls can be a case in point and are often operated as charities or by trusts.
- Special VAT treatment in some cases, but it is not always simple. You should investigate this where you are running an event through the trading arm of an umbrella charity.

There are some fairly fundamental points of law that were put in place by the introduction of the Charities Act 1993 which updated and consolidated aspects of earlier legislation and most of the Charities Act 1992. If you need to look at the detail the Charity Commission (see Resources at the back of this book) publishes a series of accessible and succinct pamphlets designed for the voluntary sector.

Paying for professional fundraisers

Finally, a point about employing professional fundraisers. Whilst the majority of professional fundraisers do a very good and valuable job, there have been unscrupulous individuals who have entered the business for the express purposes of lining their own pockets. The problem was addressed in the Charities Act 1992 Part II which came into force in 1995. The Act states that it will be an offence for any professional fundraiser to solicit funds for a charity unless they have signed a formal agreement as prescribed by the regulations.

If you are considering employing a professional fundraiser you should take advice from a contract lawyer about payment – percentages, commission or set fees, control of funds and insolvency. Whatever you do, don't employ anyone without following up two or three references.

6

Making it legal

This chapter covers the following topics:

▶ Public Liability insurance cover
▶ Employers' Liability insurance
▶ Tax and VAT issues
▶ Public Entertainments Licences
▶ Liquor or Justices' Licences
▶ Street Collection Permits
▶ Lottery registration
▶ Bye-laws in public areas.

Public Liability insurance cover

It is most irresponsible to run an event or show without Public Liability insurance cover.

By far and away the most popular events in the UK during the summer months are fetes and car boot sales and even the smallest of school fetes or the most insignificant of sales should be insured. You might just get away with ignoring a coffee morning in the Vicarage garden but even then a hot water urn can blow up or a garden seat collapse and you could be liable if anything like this happens.

Public Liability insurance covers you for claims made against you by members of the public or businesses who can prove that their accident or injury was as a direct result of the event organiser's acts or omissions. If an individual suffers as a result of not taking reasonable care for his/her own safety there is likely to be no claim, or the responsibility may be shared between the individual and the organiser.

You are not obliged by law to take out insurance cover but for about £50 premium you could save yourself or your club from a crippling financial burden not to mention the anxiety that goes with being legally pursued.

The many companies that used to provide insurance cover for small- and medium-scale events have all but disappeared. There are now a very few specialist event insurance companies that offer such cover. Events Insurance

Services is one such company; consult their website for their sliding scale of charges based on numbers attending. Another company, whose policies are intended for charities only, is Ansvar (see Resources at the back of this book).

Employers' Liability insurance

In addition to Public Liability you can also insure for Employers' Liability (even if you are not paying wages) and cancellation, be it due to poor weather or failure of the main act to show up. If you are employing people you are obliged by law to take out Employer's Liability insurance.

You might like to look at an 'all risks, money and personal assault' policy. This covers damage or theft to property associated with the event, theft of money and attack on volunteers, helpers and other organisers.

For more unique events it is worth investigating companies that specialise in certain areas, such as art exhibitions, horse shows or music festivals.

Key points:

- Always take out Public Liability insurance.
- If you employ people, you must also take out Employers' Liability insurance.
- Consider cancellation and all risks cover.
- Look for companies on the Internet but maybe use a broker to get the best deal for you.

Tax and VAT issues

Event-based fundraising is usually only concerned with one type of tax, VAT. Issues of tax relief for personal and corporate donations through Gift Aid, and issues of taxable trading, etc. are unlikely to cross the path of the events organiser. However it is best to make sure you don't fall foul of the very complex areas of tax, excise and charity law.

Use a tax adviser and make use of the Revenue, Excise and Charity Commission websites for succinct guidance,

One-off or annual fundraising efforts are usually exempt from VAT. However if you choose to run your enterprise as a shop, even if you open for as little as once a month or run your events as part of a series, you will have to register with your local VAT office (look in your telephone directory under 'customs and excise') as soon as your annual turnover reaches the £55,000 threshold. Of course if you are doing as well as this you probably won't mind having to register! But be aware that you are not automatically exempt from VAT because you are a charity, although there are some exemptions. If you are spectacularly successful at running coffee mornings or jumble sales in the same hall each week, for instance, and you reach the registration threshold you are unlikely to be accountable for VAT as it is thought that the risk of competition to local business is marginal.

A final word if you are fundraising for a school: make sure that your purchase orders are on official, numbered LEA (local education authority) order forms (unless your school is separate from the LEA). You will be charged VAT on all invoices and county councils can claim this back, but only against official orders. Use the appropriate forms for hospitals, museums, sports clubs, etc. in the same way.

Key points:

- On the whole, small- or medium-scale events will be unlikely to be liable for VAT but always check that you are exempt.
- Charities, schools, hospitals etc. may be able to claim back VAT so use official purchase orders where possible.

Public Entertainments Licences

The law (Local Government, Miscellaneous Provisions, Act 1982) states that where two or more people are performing and /or dancing is involved, a Public Entertainments Licence is required. The main areas of concern are:

- the safety of the electrical system;
- any potential fire hazards;
- the availability of fire escapes;
- exit procedures for emptying the building;
- noise pollution;
- provision of WCs.

Inside and outside events may be treated rather differently but the concerns will not change.

Shows that include a hypnotism act or live animals may be banned or restricted in certain local authority areas; it is worth getting advice if you are hiring a council-owned venue as inclusion could affect the granting of a licence.

Inside events

These tend to be potentially more hazardous when held in a previously unlicensed building. If, however, you have chosen a public building in which to hold your event such as a church hall, pub or community centre then you may well find that the building already holds a Public Entertainments Licence and all you have to do is comply with the terms previously agreed. For something like a ceilidh held in the local farmer's barn or a concert in a marquee, a temporary Public Entertainments Licence will have to be sought. Interestingly places of worship are exempt so you could hold an unlicensed event inside a church quite legally but I would strongly advise against it as the checks are for the safety of everyone concerned and churches are not known for up-to-date maintenance or for having several appropriate fire exits. Wherever you choose, you will need to apply at least three months in advance to allow for re-submission if you are at first unsuccessful.

Do not even think of applying if you cannot guarantee several fire exits or if your venue backs on to a noise-sensitive building such as a hospital or sheltered accommodation.

Outside events

Generally speaking if musical entertainment is not the main attraction, the authorities are not really interested. If you are expecting a crowd of more than a few hundred people it might be prudent to take advice; it is just possible that in urban areas complaints will have been made before and the environmental protection officers may be more sensitive than usual.

If you plan an event to comprise largely of performers you will certainly have to apply for a Public Entertainments Licence and, as for inside events, plan to apply for this at least three months in advance.

Key points:

- Ensure that public safety is not jeopardised and that you are not infringing people's basic rights.
- If you are holding an event where singing or dancing is the main attraction you may require a Public Entertainments Licence.
- It is easier to stage your event in a venue already licensed for Public Entertainments.
- Check before you apply for a licence that your show is not likely to run into problems. You will have to pay the application fee whether or not your licence is granted.

Liquor or Justices' Licences

If you wish to sell alcohol, or intoxicating liquor as it is legally called, at your event you will have to be licensed. The decision to grant a licence is made by the local magistrates' court who take advice from the Police. If you are holding a show in a building that already has a licensed bar then, provided that the licensee is in charge of the bar during the event, you should have no problems.

Outside, or in an unlicensed building, a landlord already in receipt of a Liquor Licence can apply for an occasional Liquor Licence for about £10.00 and s/he can hold up to four events in 12 months on that licence. As a non-profit making organisation you can personally obtain a licence to sell alcohol on unlicensed premises by applying for an Occasional Permission. This makes provision for non-licence holders to run bars at one-off public events; the number in any 12 months has been increased from 4 to 12.

Applications are made to the magistrates' court and you should give about one month's notice, though in practice, if you are desperate for a licence, you could be given a decision in 48 hours. Most courts sit twice a week and you should be informed fairly promptly. The government is looking in detail at the Licensing Act 1964 and a new act is due to go through Parliament in the next year or so and we can expect major changes. The licensing officer at your local constabulary will advise you.

You could be asked many searching questions and might be restricted to wine or beer only. If there is any doubt as to your suitability or the suitability of the event the licence will be denied. I feel that the best way of obtaining permission to open a bar should be to approach a licensee who already holds a full 'on-licence' and ask him/her to apply for you, although you will have to come to some financial agreement for his time and effort. This is quite legal and indeed the police welcome this action as the landlord is, in effect, asking to extend the area of his/her pub for the duration of the event. You will also have access to wholesale priced liquor.

Key points:

- If you are selling alcohol you will need a Liquor Licence.
- It saves running into problems if you approach a licensee to obtain the licence and run the bar for you although you can obtain an Occasional Permission for yourself.

Street Collection Permits

Some ten years or so down the line from the Charities Act 1992 and the promised new legislation regulating what will be known as 'Public Charitable Collections' has still to materialise and there is no sign of it on the horizon.

The new regulations, when published, are likely to cover matters relating to the keeping and publication of accounts, prevention of annoyance, wearing of badges and carrying of certificates by collectors who must be over certain ages. For the time being we still have to work with an amalgamation of two or three different Acts; differences do occur in the different countries of the United Kingdom and indeed in different areas within each country, so it is as well to consult your local authority in order to familiarise yourself with requirements, before you plan too far ahead.

Some councils have started to anticipate the new regulations and are bringing in quirks of their own. For instance, in Dudley all collectors are required to carry their permits with them, while in London or in Northern Ireland you are not allowed to collect whilst accompanied by an animal. Minimum age requirements for collectors can vary from area to area, being anywhere between 14 and 18 years old.

Terms and details of how to apply for a permit are covered in Chapter 3 (Event 22) but essentially you will be required to apply, in writing, to the administration or licensing department of the district council covering the area in which the collection is to be held at least one month before the event. You may need to apply a great deal earlier than that if you want to be sure of booking the day you need.

After the collection you will be asked to complete a form giving the council information including the total amount collected, who counted it, and a list of all the collectors, etc.

Key points:

- Don't forget to register well in advance if you want to have a collection on public property.
- Establish requirements peculiar to your area and abide by them.
- Keep your paperwork and accounting clear so that you will be able to satisfy the post collection return properly.
- Be aware that new regulations are in the pipeline.

Lottery registration

A lottery is a game of chance for which tickets are sold enabling the holder to qualify for the potential to win a prize or money. Games of chance are covered by the National Lottery Act 1993 and this Act made significant changes to the Lotteries and Amusements Act 1976. All the changes are now in effect.

The definition of 'lottery' can include raffles, sweepstakes, tombolas, etc. When you introduce an element of skill such as in 'Spot the ball' or 'Guess the weight of the cake' it then becomes a competition rather than a lottery and is not subject to such rigorous regulations.

One other area not covered by legislation is the 'free prize draw'. As long as all tickets, or chances, are offered on the basis of a voluntary donation only, your lottery is completely unrestricted. You must be very careful in your wording and all advertising and tickets must include the words, 'No donation necessary'. You cannot even suggest a donation or stipulate a minimum donation – a risky business when it comes to budgeting and the cost of promoting the lottery. A lucky number on a free programme (with a voluntary donation, naturally) is an example of good use of this unrestricted game of chance.

In simple terms there are now five different types of lottery covered by the legislation:

- Small lotteries.
- Private lotteries.
- Society lotteries.
- Local Authority lotteries.
- National lotteries.

No registration is necessary for Small lotteries and for Private lotteries. Registration with the local authority is required for Society lotteries of a value not exceeding £20,000. Registration with the Gaming Board for Great Britain is required for all other lotteries but these are not covered here.

On the whole the regulations covering raffles and similar games of the sort that we enjoy at community events in every town and village on every day of the year are relatively straightforward. The simplification of rules and the increase in value limits have made the operation of such events within the law easier to achieve. However, the details covering the regulation of society lotteries and others are very technical and complex; don't be afraid to ask for help.

Small lotteries

These must not be the main attraction of the event. They must be incidental to an exempt entertainment such as a bazaar, sale of work, fete, dinner dance, sporting event, etc. The lottery must then take place on the premises (but not charity shops) where the main event takes place and there must be no element of private gain in the running of the lottery or the entertainment. Money spent on the purchase of prizes must not exceed £250; this is at the whole event – not just one bottle stall, for instance – however prizes of greater value can be donated by supporters as long as no money prizes are awarded, although gift vouchers are permissible.

Interestingly it is still lawful to offer bottles of alcohol at an exempt entertainment even if that entertainment does not hold a liquor licence; whether you are then allowed to open the bottle and drink it immediately is another question. Subject to the above, there is no limit on the size of the lottery or on the price of the tickets, although tickets can only be sold during during the actual event itself, and the lottery must be resolved before the end of the event, even if this takes place over several days, and on the same premises.

As there is no legislation covering the price of the tickets it is, within the letter of the law, permissible to sell multiple tickets at a discount and this is a frequent feature of raffles. The Gaming Board is at pains to point out that this is not good practice; in the spirit of the law, everyone should be given a fair and equal chance and this can only happen if all tickets are sold at the same price.

Private lotteries

Whilst of a more limited fundraising potential, these are far less regulated than any other type of lottery. It must be confined to members of a club or society, promoted by a member of that club with the net proceeds of the lottery being used to provide prizes or to further the work of the society. The only deductions allowed are for the printing and stationery. This means that you cannot hire and pay a manager (even another member of the club) to run the lottery.

The lottery can only be advertised on the society's premises and you cannot send the tickets through the post – so no sending a raffle book out with the minutes – but there is no limit to the size of the lottery or the price of the tickets. Indeed there is no requirement to have actual tickets; a sweepstake would be perfectly in order. However, the price of every entry must be the same and the chances can only be allocated by way of sale and, as stated, this must be done in person.

Society lotteries

For a more effective lottery involving the sale of tickets over a period of time you will need to go through the process of registration with the local authority (usually the licensing or administration department) at least two months before the lottery takes place. This is only cost effective if your group is to hold regular lotteries. The fees have not been increased for many years and still (correct in 2003) stand at £35 for initial registration and a further £17.50 on renewal each New Year unless a cancellation note is received.

There have been substantial changes governing these lotteries since the Charities Act 1992 regulations came into force, and whilst I will outline below, in very simplified terms, the requirements to get you started, you would be well advised to ask for more detailed information from the licensing officer at your local authority.

Any promoter wishing to look into a more lucrative form of lottery, perhaps with a value exceeding £20,000, is advised to ask for more information from the Gaming Board for Great Britain at the address listed under Resources at the back of this book.

Registration is only possible if you are already an established group, the primary purpose of which is fundraising for charitable reasons in ways other than games of chance. Essentially this means you cannot set up an organisation (charitable or not) for the sole purpose of running lotteries.

The total value of tickets in one lottery must not exceed £20,000; the total value of the tickets offered for sale (even if they are part of different lotteries held by the same organisation) in one calendar year must not exceed £250,000. If you wish to exceed these limits you must also be registered with the Gaming Board for Great Britain who charge a fee according to the number of ticket sales. This will almost certainly be many hundreds of pounds (see their website for the scale of charges).

Prizes may only be offered up to £25,000 in amount or value or 10 per cent of the total value of tickets sold, whichever is the greater (i.e. a maximum of £100,000), no single donated prize must exceed this limit. Not more than 55 per cent of the actual proceeds can be used to provide prizes. There are further rules that affect the value of donated prizes which can be taken into consideration but this is a complex area and study of the Gaming Board's web site or booklet on 'Lotteries and the Law' is recommended. There is a very clear flow chart that takes the first-time promoter through the minefield.

Expenses may be appropriated providing they are accurate and not more than 35 per cent of the proceeds. However, the maximum percentage of the proceeds which may be deducted for expenses and prizes together is limited to 80 per cent. This means, in effect, that in any lottery at least 20 per cent goes to the good cause.

The maximum price of each ticket or chance has been increased very recently to £2.00, and not before time, having stood at £1.00 for many years. Every ticket should look the same and show the cost on the ticket itself, the name of the society promoting the lottery, the date of the draw, the name and address of the promoter, (in the case of registered charities) charity registration number and which local authority the game is registered with. This means that you cannot offer a discount for the sale of several tickets, in other words, five tickets for the price of four is not permitted. No ticket should be sold to anybody under the age of 16.

The restriction involving the sale of tickets door-to-door was lifted in June 1996 but it is still illegal to sell tickets in the street or by way of a machine.

The restrictions on both the number and frequencies of lotteries has been removed. Although it is not covered by the regulations it is recommended that no lottery is held with the draw on the same date to avoid confusion. Afterwards, the promoter must make a return to the Local Authority on the form provided within three months of the end of the lottery. Lotteries held by the same group but on different dates must have their accounting records kept separate from each other.

Competitions

Lotteries seem the more popular form of additional entertainment at many events. When you consider the regulations and restrictions that surround them it is surprising that competitions are not more popular.

Competitions include any activity where the outcome of the event is decided by the skill or judgement of the player. Although there is a mixture of skill and luck this is still classified as a competition. A draw to win a boat is a typical example. The draw alone would not be legal if the prize is worth more than £25,000 or 10 per cent of the total value of the tickets or chances sold. But introduce a tie-break sentence for the two potential winners pulled out of the hat, and you now have a perfectly legal competition.

There are no restrictions on the amount of money taken or any limit on the value of the prizes. Indeed you are at liberty to offer cash prizes. So my advice is to forget lotteries; go for competitions every time unless you plan the draw on the day and during the course of your event.

One word of warning; for all the above, Section 14 of the 1976 Act details legislation covering competitions and in particular competitions run in newspapers and for commercial profit. However, in my opinion competitions held at charitable events will be exempt from this section. Again, and as always, if you are in doubt, check with your Local Authority.

Bye-laws covering public areas

Public areas and footpaths are often covered by local bye-laws and if there are conditions covering these they will be pointed out in the contract if you are hiring a council-owned venue.

The sort of bye-law that may affect you is whether you are allowed to fence off a footpath or indeed an entire public area (usually provision is made within the bye-law for a prescribed number of days closure per year). Or you may be advised that no event can be held between certain hours or, understandably, that you have to leave access to the children's playground free for public use.

Existing concessionary cafés or shops can also cause problems, sometimes entailing restrictions on your use of extra caterers or food vans. Most recreation departments will cover these points for you but you do need to be aware of the types of complaints that may arise.

If you plan to use the river, or other expanse of water, on your site for entertainment, perhaps a raft race or boat procession, it may be that you will need permission from the local office of the Environment Agency. If the water is navigable you will certainly have to speak to them before you plan anything. Your local council can advise you where to go for help as they will be in constant communication with the correct organisation and will know the potential problems.

Key points:

- Make yourself aware of any local bye-laws that may affect you or the site in question.
- Ensure that you have adequate insurance cover.

7

Publicity

This chapter covers the following topics:

▶ Why do people go to an event?
▶ Marketing – or generating an audience
▶ Pricing and promotion
▶ Selling tickets
▶ Advance ticket sales
▶ Selling tickets on the day
▶ Choosing and printing tickets
▶ Public relations
▶ Advertising
▶ The importance of design and print
▶ Pre-event events (tasters)
▶ Signage.

Why do people go to an event?

There is an old saying that tells us we can't afford not to advertise – and nowhere is that statement more true than in planning one-off events.

Today's public is sophisticated, critical and independent. People make up their own minds about what to do for the day. The works outing and annual visit to the circus is a memory of past generations. According to the last national census, around 72 per cent of households own at least one car or van and increasing numbers of families take a foreign holiday once a year. A frightening number of people are illiterate but nearly everyone has someone in their family who can read English and with over 90 per cent of households having access to a television, they be entertained without even leaving their armchairs every single minute of every day.

There is, however, something unique and special about going out for your leisure entertainment, especially to an outdoor show. You cannot share the television with hundreds of other people, or at least, not all in the same location (except, perhaps, in a pub). You cannot convey on TV the atmosphere, the special noises and smells that are associated with an exciting, raucous, thrills and spills visit to the fair on a warm summer evening. Even something as proper and quintessentially English as a tea dance held on a weekday afternoon in the local village hall offers the kind of companionship and shared enjoyment that cannot be found elsewhere.

Indeed this shared experience is so important to human beings and such a necessary part of living that, however brilliant the technology of personal computers and home entertainment systems, we will always seek to rub shoulders with others and gawk and gasp at something entertaining together.

These moods are peculiar to the individual event and it is the anticipation of experiencing heightened emotions that is going to attract your customers. What you are offering is live, shared entertainment and usually, just a single opportunity. It is your job to foster that anticipation and hint of the excitement to come and the skill is to condense it into something two dimensional and poster sized. Enough of my homespun psychology, but it serves to remind us that there is more to selling events than just a title stuck on an A4 sheet.

In the following sections of this chapter you will find some basic marketing ideas for your event. It is a lengthy subject and one that is really too involved to do full justice to within this guide. Marketing should be absolutely unique to each event and a separate marketing plan should be drawn up for each one. Some good books for further reading on the subject are given under Publications at the back of this book.

Marketing – or generating an audience

All the methods you can think of that are going to generate an audience for your event can come under the blanket title of 'marketing'. These include studying your market, pricing, public relations, merchandising, sales and promotions, media, printing and design, pre-event events ('tasters'), signage and probably more that I have yet to come across.

I shall tackle advertising, printing and design, tasters and local signage separately and in greater detail later in the chapter.

Study your market

Before putting on any event you have to study your market. It is impossible to satisfy all of the people all of the time but you will have to identify your 'attenders' (the people who will almost definitely come). If you aim to widen your audience, you need to know who might come if the price or other circumstances were right. These are your 'intenders' and they are the most important group to aim for.

It is also important to know who definitely will not come even if given free tickets and a minibus from door to door. You don't want to waste money and effort in including them in your advertising plans.

The one person who knows your potential market is you; you also know where to find them. If you don't, then you must go back several steps and conduct some basic research before you even begin to decide on an event – in other words, use the decision ring as described in Chapter 2.

One way to begin studying your intended market is to think of your potential audience in groups, for instance:

- socio-economic group;
- geographic area;
- religious affiliation;
- ethnic background;
- age;
- family status, etc.

In addition, it is particularly important to identify which newspapers and magazines they would read; this gives you a pretty good idea of where to place your press advertisements for a start. Then look at the advertisements these publications are already running, especially the classified section; this can direct you to special interest clubs or weekly meetings to which you can advertise direct.

Keep a picture of the typical member of your audience in mind all through your marketing campaign and if you don't waver from your original decision you won't go far wrong. Above all, remember they may not be like you.

Pricing and promotion

Pricing is possibly the most important, and the most difficult, aspect of attracting your intended audience. Get this wrong and you either get plenty of people to the show but you don't make any money or you get too few because they can't afford the tickets. Either way you can end up with egg on your face and the problem of not knowing how your expenses will be covered.

You can only tell if you have got the price right if you do your sums properly (see Chapter 5). Very simply: you should add all your estimated expenditure together, don't forget a single thing, work out how many tickets you are likely to sell (go to similar events to get an idea of this and look at other pricing policies). Then multiply numbers by ticket price, remember to include the concessions, and check the profit margin. Prices might vary around the UK or between town and country so cut your cloth accordingly. There is no point charging what you think the show was worth in the Home Counties at £8.00 a ticket, if you know that the local public in Merseyside is used to spending £5.00.

The only exception to the rule is where you are holding an annual event that is a 'Spectacular'. The public get to know that each year is bigger and better, they had value for money on the last occasion and look forward to another visit on the same day the next year. At this stage you can begin to charge at a different rate from your competitors.

> ### Checkpoint
> The golden rule is to charge as much as you think you can get, which doesn't mean, charge as much as you like. As Keith Diggle points out in his long-ago published but still excellent *Guide to Arts Marketing* (available from the address at the back of this book under Publications) 'If we charge more than people will pay, then we get nothing'.

Concessions

Many local authorities will only allow you to hire their property or venues if you agree to considerable concessionary reductions for members of the community on income support, state pensions and so on. If you had not thought this was part of your plan it is yet another reason to read your local authority contract carefully. Of course as well as being morally ethical this can work to your long-term advantage. If you attract a wider audience, including people who would not traditionally be interested in your specialist event, through wise concessionary pricing bands, you may make some converts and increase your potential audience for future events.

In a few limited situations it may be possible to offer sales or discounts on tickets and entry fees for more than one event, especially if you are running a series of connected shows. Other incentives might be for a free drink in the interval with a voucher in the programme, '£1.00 off' leaflets, or discounts for large parties. The permutations are endless and you only have to walk round your local supermarket to see ideas that can be adapted.

Many sites are too large and impractical to fence off, making it impossible to sell entrance tickets. Mobile events such as parades are also impossible to ticket because of the transient nature of the crowd and, you hope, the high numbers, so in such cases you need to be sure of making your money elsewhere such as street collections, sponsorship, selling trade plots, raffles, programmes, etc.

Is all this marketing? Yes it certainly is. And you also need to price your programmes, raffle tickets or stand plots with a similar eye to your audience, to encourage people to buy. Most importantly, by getting your pricing right you are contributing to the atmosphere by allowing people to enjoy their day out without feeling, at the back of their minds, that they have spent more than it deserved.

Selling tickets

You can sell a ticket in two different ways.

- Days or even weeks prior to an event.
- On the door as people arrive for the show itself.

A large proportion of indoor shows sell advance tickets, but a far lesser proportion of outdoor events do so. There are advantages and disadvantages for both methods and you will need to work out your own needs and situation to choose which is best for your event.

Advance ticket sales

The simplest way to sell tickets in advance is by mail order on receipt of a cheque or postal order. You can then do away with the need to staff a sales point.

If you are selling tickets for a one-off fundraising show you will not have, or need, permanent box-office facilities unless you are using a purpose built theatre. For both mail order and face-to-face selling of advance tickets you will need to arrange a ticket sales point and advertise it well.

A shop or pub is a good place to sell tickets from especially if the owners are contributing to the show by sponsorship or providing the bar. Your local tourist information centre might be prepared to sell tickets on commission as might your council especially if the event is to be held on council property. Bookshops are often happy to be associated with arts events and the chamber of commerce might help with a trade show. Try to choose an outlet that is related to the type of event; not only are they more likely to assist but you will mutually benefit from like customers.

The advantages

- You have a longer time in which to sell tickets.
- Money is paid in advance.
- You can control sales for a limited space.
- You can make decisions based on real sales and not rely on predicted sales.
- If you 'sell out' in advance you can avoid queues of disappointed customers being turned away.
- It is usually easier to keep track of advance tickets and money as you have

smaller quantities at a time to deal with.

- You can make tickets available to the convenience of your audience and allow them to buy them when the mood is upon them i.e. NOW!

The disadvantages

- You need to have someone available to sell tickets for a lengthy period, although you can use retail outlets or an answerphone.
- You need to make frequent arrangements to collect and bank money and an account in which to deposit it.
- You need one or more separate selling points if you are not using mail order.
- You need to print official tickets.
- Tickets may be copied and sold illegally.

Selling tickets on the day

The advantages

- You only need sell tickets for a limited period.
- You can use pre-printed raffle tickets or, in some cases, no tickets at all.
- You can control entry to known troublemakers.
- There are no arguments about lost tickets, etc.

The disadvantages

- You may have a long and at times impatient queue.
- You will have to cope with large amounts of cash.
- It can be hard to keep track of sales.
- Concessions are often given on trust. It is impractical to check UB40s or pension books in front of a swiftly moving queue.

Choosing and printing tickets

Having decided how you are to sell your show you will need to decide if you need tickets at all and if so, what they should be.

Tickets for advance sales

Tickets designed for advance sales are rather different and need to be 'official'; by this I mean pre-printed onto rolls or books. These tickets should also be security numbered to deter counterfeiters (especially for popular shows) and there are specialist printers who will do this for you.

In addition the ticket should show the name of the show, the date, the price paid and the seat number if necessary. It is also helpful if you advertise a contact telephone number for any enquiries. I favour tickets in books as you can keep the stubs together and give different books to each outlet. This also helps when it comes to reconciling the sales over a period of weeks.

Tickets to be given on the day

In my opinion you do need to have some sort of record of sales for every event, even if you are collecting 10p on the door for a village hall jumble sale. So if you decide on no actual tickets, make sure you keep the entry money separate from any other; you can then work out your gate at the end when you cash up.

If you want to extrapolate information from your current audience to help plan for future events, then you will need to give tickets of a sort. You can use readily available cloakroom tickets of different colours to give you figures for car parking, OAPs, children, people in wheelchairs or any group that you want to research for further reference.

Public relations

A one-off event may not offer opportunities to get involved in serious public relations, but the way you and your committee conduct yourselves and handle the event will add to the public's perception both of your ability as organisers and of the cause for which you are raising money.

If you are planning to work again as an operational group and/or hold the event as an annual occasion then that all-important first impression has to be a good one. You need your colleagues and the public to trust and believe in you. Make the effort to construct a marketing plan and allow more time than you think to implement it.

If you were planning an eco-festival to promote the importance of conservation, vegetarianism and environmental awareness, for instance, you would raise your credibility if all your stationery, posters and tickets were printed on recycled materials. Your 'street-cred' would be severely damaged if you then allowed a hog-roast to take one of the stands or had a thousand plastic bags printed to hold the freebies. You would need to check the approach taken by every element of the festival, down to the last veggie-burger; the chief organiser of such a show has to have a complete overview and understanding of the aims behind the fundraising.

The role of local radio

The media can play a big part in your event if you let them and local radio is one of the most helpful media, especially if you have an individual presenter as one of your supporters.

Start by sending out, about a month in advance, a package containing a press release, some hand bills and an invitation with a covering letter explaining any local angle or connection that the local radio station might be interested in. This angle or connection could be a popular VIP, a local project or something unique to the area.

Always include with your package two contact names with their daytime or mobile phone numbers and suggest that you will make a follow up call in a week's time. More often than not you will get a call asking you to explain your event a little more or, better still you might be invited on to the show to explain the event to the listeners. Come to the interview well prepared with some notes for yourself if necessary, some more handbills to leave behind and your own name and position on a piece of paper for the presenter to have in front of her.

The role of local TV

If you think your event might have local television impact then you can follow the same procedure as above for the regional TV news station in your area. They will be less likely to contact you and you might well have to make a follow up call. Do remember that even if you get as far as being interviewed there is no guarantee that it will be broadcast. Television is very immediate and your event will not be able to compete with part of the pier falling into the sea at three that afternoon. But given that summertime is known as the silly season in journalism, you might just get lucky.

The role of newspapers and magazines

Newspaper and magazine articles are often read by hundreds of people, so cultivate a features writer and keep the ink fresh by sending in press releases and photographs. Suggest running competitions with the paper or allow them to compile an advertising feature on the back of a free programme pullout. You should arrange to let them have a list of trade stands and sponsors so that they can sell advertising space to make it pay. You may even find that in return for the words 'in association with ...' on all your publicity you can negotiate free press advertisements. This is well worth the effort!

Advertising

Advertising is communicating. You can make people hear about your event if you hire the town crier and he cries out your event from the street corners; but shoppers might be too busy to listen and no communication has therefore taken place.

You need to place your publicity where it will be seen or heard otherwise it will be a complete waste of time and money. Having got people to notice it and so attracted their attention, you need to make sure that you are telling them everything they need to know.

The three golden rules for event advertising

These rules are:

- What is it?
- Where is it?
- When is it?

From these three things your potential audience knows what to expect, where to find it and at what date and time to be there.

For perfect communication you can also add the following elements:

- The name of the organisers and a contact name and telephone number (and in fact this is mandatory, if you are a registered charity).
- What is it for? (i.e. the cause for which you are fundraising.)
- How much do they have to pay to get in?

Where do you advertise?

Absolutely anywhere that your potential audience might be. It is helpful to think of getting value for money from each flyer and poster. If you hand deliver leaflets through letterboxes they have to be the right letterboxes as they will have a limited readership. However, if you put your poster up in the community centre or village hall you will get many different people all looking at your one poster.

Other places to think about for posters and handbills are:

- inserts in the local free paper (potentially expensive, but might be worth it – a press advertisement might be better value);
- the central library – libraries often do a countywide distribution service to all their branches;
- health centres, doctor's surgeries – again the local NHS Trust might run a distribution service around doctors' and dentists' surgeries;

- hospitals;
- pubs, restaurants;
- council poster sites;
- bus stops, stations, taxi lines, public lifts;
- company canteens;
- council offices;
- tourist information centres;
- local tourist attractions;
- other appropriate events.

Of course you need not restrict yourself to posters and flyers. Look at the section above, under 'The role of local radio' for advice on how to negotiate press publicity. For an arts event, why not think about printing card bookmarks with your other publicity and ask the library to give one away with each book borrowed or with each sale at a sympathetic bookshop? What about beer mats in the pub for a beer festival? Or table napkins in the local restaurant for a medieval banquet (on a date that the restaurant is closed, of course!) Get permission from the council to fly a flag, hang a banner over the street or paint footprints on the pavement using washable paints showing the way to your show.

The importance of design and print

How you choose to design and print your publicity material can help to form those all-important first impressions.

Designers seem expensive but they needn't be. Most enjoy working on publicity material; it is quick and they can let their imagination loose. They also know how to keep to a budget if presented with a maximum figure for the likely print costs as well as the design fee. So although it is tempting to get young Harry, who is pretty clever with a DTP programme on his computer, to design all your publicity, this is not always the best, or even the cheapest, option. One source of exciting design talent that I have used in the past is the local art and design college. They will almost certainly have a print shop in which they may be prepared to make the finished posters, for a fee, but they will need notice to fit it into the term's work.

Printers are very competitive and you would do well to ask for several quotations. If you like what one printer produces, but prefer another's price, then negotiate until you get what you want. Remember to ask important questions such as what their lead time is and whether you can have a discount if you collect direct.

> **Checkpoint**
>
> Make sure that you understand the prices of coloured paper or extra ink colours. Sometimes if you give good advance notice you might be able to have an extra colour printed back to back with another job in the same ink.

Pre-event events (tasters)

Some events are just crying out to be given a taster session. By this I mean going to your potential audience and giving them a little hint of what is to come, rather than waiting for them to read the publicity flyers and decide to come to you. It can be as low key as sending a couple of jugglers to the town square before a circus skills workshop. Or you could take half the cast of the pantomime to the local department store to act out some of the scenes followed by an autograph signing session and interview with your local radio.

At Stevenage I once planned to drive a horse-drawn hearse complete with black plumed horses and draped coffin, all around the town with no other explanation than for a 'mourner' telling people to be ready – ready for what? – at the Gordon Craig Theatre that night at 7.45 pm. Sadly I couldn't find anyone near enough to supply the hearse but three lugubrious characters dressed up in black suits and top-hats did the job in a very sinister fashion and managed to drum up a good late audience to a spoof Dracula show.

Use your imagination and be as off-the-wall as you dare. Tasters are a very immediate form of marketing. You can even have a temporary box office in a caravan nearby selling tickets.

Signage

It does not matter how well you think your venue is known, there are bound to be people who have never heard of it so signs are always useful.

Large events

For a large event it may pay to ask the RAC or the AA to do road signs for you. Both organisations are experienced in this work and cover the whole country. They offer very much the same service but it might be worth asking for a quotation from each as costs may vary from area to area.

Road signs need planning permission and you must make contact with either of these organisations a couple of months in advance of when you want the signs to be put up, usually 48 hours in advance of the event. You do not need to be a signs expert as their signs officer will help you with suggested wording for the notices, the location and how many signs you will need.

Smaller events

For most events you will not need to go to such elaborate lengths, but for any show, signs on the roadside e.g. on a council-owned verge, will probably need temporary planning permission as they could cause a distraction to motorists.

Signs on trees or on posts overlooking the road but situated on private property such as fields or gardens are however exempt from planning permission.

Checkpoint

Don't attempt to put too much on a notice: the name of the event and an arrow may be all that is needed. Think hard whether you will need to include a date. If they are dated and you wish to repeat the event next year they will have to be re-painted. The day of the week may be all that is necessary.

On-site signs

Signs within the site are a different matter and are entirely up to you. The sort of signs that are useful are directions to the car park, toilets, refreshments, first aid post, lost children's gathering point, secretary's tent or crèche. Other events might need signs to grouped trade stands such as crafts, clothing, toys, etc.

Sign construction

The best signs are painted on wood or metal and mounted on wooden stakes, hammered securely into the ground. However as long as it is weatherproof and reasonably rigid, any material will do. If your event is to become an annual tradition then it could be worth getting the signs screen printed with a more permanent design for use year after year.

Key points:

- You cannot afford to give marketing a miss.
- Identify your attenders and intenders.
- Bring the flavour of your event into your publicity.
- Consider all aspects of marketing as outlined above.
- Make a marketing plan that is unique to every event.
- Target your publicity.
- Remember that there are more ways of making money than relying on an entrance fee.
- Ensure that your event suits your sponsors, landlord and cause.
- Always use the golden rules for advertising.
- Negotiate prices for everything.
- For larger events use the professionals to take the chore out of signing.
- Consider pre-event activities and launches.
- Work to a time scale and stick to it. Allow more time than you think is strictly necessary.

8

Your safety responsibilities

The whole question of safety responsibilities used to be left to discussions of the running of professional events – but no longer. Legislation has toughened up in recognition of the increased role that the voluntary sector plays in all our lives, not just fundraising. This has resulted in a bit of a paradox. On the one hand volunteers need to take an increasingly professional approach and on the other, with the devolution of funds, more and more voluntary organisations are being created and more and more volunteers are working in the marketplace, sometimes with little or no experience.

Because health and safety law has been written primarily for the paid employment sector there are some areas affecting the voluntary sector that are confusing or ill-defined. Never let it be forgotten that, even if you truly believe that an area of law does not affect you or your event, we all, nevertheless, have a duty of care.

This chapter covers the following topics:
▶ Health and safety at work
▶ Risk assessment
▶ Fairgrounds and related safety certificates

Health and safety at work

The Health and Safety at Work Act 1974 is not only concerned with people in a formal place of work engaged in paid employment for a registered company or individual. It is a 'catch all' law intended to secure the health, safety and welfare of people at work, whether paid or voluntary. It is also particularly concerned with protecting third parties, for example the innocent passer-by who has something fall on his head from above. If an accident occurs as a result of activities taking place because of your event the investigating authority will be looking for someone on whom to pin the blame and prosecute. That will almost certainly be a member or members of the organising group of the event.

Any activity that involves scaffolding or building work of any kind will be classified as 'the assembly of a structure' and the laws surrounding this work are very stringent. If you are using scaffolding towers, even to make a small grandstand for instance, you are required to have it erected professionally, thus taking the onus off yourselves.

Any group organising any event other than a few stalls or teas and games should study a very readable and clear government publication called *The Event Safety Guide: Essentials of Health and Safety at Work* published by The Stationery Office (see Publications at the back of this book). All types of work and activity are covered and it gives very practical and easy-to-use guidelines and illustrations on avoiding hazards and what to do in emergencies. It is a sobering thought that every year over 500 people lose their lives whilst engaged in work activities and thousands more are injured or suffer work-induced illness.

Be aware that any area of your event could potentially give rise to a claim and it doesn't have to be covered by specific legislation. You have a duty of care to all people, animals and property and if that duty is considered to be neglected, a claim against you can be brought under the law of negligence.

Risk assessment

Risk assessments are nothing more than a careful examination of what, in your work, could cause harm to people so that you can weigh up whether you have taken sufficient precautions or should do more to prevent harm occurring.

Professional event organisers, schools or workplace leisure officers would not dream of organising any event without carrying out a detailed risk assessment and recording it. It would be professional suicide to be so negligent and, in any case, it is a requirement of the Management of Safety at Work Regulations 1999.

As a voluntary group you may not be required to carry out a risk assessment by law unless you employ more than five people (under five people employed and you don't have to record your findings) but you would be strongly advised to do so.

Where to start

Start by making some observations which, in simple terms, you then divide into two groups. You are looking for:

- potential hazards;
- subsequent risks.

For each identified risk (i.e. who might be harmed and how) you should assess whether it can be reduced or eliminated – existing precautions may be adequate. Record your significant findings and your actions. For each risk, you should then decide when next to review your assessment.

Sources of help

When you are new to event organising, it is unlikely that you will have enough experience to carry through a carefully detailed and thorough risk assessment. You would be well advised to ask for direction and specialist help from the Health and Safety Executive (HSE). Your local office will be listed in the telephone directory under 'Health and Safety Executive'. You could also contact your local environmental health department.

You will also need the cooperation of those people in your group who have special responsibilities such as running the bar and catering, loading and unloading equipment, erecting infrastructure and so on. Alert the people involved to the fact that they will need to help make assessments in their particular areas. As well as achieving a more accurate assessment you are also more likely to get a more committed response if you ask for opinions and keep people involved in the process.

A unique risk assessment should be carried out for each of your activities or events and whenever you are aware of any new practices. You have a moral, if not legal, obligation to provide the general public, and your volunteer staff, with the same level of protection that they can reasonably expect from any professionally organised event.

In a fundraising book covering such diverse areas there can only be room to stress the importance of certain considerations and I suggest that you look carefully at a detailed guide, *The Health and Safety Handbook for Voluntary and Community Organisations* published by DSC (see Publications at the back of this book).

Electrical supplies

When using any electrical supply, and in particular three phase (see Chapter 9), it is prudent to have a qualified electrical engineer check all the connections, leads and equipment. You have a responsibility to protect the public and you may be required to have the site checked by a qualified inspector by the terms of the contract or insurers. Your local council will hold a list of qualified inspectors.

Fairgrounds and safety certificates

Most fairgrounds are owned by professional showmen and women. You can sometimes book individual rides but more usually you employ the whole works

– rides, stalls, candy floss pitches, fairground personnel, everything. You can let them come on to the site free of charge if you wish to offer an added attraction, but most showmen will think it worth their while to pay £500 and more for the pitch depending on how good it is. Some showmen and women can be intimidating if you have never worked with them before and you need to be clear what it is that you require from them and what they will expect from you and what your rights and legal requirements are.

Traditional fairs are frequently family run and culturally they operate a matriarchal society, which means that although the men will talk big, you will often do your financial business only with the women.

Many showmen prefer to work the sites that they are familiar with and, in the main, they are likely to turn up as planned if they are not going somewhere new, especially if they have paid a pitch fee in advance. It goes without saying that there are fairground operators who always behave honourably, but speaking from many years of personal experience, it is worth noting that there are some you cannot always rely on.

Site safety

If the event is organised by you or your club and a fair is present at your invitation it is up to you to provide a safe, firm, level site to park the fairground. It will be your insurance which has to pay up if there is an accident.

You will also have to ensure that the site is safe after the fair is set up a few hours before you open to the public and for this you will need a site inspection from a member of NAFLIC (National Association for Leisure Industry Certification). You can ask for a list of qualified inspectors from your local HSE office or you can look on the NAFLIC website. This is not a very easy site to use; you will have to look through the whole list of member inspectors as they are arranged (the last time I looked) in alphabetical order and not by region or county. Make sure you book someone well in advance because, in some areas, the inspectors are thin on the ground and some days are more popular than others.

The inspection is arranged at the showmen's expense and they know that they will have to pay the engineer before they can be issued with a site Safety Certificate. In addition every ride has to have an annual inspection, rather like an MOT, and is given a certificate if it is safe. You have the right to see all the certificates.

You might like to give the site the once over before the inspector comes so that you can point out anything that worries you. Here are examples of the sort of things you should be looking for.

- Are the gangways clear, and wide enough to get emergency vehicles through if needed?
- Are all the cables heavy duty and weather proof?
- If cables cross gangways do they need to be 'flown' over (above seven feet) or dug into the ground so they cannot cause people to trip.
- Do the rides look well maintained or are safety rails missing or moving parts unprotected?

Be aware that the inspector has the right to close any ride or indeed the whole fair if it is deemed unsafe although it is highly unlikely that any fairground operator will allow himself to lose his livelihood due to wilful negligence

If you are unhappy with any aspect of your fair or the behaviour of the showmen running it you can complain to the Showmen's Guild of Great Britain – your local section secretary will be listed in the telephone directory.

Key points:

- Remember that the Health and Safety at Work Act covers ALL activities that take place in the public domain.
- Conduct a risk assessment for each and every one of your activities.
- If you are using a commercial fair make sure that every ride has its 'MOT' and that you obtain a Safety Certificate for the whole fairground.

PART THREE

ON THE DAY AND AFTERWARDS

Infrastructure

Where does all that equipment that you see in use at events and shows come from and how does it get there?

Even for a small 'do' in the village hall or a bring-and-buy sale in the back garden you need a certain amount of equipment. For very small scale events you may be able to supply all that you need from your own and friends' houses, and the tables and chairs that you have borrowed are probably small enough to go into the back of a few trips of an estate car or private trailer. For larger events with greater numbers of people attending this may well not be possible.

This chapter covers the following topics:
▶ Basic equipment for indoor events
▶ Basic equipment for outdoor events
▶ Ticket booths
▶ Utilities
▶ Car parking.

Basic equipment for indoor events

If your show is to be in a public building such as a community centre, church or sports hall, most of what you will need is very likely to be available on site with or without an extra charge. You can expect chairs, tables, benches, podiums, stage risers and lecterns all to be fairly common requests. If an official 'cash desk' does not exist, then a very effective filter system can be made between a sales person sitting at a table and another opposite on foot to control the line.

Basic stage lighting and public address systems are often 'in situ' but a full stage lighting rig might pose more of a problem. Most suppliers are listed in *Yellow Pages* under 'theatrical services or supplies'. Any suppliers of lights should also be able to provide a sound system if necessary.

Setting up a barn

For an event in a barn you will have to provide everything required, transporting it both to the venue and removing it afterwards. And before you decide on holding an event in a barn, think of the possible fire hazards. They are really only a safe venue if brick-built, scrupulously swept clean of all combustible materials, such as straw and hay, and cleared of all chemicals and farm equipment. If your barn is part of a farmyard complex, ensure that other buildings are locked and that all farm equipment and animals are inaccessible and safe.

If a barn really is the only option, then you should provide proper equipment like decent seating facilities. Never, never use bales of straw. Not only are they incredibly dangerous due to their flammable nature, but their use could invalidate your insurance. Make sure that numerous buckets of sand are available for stubbing out cigarettes and provide fire extinguishers, suitably and prominently signed. In a climate of increasing health awareness it may even be acceptable to make the barn a smoke free zone and request that smokers indulge their habit outside in a designated area away from other farm buildings.

Sources of tables and chairs

For all events, if you cannot provide enough tables, trestles and chairs through your own contacts then possible sources might be schools, village or church halls, community centres or marquee firms. Some areas might have companies, again listed in *Yellow Pages*, who specialise in hire services for functions.

Some education authorities sell off old school chairs at regular sales and this can be a good source of chairs, tables and desks if you don't mind them being a bit tatty and you think you are going to have regular use from them.

Basic equipment for outdoor events

Events outside tend to pose more of a challenge. You have to build your own walls, doors and floors, as it were, before you start. Your 'walls' will include:

- fencing (if it is used);
- parade rings;
- crowd control barriers;
- the shape and placing of stands and marquees;
- bumbling pins and ropes (bumbling pins are thin metal stakes with the tops curled over like a pig's tail to guide a length of rope – they are a very flexible and cheap form of marking out an area).

The box office, entrance gate or ticket booth are your 'doors' and the 'floor' is usually grass. Bear in mind that because grass is subject to the vagaries of the British climate its appearance when you chose the site in April may be quite different when you come to set up the event in July. Remember also that it may need to be cut or protected with matting if the weather has been wet or if you have had a drought. Slippery grass is also dangerous and needs to be covered to prevent accidents. Matting or flexible plastic weather boarding is available from tent hire companies. You can find such companies from *Yellow Pages* or the *Showman's Directory*.

General fencing

The first thing you must decide is the type of job you want your fence to do. This dictates the nature of your fencing.

If all you need is a demarcation line marking the boundaries of, perhaps, a car park, then stakes and a rope will be quite adequate. However, if you are selling entry tickets you will need to be able to keep out those people who are determined to get in for free. Here two-and-a-half metre chestnut paling at the very least will be necessary, especially if you have limited alternative security. This may be available from the estates department or direct labour organisation of your local council or possibly on hire from builders' suppliers, building or highway contractors or – at greater cost – from fencing services companies; again try *Yellow Pages*.

If you intend to erect the chestnut paling yourselves, you need as many volunteers as you can muster, some large sledge hammers (they are often available with the fencing) and at least a day to do it in. It is very hard work and best left to contractors.

Fencing for parade rings

The safest fencing for parade rings, if you are showing horses or stock, is to use good quality, interlocking crowd control or stock barriers. They have the added advantage of operating very satisfactorily as gates which enables the whole ring to be sealed quickly if an animal gets loose. I have known this happen more than once at a Heavy Horse show during the young handlers and foal classes. A shire yearling, loose and going at full throttle is pretty unnerving and it definitely helps if you can keep it contained! On the other hand you might want to remove an animal urgently from a ring and barriers allow you to make a gap anywhere you like.

Crowd control barriers can be hired from your local council or, failing that, from a national supplier. If you have any problems finding a supplier your local police station may be able to help. Give several weeks' notice and don't forget to give a delivery address; you don't want to end up with 300 barriers in your front garden! Be aware that barriers and their feet are often delivered dismantled and you will be required to put them together, which takes more time on the day. For high security sites you can use a two metre high fencing called K/Fence. This fencing is only really necessary at high-risk music events and is available from specialist event service companies as listed in *The White Book* or the *Showman's Directory* (see Publications at the back of this book). It is pretty costly.

Tents and marquees

Again you might be able to borrow tents from the local authority but you have a wide choice of hire companies available. Traditional canvas marquees with a ridge pole and guy ropes are a bit of a thing of the past; they always look attractive but take up more space and need considerably more people to erect than the more modern plastic coated, free standing rigid frame tents.

A more interesting way of tackling the weather problem is to use temporary inflatable buildings or the spectacular canopy tents that are increasingly available known such as the beautiful Pagoda or more subtle Sheltent which look like giant sails or birds' wings. Many marquee companies advertise in *Yellow Pages*.

For very small spaces or stands you could use a telescopic 'mini marquee' that you can put up in a couple of minutes.

Ticket booths

Most events can get away with no ticket booths at all; a large number operate using a good filter system made from crowd control barriers. Another way of organising a filter system is to direct the queue to walk through an open-ended tent furnished with an appropriate number of trestle tables and ticket sellers. This is particularly effective if you are running a large event and expect a large crowd in a short space of time, or if it is dark outside or raining. (See Chapter 10 under Security for more information on the numbers of ticket sellers required.)

The simplest form of ticket booth is made from folding 5cm x 5cm frames covered by plywood sheets or canvas to protect a free-standing table or chair within.

Your decision as to which system to use may largely rest on what sort of an event you are planning. Shows that are on the arts end of the spectrum are traditionally entered through a box office. Fetes and fairs use crowd control barriers and sports events may well use a turnstile system.

In the end you may find that the decision comes down to one of finances, or aesthetics or availability, or all of these considerations. Provided the cash raised from ticket sales is removed regularly to a secure store you should not have a problem whatever system you use.

Checkpoint

When they are looking forward to an event, people are happy to stand in line as long as the queue can be seen to be progressing. If you know you will have a problem at peak periods, try keeping the crowd amused with buskers or at least display signs to indicate, say '10 minutes from here'. They can then make their own choice to stay or come back later.

Another useful idea is to display a site plan next to the queue to tempt the public into dispersing quickly once inside and help prevent the inevitable bunching that occurs just inside the gates whilst people decide what to see first.

Utilities

If you know that you are going to need electricity, gas or water on site then you need to check for availability. However, it's not the end of the world if you get there and find that your otherwise perfect venue is without the utility you need as you can, if necessary, bring it with you.

Portable electricity generators

If you are using public property, a metered all weather electrical supply may well be connected and ready for use. If not, almost all tool hire companies will stock portable generators of varying sizes suitable for most electrical needs.

As some 'portables' are exceedingly heavy you may have to arrange delivery; make sure that the generator is left exactly where you planned, as you may not be able to move it yourselves. Small portable and semi-portable generators will probably run on petrol, the larger and more powerful ones will need diesel. Check with your supplier that you have enough fuel on site for all your needs and store it safely away from fire and out of the sun. Remember too that you will need an alternator (although this may be integral, but don't count on it) to convert your 'homemade' power into something your equipment is more used to. Modern generators are much quieter than they used to be but you still have to make sure that you have enough cable to place it far enough away from the entertainment to ensure that your crowd can hear the announcer, for instance.

For small- and medium-scale events it is unlikely that you will need a three-phase supply; however you may occasionally find that for certain types of usage it can work out cheaper than using single phase.

If you use a generator capable of producing three-phase electricity you will have the advantage of having both single and three phase available if necessary. If a three-phase supply is not on site you could hire a generator instead or ask the local electricity board to connect a temporary supply. Don't forget your responsibility to protect the public and have the site checked by a qualified electrical engineer (see Chapter 8).

Mains gas

Whilst virtually all buildings will be connected to mains electricity and water, not all will have a mains gas supply and, unless there is a cafe or clubhouse on a sports field or recreation ground, your outside venue will almost certainly be lacking a gas facility. Cooking, refrigeration and heating are the main needs for gas and can all be adequately provided for using Propane or Calorgas. Suppliers of LPG (liquid petroleum gas) can be found in the *Yellow Pages* under 'bottled gas'.

Water supply

Water will be necessary if you are supplying refreshments or have animals as part of your show. Horses especially are very thirsty, particularly in the summer, and for a horse show you will need gallons of fresh water available. A standpipe is ideal, but it is not always possible to provide or it may be too far to carry buckets back and forth from one pipe on a very large site. Hose pipes are not adequate or reliable and are too susceptible to damage. If a mains water supply is impossible then you will have to have clean tanks filled by a bowser (a large trailer-tanker pulled by a tractor or similar). Most parks departments have access to water bowsers or, if you are in the country, a sympathetic farmer may come to your rescue.

Catering companies can be expected to make their own water arrangements but they need to be warned if none is available on site, If you are providing the refreshments then ensure that you are able to provide adequate supplies of water to drink.

Key points:

- Try to think of all the equipment and facilities that you might need well in advance.
- Remember to arrange for transport if extra items are not delivered.
- Think hard before you decide to use a barn. They are potentially dangerous.
- You may be able to hire or borrow much of the equipment from your local council but you will find commercial suppliers listed in *Yellow Pages*. Tool hire companies can be a good source.
- Remember the grass may need cutting or protecting.
- Ensure that you understand the needs and dangers of any generator that you might hire. Have a qualified electrician check all the connections and lighting rigs before you open. Store the fuel in a safe place.
- Check Chapter 8 for how to conduct a risk assessment;
- A standpipe might be vital if you involve animals; failing that, you must be able to supply clean water by using other means;
- Make sure that all caterers are warned if water is not available on site.

Car parking

For any event be it indoors or out, in the country or in a big city, you will have people arriving by car. This can be a good opportunity to make some extra money, although the added attraction of a free car park can swell the crowds. If you wish to control parking, due to restricted space, you can just charge for car parking and have no entrance fee. This encourages more people to use one car and you can maximise your profit by using clever pricing elsewhere on site.

Any space that you choose to use for a car park will have to offer a suitable surface. Parking on a beach, for instance, is unwise as cars may not be able to get out easily. Similarly, if you have days of rain, the meadow that you had planned to use may be too boggy. On the other hand drivers do not expect acres of tarmac, beautifully marked out and most are prepared to park on grass and walk several hundred yards although they will need it reasonably dry and firm underfoot.

In urban areas you will not be able to make money from official car parks but parking might still need to be controlled, usually by the police (see Chapter 4).

Making it pay

It is usual to charge for the car and not for the passengers. You will need to fence the area and allow only one entrance so that you can charge each car as it approaches. Frequently, after the first few hours, you can let the car park look after itself and open another access as a second exit as the small number of cars coming towards the end of the show will not warrant keeping someone on the gate.

As long as it is fairly obvious where to park – placing a few staff cars in prominent places can help start the lines – or the field is very big you will not need stewards.

If you are expecting a great many cars or think they will turn up all at once due perhaps to a particular time for the start of a performance it might be prudent to have several stewards directing cars and taking money at the same time. In this way you can avoid a hold up in the road as they turn into the entrance.

If you provide a coloured ticket to display in the windscreen then you can have stewards patrolling, directing and taking money without fear that you will miss some cars.

Just getting 'em parked

As a rough guide, you need a 5m × 2m space to park one car and allow room for passengers to get out without hitting the car beside them. If you have cars parked nose to nose with a 6m lane to use as a turning circle behind each double row you will not go far wrong. Coaches need a space 14m × 4m and you would be advised to keep them to a single line if possible and separate from the cars.

It can help to reserve one section for cars with passes even if you are not charging for parking. It is embarrassing if the Mayor or VIPs cannot find a space reasonably near the entrance.

It isn't usually necessary to have marked and numbered spaces for small or medium scale events. These are only used if you are selling reserved spaces in advance or your event is based around the cars you are parking, such as a vintage car rally. In this case you will need considerably more space around each vehicle and you get better visibility if parking is arranged on the diagonal.

Checkpoint

The easiest way I know to get cars parked quickly and efficiently is to ask the Lions Club, Scouts, or similar to help. You can usually arrange a mutually beneficial arrangement: something along the following lines for instance. The Lions keep the car park money but provide stewards for the whole event; or, the event organisers keep the car park money but the Lions receive a percentage as a donation; or, the organisers keep the money but allow the Lions some other money making facility such as the tea tent or another activity that the Lions want to bring along. Doing it this way takes the pressure off you on the day.

Clubs such as the Lions, who are experienced at parking cars, often have their own pre-printed vests to wear. It is thus clear who the stewards are and you do not have the added expense of having to hire special coats or print armbands.

Competitors'/peformers' cars

If you are running an event where there are competitors or performers it is probably prudent to keep a separate area free for their vehicles. When it comes to horseboxes or stock lorries it is also a matter of safety to keep them away from the public. Look at the ground carefully if you expect heavy lorries – and some can be very heavy! I remember one summer when the river at the bottom of the competitors' car park had flooded the week before a Heavy Horse show and although the ground seemed firm enough in the morning, by the end of the day trailer after trailer had difficulties getting off the site. One particularly heavy horsebox eventually had to be towed out and I was not popular.

Security equipment for after dark

It is possible that an event might finish after dark. This can present special security and safety problems that are not necessarily present during daylight. In this case you will need to provide a few mobile floodlights so that pedestrians crossing the car park are not in danger and to deter thieves. Be very vigilant about trip hazards especially if bumbling pins and ropes are used to fence the park and make sure the exits are clearly signed in direct light.

Key points:

- Decide whether you want to make money from parking cars or not.
- Estimate the number of cars that may come and plan your area carefully and think about the surface.
- Separate visitors' and competitors' or performers' cars.
- Consider asking another organisation to run the car parking for you.
- Light the area at night.

10

On site

This chapter covers the following topics:

▶ Running times and orders for performances
▶ Security
▶ First aid
▶ Loos and litter
▶ Final instructions and checks
▶ Useful items to have to hand.

Running times and orders for performances

You will need to have worked out a running order well in advance, probably down to the minute. Plan to pack things together tightly and have plenty going on at once. Events are best when there is a sense of urgency about the day. They really seem tedious when you have to wait 15 minutes between each item.

It is strange but on the day, when performers are good and a show is going well, everything seems to speed up. (The exception to this rule is pantomime, the performers get so carried away that several minutes can be added in the form of off-the-cuff responses to the audience). The adrenaline is high and even animals move faster so you can suddenly be left with a long gap between acts. Make sure that you programme in lunch and tea breaks to bridge the gaps or allow for catching up with yourselves if you are running late. It is better to run late than early but make sure you announce the fact that you are overrunning over the PA system and restart as near as you can to the published time in the programme after the break.

The public will spend the time looking at stands or getting something to eat as long as they expect a pause but they won't stay for long if everything starts to drag.

Optimum running times

Most people will not stay at any event for longer than about three hours. Families with small children will frequently stay less than three hours, so if you plan a show to be open for four or five hours be prepared for a certain amount of turnover – which is good and swells your entrance take. This way you will catch nearly everyone who wants to come and they will be left feeling they would like a little more and might well come again another time.

Scheduling judging time at competitions

If your event is really a specialist competition that is open to the public, such as a horticultural or cat show, ensure that all the judging is done in the morning (even before you let the public in). Always get the bulk of the competition out of the way by lunch time. Of course this doesn't go for events like horse shows where the competitions are the entertainment as well as the exhibits. However in all cases any entertainment section of the schedule should always be scheduled for the afternoon.

Keep the 'best in show' for the last class of the day, and whilst the judges are deliberating, you can give the audience something rather more light-hearted to enjoy, such as a demonstration, and then end with a parade or procession if appropriate.

Security

Handling money at the gate

Unless you have a till, you will need a receptacle to keep your float and sales money in. At the very least a couple of empty ice cream containers will do. Keep them fitted one inside the other with notes in the bottom one so that they do not blow away.

Two people are needed on the door, one to tear off tickets and keep an eye on the queue and one to look after the money and give change. If one is called away in an emergency you will still have someone to sell the tickets.

For a larger outdoors event you will need several people along an eight foot table for every entrance or filter that you are using. You should keep money in several containers to prevent losing the lot if someone makes a grab for it.

Ensure that a couple of trustworthy collectors are appointed to remove accumulated notes at regular intervals throughout the day. They will need somewhere secure to take them to and a safe kept in a staffed club caravan or clubhouse is ideal. I suggest that whenever money is carried around it should be accompanied by two people.

Handling money after the event

After the event is over the bank or building society may not be open for you to deposit the income. You will need access to a safe or make arrangements with your bank to use the nightsafe, preferably during the hours of daylight. It is probably unwise to take the money home unless it really is a very small amount. But if you do, on the Monday morning, give the bank or building society a telephone call to warn them you are coming in and give them an indication as to how much you think you are bringing. They may want you to come at a time when they know they will be quiet as one cashier will be busy weighing your money for some time, especially if you have had a collection in small coins.

Handling alcohol and cigarettes

On the whole criminals at events are interested in very little other than money, alcohol and cigarettes. Alcohol and cigarettes should therefore only be sold from a restricted area or designated bar and money should be kept on site for as short a time as possible and even then kept out of sight and away from public access.

Prizes and cups

Occasionally prizes or cups prove attractive to the potential thief and it is probably sensible to keep them out of sight.

Illegal entries

One other security problem is people trying to enter your show ground or building without paying. This is almost impossible to control on a large outdoor event site but with limited entrances, reasonably substantial fencing and a couple of large people making regular patrols to repair any gaps you should be able to keep illegal entries to a minimum.

For people wanting to go off the site and return later you will need to give pass-outs; the simplest workable method is to rubber stamp their hands. A stamped hand is impossible to pass over the fence but ticket pass-outs are wide open to abuse. Because of the closed nature of a building you should have little difficulty with security but a tent may present more of a challenge. You will have to have several exits from a tent for emergencies but, unlike a building, you will not be able to keep them shut with crash bars.

To be absolutely certain you catch everyone at the official entrance you will have to put a 'bouncer' on each exit, at least until the show is well under way.

First aid

The St John Ambulance Brigade and the Red Cross are the two main bodies in Britain who are prepared to give their services free of charge to events all around the country. They need to be booked well in advance and for a small event just a couple of members on foot may be all that is required. For a large event, they may suggest bringing a vehicle or a tent and you will have to plan a space in the centre of the site. If you are indoors then a specially designated room or Portacabin close to the main building will have to be made available. You will find the local headquarters for each listed in the *Yellow Pages* for your area.

A donation is always welcomed and may be compulsory as they, like you, are working with volunteers as a charitable organisation.

Loos and litter

This section concerns itself with what a crowd leaves behind after the show is over. The problem is almost entirely confined to outdoor events as any 'do' indoors is going to be in a building that has at least basic toilet facilities (except barns) and, perhaps with a few additions, enough ashtrays and waste bins to satisfy all needs.

Getting rid of the rubbish

Let's look at litter first. It doesn't seem to matter how many bins you provide, the Great British public still prefers the ground. It does help, though, if you put the bins in the right places, i.e. right under their noses as they throw things away.

Study the site to decide which places are likely to generate the most litter and place your bins accordingly. These sites will include:

- the entrance gate if you are selling tickets or programmes;
- all around the refreshment tents, takeaway stands and ice-cream vans;
- stalls where raffle tickets are used;
- bran tubs or lucky dips;
- cake stalls where a surprising number of people are greedy enough to rip the wrappers off their chocolate crispy cakes and eat them there and then!

For small events a few ordinary domestic dustbins – minus the lids – lined with a black bag and borrowed from friends will often be enough. On a windy day you may need to weight them with something heavy to stop them blowing over. In windy weather you should also empty all bins when they are half full or provide wide wire-mesh lids for each bin. Rubbish soon starts to blow away if you allow it to accumulate.

A larger fete will need a significant number of bins and liners, which you may be able to borrow from the environmental health department of your local council or, at the very least, fence posts with a thick black bin liner securely fixed at one point so that it presents an open top. Where you are likely to have huge quantities of rubbish such as outside a multi-station burger bar you may have to go for large oil drums and ensure that they are emptied when full.

For any but the smallest show, it is judicious to rent a skip of an appropriate size so that you do not have to cart loads of garbage to the nearest tip. Even if the council has a collection service it will not be until after the weekend and food waste will attract dogs, cats and vermin.

Deciding on adequate toilet facilities

Toilet facilities come in many different forms ranging from a ditch with a telegraph pole to sit on – quite revolting and not up to legally required standards (some may remember the sort of thing from scout camp days) – to the grandeur of a complete bank of flushing WCs in wooden cubicles sited within a lined, carpeted marquee.

You should aim to provide facilities suited to your event and finances. If you need a Public Entertainment Licence because you are running a largely musical event the number of sanitary facilities may be governed by the terms of the licence.

Whatever you choose, try to make arrangements for wheelchair visitors who cannot manage steps. There may be other special needs you want to cater for: mobile baby changing facilities are available for hire nowadays, a luxury I could have done with when I first started running events. In any case, people wanting to dispose of dirty nappies should be encouraged to do so safely. Provide covered bins, at the very least, or a special, lined nappy disposal unit at best. This facility needs to be adequately signed.

If your venue has a manhole cover over a drain on site you will be able to use a mobile unit that has flushing facilities. This stands over the hole and drains direct into the main sewer. (If necessary, they can also drain direct into a deep hole dug for the purpose.) The flush is provided from a tank of water located in the roof. These mobile units are towed onto the site complete with full tank and left free standing. They are, very simply, a rectangular caravan with an internal division and a door at either end providing discrete male and female facilities in the one unit. The large mobile loos can probably accommodate four or five cubicles in the Ladies and one cubicle and a six foot run of urinal in the Gents. Both sides have hand-washing facilities and some may be fitted with battery powered lights. Arrangements have to be made to supply them with soap, paper and towels throughout the day.

The next best loo you can use is a 'tardis' affair with one loo and a tiny basin in a rigid box. These come with and without flush and use sanitising chemicals designed to last a whole day, or more, without being topped up. They are often arranged in rows on more than one area of the site. The same system can be hired for less money if you go for a tent surround but this comes without the hand basin. You will need at least two of these single units.

Finally, (and frankly only one stage better than the telegraph pole) you could use a tall canvas surround, placed over a hole in the ground. Around the hole goes a kind of shower base with a hole cut in the middle to provide 'croucho marks' as one member of my family succinctly observed when describing certain French motorway facilities! Care must be taken when filling in these holes at the end of the day and a dose of lime might not go amiss.

Hiring loos

You can hire all types of toilets from builders' suppliers or marquee firms. The single units might be available from tool hire companies and your local council may be able to supply the larger units and disabled loos (sometimes free of charge) themselves or put you in touch with a supplier.

Legal requirements of loo provision

The law is rather open ended about the supply of toilet facilities for outdoor events. Legally you are not obliged to supply anything unless it is within the terms of Public Entertainments Licence (see Chapter 6), but if you chose to do so – and you would be well advised to – you must supply facilities to a certain standard. Guidelines are available from your local environmental health department and an officer will always be prepared to advise you. *The Event Safety Guide* published by the HSE has a good chapter on suggested provision (see Publications at the back of the book).

How to work out the number of loos

Very briefly the figures I have always worked to, based on a four to six hour show are as follows:

Female conveniences: 1 loo per 150 females (100 if it is a family event)

Male conveniences: 1 loo per 100 males

3 loos per 500 male

5 loos per 1,000 males

1.5 m of urinal accommodation per 500 males

Unisex accommodation can allow greater flexibility and even a reduction in numbers of loos, but you should increase maintenance supervision. You should also increase provision if the event is longer than six hours duration.

Key points:

- Allow enough rubbish bins and /or liners for the expected number of spectators.
- Put bins in area of most use.
- Arrange for collection, a skip or to dump the rubbish yourselves.
- Suit the type of sanitary provision to your budget and event, but make sure whatever you choose is up to standard.
- Check the terms of any licences.
- Ensure that the loos are cleaned and maintained throughout the day and arrange for them to be in a hygienic condition when you leave unless otherwise arranged.
- Remember to provide facilities for disabled people and mothers with babies. Think about hygienic nappy disposal.

Final instructions and checks

So, now you have got to the day itself. You will feel a mixture of excitement and apprehension; a form of stage fright. You deserve to be congratulated for coming this far, many lesser mortals fall by the wayside under the weight of regulations, unhelpful suppliers or when the full enormity of what they are taking on dawns on them. But you are not out of the woods yet.

If your event is small or able to run with only the committee members on the day then, hopefully, you will have been present during the planning and know what your separate responsibilities are. However, for larger shows you will now be facing a line of volunteers and it is your job to make sure that everyone knows:

- what their job is;
- what the emergency procedures are;
- who has mobile phones and what their numbers are;
- where the first aid post is positioned;
- where the fire exits are if you are indoors;
- what you will be doing in case they get stuck and need to find you.

Keeping in contact

If you need to keep in contact you should have already decided if it is to be by mobile or by radio. If the latter, now is the time to hand them out and make sure that everyone knows how to use them properly. Remember to remind the operators where spare battery packs and the chargers will be kept.

Decide where your base will be – preferably a room where you can lock away the entrance money when the show starts – and ensure all your helpers will know where you will be. If your event covers a large site and you are not in touch over the ether, ensure that your public address (PA) system covers all the important parts of the show-ground: the arenas, beer tents, main seating areas, etc. and even the car parks.

Appropriate dress

You do not need to wear uniforms unless you are official stewards in a show-ring, in which case it is traditional to wear a dark suit and a bowler hat (even the women). However it helps for you, at least, to wear something distinctive – a brightly coloured tracksuit is fine; arm bands are not so good as they cannot be seen easily and in my experience often fall off anyway. A printed waistcoat or vest is ideal.

Cloakroom provision

It is worth remembering that people will want somewhere to leave their coats if there is no room by their seats or if it is a party; they might feel happier about leaving their belongings if you have a cloakroom attendant or two. As with outdoor events, it helps if all 'staff' are dressed in a similar way but if the whole show is a fairly intimate affair, badges might be adequate.

The importance of a site plan

I find it helpful to issue everyone with a site plan, which includes a police emergency number and running list, and spend five minutes talking it through with everyone involved. Arrive having worked out what needs to be done beforehand and offer jobs around rather than dole them out. Helpers tend to volunteer for the jobs for which they are most suited or like best so are less likely to get bored and wander off. If there is a particularly unpopular job, suggest that it is job-shared.

Making a final check

However many times you have checked things before, make a final check over the whole site or building about 15 minutes before you open. You will be surprised how many things have been moved or lost at the last minute.

Useful items to have to hand

A clipboard

It might seem stereotypical to be seen running around with a clipboard under you arm but it is the only way I know of keeping all your information together and instantly accessible without it getting lost or blowing away. You can keep extra running order sheets if others get lost, any extra piece of information that you are handed can be quickly secured and you have a constant reminder of important items in your hand.

If you can find a clipboard that has a fold-down waterproof cover, all the better. Some even have little pockets to keep small items which can be very useful and I always attach a pencil with a piece of string so that I never have to waste time looking for one.

An 'emergencies box'

Keep an 'emergencies box' in your car or office adjusted to the size and style of your event. This could contain:

- six to ten sheets of A4 stiff white card;
- permanent thick felt pens of varying colour;
- a stencil if you lack confidence as to your sign-writing prowess;
- two balls of string – one thick, one thin;
- a pair of serviceable scissors;
- Sellotape;
- thick insulating tape or duct-tape;
- a heavy duty staple gun;
- a tape measure;
- a basic tool kit;
- a first aid kit;
- a small portable fire extinguisher;
- something to eat and drink.

If your event is outdoors, you could add a hand-held megaphone and even a change of clothes and a sun hat. I once was helping to put up a marquee on a river bank when the man hauling a guy rope opposite me saw his wife walking down the towpath the wrong way. He let go of the rope and ran to head her off. The ridge pole fell down and the weight of canvas knocked me in to the river. I spent the whole of the rest of the the event in a borrowed track suit, three sizes too big, in baking sunshine!

With the help of the above kit, you should be able to design notices at the drop of a hat, make running repairs, put out minor fires, aid the injured, shout instructions, keep yourself in good working order and keep the sun off your head if you know it affects you. Eight hours outside without respite can be very demanding.

Key points:

- Enjoy the day and try to have everything precisely planned before you arrive.
- Inform all your helpers of the running order, all the tasks and clearing up jobs before you start. Allow them to choose what they will be doing.
- Ensure everyone knows where the nearest first aid kit is and who has telephones. Give out emergency numbers if necessary.
- Check everything 15 minutes before you open.
- Keep your show tightly packed with activities and remember to plan meal breaks where appropriate.
- Keep the public informed of changes to the advertised programme.
- After the entrance money has been collected for an indoor show remove cash to a safe area.
- Remember to bring an 'emergencies box'.

11

Catering

This chapter covers the following topics:

▶ Including food in your event
▶ Do food regulations apply to the event?
▶ The Food Premises (Registration) Regulations 1991
▶ Food hygiene
▶ The Food Safety Act 1990
▶ The Food Safety (General Food Hygiene) Regulations 1995 and the Food Safety (Temperature Control) Regulations 1995
▶ Food labelling.

Including food in your event

The offer of good and varied food is a very attractive part of most events. There is usually some way in which you can choose the food to fit your theme, perhaps Elizabethan apple pastries for an early dance exhibition or food from around the world for an ethnic cultures trade festival. And of course even your local fete would be lost without the traditional WI stall to offer its delicious supplies of fresh cakes, breads and bottled fruit, jams and pickles.

But the inclusion of food in an event can be a real problem. Where to keep it until it is wanted? How to keep it cool? How to keep it hot? What to do with the leftovers? How to gauge the demand correctly? What to do with the dirty dishes? Where to prepare it in the first place? But above all: how to keep food safe to eat?

In the following sections I hope to improve your knowledge, or remind you, of the good hygiene practices that you should use and the regulations that cover the provision of food at events and shows. (By food, I mean both food and drink throughout the chapter.) Good food hygiene may not be such an issue if you are holding your event indoors, especially if you have access to a purpose-built kitchen that includes sinks, a fridge and a good food preparation area recently inspected by an environmental health officer. Of course you should still use safe preparation techniques as outlined in the 'ten golden rules' (see below) but basic facilities such as fridges, separate sinks and easily cleaned surfaces should all be available.

Outdoors it is a different matter altogether. Most events take place in the summer at a time when we all hope that it will be warm and sunny, in fact perfect breeding weather for food bacteria, so caterers will have to be especially vigilant.

Do food regulations apply to the event?

As with all aspects of running events, you have a duty of care to ensure that the food and drink you provide is safe and of a reasonable standard whether on sale or available free of charge.

The important point to remember is that, although many of the relevant regulations are a 'grey area' when it comes to fundraising events, it is absolutely clear that:

- if someone becomes ill or dies as a result of your actions, whether or not you feel you are covered by the law, you may be found negligent and prosecuted as a result.

Clearly, then, you should comply with the regulations since they exist to promote good hygiene practice and safety.

Is the provision of food a 'business'?

You will have to decide if the food provision service you offer could be described as a business. In the terms of the regulations covering aspects of food handling the word 'business' is extended to include 'the undertaking of a canteen, club, school, hospital or institution, whether carried on for profit or not' and probably includes only undertakings where food is sold. In the case of canteens and clubs etc. the organisers of any event will clearly have to comply with the regulations detailed later in the chapter.

However, in many cases voluntary organisations will not need to comply. For instance, if you were to throw a party for your friends but asked for £5.00 a head to go towards the cost of the food and drink, no enforcing authority would care two hoots. But, when you get into the realms of taking a stall on the local market to sell your cakes for a profit, even if that profit is for charity, then your activities may be viewed in a different way.

In general the more commercial the operation appears to be, especially if you are acting in competition with other traders, the more likely it is that the relevant authorities will be interested. If you are providing foods at a very low key event such as at a church fete, officers are only likely to show an interest if there is illness caused by a hygiene or storage problem.

The Food Premises (Registration) Regulations 1991

As from 1991 all premises used for the purposes of a food business and the premises at which mobile food vehicles operating as a business are kept, now have to register with the local authority. This requirement covers the area of the premises or, in the case of a vehicle, where it is garaged at night.

If you are selling pitches for food vans it helps to ask for payment well in advance; you can then compile a list of all the business addresses and check for registration yourself or send the list on to the council if your event is held on council-owned land.

If your committee is organising the provision of its own food on a one-off basis you do not usually have to register with the local authority. However, as emphasised above, you should always observe good hygiene practices and advise and encourage those preparing food to keep records of systems of control, cleaning regimes, and so on. This gives weight to a defence of due diligence if a case against you is ever brought.

If you are preparing food on premises (including any stands, marquees, tents, mobile canteens, vending machines or any site or pitch from which food is provided) that are used over a period of weeks or consecutive days you may be required to register unless you are covered by the exemptions detailed below. You should take advice from your local authority. There are certain food premises, stands, stalls, vehicles etc. that are exempt from the requirement to register.

Exemptions

Registration does not apply:

- to the supply of beverages, biscuits, potato crisps, confectionery or other similar products ancillary to a business which is not the sale of food;
- to premises controlled by a voluntary organisation or the trustees of a charity which are used only for their own purposes and where no food (other than dry ingredients for the preparation of refreshments such as tea, coffee, sugar, biscuits, crisps and other similar products) is stored for sale;
- if the premises are not used for a food business for five days or more in any period of five weeks;
- where the premises are domestic premises but the proprietor of the business does not live there. By this you can suppose that the proprietor of the business might be the proprietor of the charity itself and simply means that volunteers preparing food for sale for charitable purposes might well be able to prepare food at home without registration.

Food hygiene

Anyone who is to work with food to any extent is advised to study the Basic Food Hygiene Certificate course provided by your local environmental health department. The Basic Certificate usually takes six hours tuition followed by a multiple choice examination and the qualification is recognised nationally. Display your certificate with pride on your stall and suggest that other regular helpers also study for the certificate.

The government does have power, under the Food Safety Act, to introduce compulsory food hygiene training via the local environmental health department for those involved in food businesses if it is deemed necessary. This gives you some idea of the importance that is attached to proper training in areas of food preparation, transport and storage.

If you are a member of the WI you may well be able to obtain training through the Institute itself as they have their own tutors. Annual refresher training is recommended because hygiene regulations and best practices move on. The *Industry Guide to Good Hygiene Practice* is the latest publication recommended by environmental health officers (see Publications at the back of the book).

Ten golden rules for good food hygiene

- ALWAYS wash your hands before handling food and after going to the toilet.
- TELL your boss, or supervisor, at once of any skin, nose or throat or bowel trouble.
- ENSURE cuts and sores are covered with waterproof dressings (preferably blue).
- KEEP yourself clean and wear clean clothing.
- DO NOT SMOKE in a food room. It is illegal and dangerous. Never cough or sneeze over food.
- CLEAN as you go. Keep all equipment clean.
- PREPARE raw and cooked food in separate areas. Keep food covered and either refrigerated or piping hot.
- KEEP your hands off food as far as possible.
- ENSURE waste food is disposed of properly. Keep the lid on the dustbin and wash your hands after putting waste in it.
- TELL your supervisor if you cannot follow the rules.

Do not break the law.
(Information provided by Food Sense booklet No. PB0351)

Something similar to this is available by all local environmental health departments. Contact your local council.

The provision of picnic areas

Providing a picnic area is a great way out of having to prepare food. Invite people to bring their own. You could, of course, provide a picnic area anyway for the takeaway food provided on the site. The advantages are that you can control the litter and restrict food being taken into exhibition areas.

Any adequately roped-off grassy space away from traffic or animals would be suitable. Provide lots of bins and a few tables and chairs and let the public do the rest.

The Food Safety Act 1990

This Act goes slightly wider than the regulations discussed above and covers all food; not just that prepared from a food premises. Local government inspectors now have greater powers than ever and are quite within their rights to inspect any premises (registered or not) in which food is prepared for the general public.

Unfit food

The Food Safety Act 1990 governs the condition of the food itself. If you are found to be offering food for sale which is unfit for consumption, or your food is falsely or misleadingly labelled you could be fined a maximum of £20,000 and/or imprisoned. So you need to be aware of where you might be contravening the law.

Unfit food could include food that is infected with bacteria or that included foreign bodies – anything from insect larvae to nails. Some foods are more likely to grow food poisoning organisms than others and particular care should be taken when preparing those foods classified as 'high-risk' such as: meat, fish, shellfish, dairy products and pastries or cakes containing fresh cream, egg dishes and cooked rice.

It is as well to realise that this regulation is exceptional in that it covers *any* supply of food that is not safe, even when there is no sale, so long as the supply is part of a business, in the broad sense of 'business' as explained before. So the regulation applies even if the food is free. It also applies to anything that might be prepared for prizes or given away to the general public at a social gathering of almost any kind. Barbecues can be especially at risk (see Chapter 3, Event 2).

An environmental health officer is entitled to inspect any premises if s/he suspects that an offence has been committed, including a domestic kitchen. This would almost certainly happen if he had been alerted to a possible problem by a complaint about say, a piece of glass being found in the middle of a homemade cake. However, in the case of domestic premises officers are not permitted to make an inspection (except with a magistrate's warrant) unless 24 hours notice in writing has been given. At the very worst, the cook could find him/herself prosecuted under the Food Safety Act for a foreign body and under the Hygiene Regulations for having a kitchen that was below the recommended standard. In practice this is highly unlikely to happen unless the complaint is very serious.

The Food Safety (General Food Hygiene) Regulations 1995 and the Food Safety (Temperature Control) Regulations 1995

These regulations cover all food which is produced commercially for profit as well as food produced by voluntary organisations. This means that all outside caterers or mobile food vans that you might employ have to comply. If you are not happy that they are carrying out their business properly then you can complain to your environmental health department.

This law covers permanent premises, equipment and food handlers associated with the preparation of food for consumption by the general public and includes all stages of that process from transportation, storage, packaging and even the seller of the food if that person comes into direct contact with the products.

Essentially the areas to be aware of are that high risk foods (as detailed above) should be kept refrigerated below 8°C, kept hot above 63°C and frozen at below –18°C unless otherwise specified on the product. There should be daily records kept of the gauges of fridges, freezers and hot plates. Your local environmental health officers will have the current leaflets produced by the Health Publications Unit to help you.

Food labelling

It is very hard to pin any of the professionals down on this subject. They know what the law states and as far as commercial companies are concerned they are prepared to follow it to the letter and throw the book at anyone who may be operating outside the law.

However, and I think this is because of the 'it has always been so' factor involved, small fetes, WI stalls, charity stands in the church hall and the produce left for auction after a garden produce and horticultural show tends to be treated rather more leniently in practice if not in theory. But you will not find any trading standards or environmental health officer in the country admitting this.

In many cases the food labelling requirements will not apply due to exemptions which cover prepared meals, sandwiches and un-packaged food. However, and I am sticking my neck out here, even where labelling might be considered necessary, I honestly do not believe that any inspector is going to prosecute if food offered for sale is not labelled absolutely correctly as long as it has been prepared hygienically, transported and stored responsibly, and offered for sale within a reasonable period suitably protected by a wrapper or other container.

The importance of labelling where there is a complaint

Of course, if there were complaints the manufacturer may still be liable under the Food Safety Act as shown in the earlier example of glass being found in a homemade cake. One of the requirements is to state the producer's name and address on each product and if this was missing from an item which was the subject of a complaint your organising group might find themselves the target for prosecution in the absence of proof of the true perpetrator.

In the light of this responsibility you might consider insisting that you accept no food product for sale that does not bear the name and address of the person who made it. On the other hand there is the very real danger of putting genuine volunteer cooks off the idea of producing food if it has to carry their name and address. Perhaps a way around this understandable stumbling block is to keep a record of all items and their manufacturers or use a producer code. You would then be able to trace produce back to source if there was a complaint.

Labelling pre-packed produce

The strict letter of the law insists that the following information is stated on a label attached to each product:

- The name of the food (which must not be misrepresented in any way).
- Description of what it is, if not covered by point 1.
- Name and address of manufacturer.
- 'Best before date' or 'Use by date'.
- Any specific storage instructions.
- List of ingredients starting with the greatest first by weight and including any additives.
- The quantity of the food in metric measures, using abbreviations and lettering as laid down by the Weights and Measures legislation.

If you follow the above rules you will be seen to be doing all you possibly can to conform, although just the first three instructions should be enough to cover most low-risk foods. Some other products must list specific percentages (e.g. cooked meat products and jams must list the amount of meat and fruit respectively) but I can't see how that can be applied to volunteer cooks preparing food in a domestic setting.

Nut allergies

One final point about labelling: in a world of increasing risk due to allergic reactions it would be very sensible to label clearly the presence of any nut product.

Key points:

- Do not be put off including food within your event as it can be a vital attraction but make sure your committee is aware of all the legal requirements.
- If you are at all concerned or confused ALWAYS talk to your local environmental health department or trading standards office well in advance.
- If someone is regularly preparing food for public consumption it would be sensible to suggest they take a Basic Food Hygiene Certificate course.
- Remember that it is not only food offered for sale that is covered by the Food Safety Act, it covers produce offered to the public whether money changes hands or not.
- Be aware of high-risk foods and be especially careful.
- It is unlikely that you will have to register your premises with the local authority unless you are operating on a regular basis, but check if you are unsure.
- Ensure that your group is aware of the laws surrounding food labelling and make yourselves familiar with the policies in practice in your area. Take advice if necessary.
- Use the 'ten golden rules of food safety'.

12

Specialist information

It is a sad fact of life that the needs of people who use wheelchairs, people who are visually handicapped or deaf, and children and their carers, are sometimes forgotten or at least only given cursory consideration during the excitement and enthusiasm of setting up an event.

This chapter covers the following topics:
- Access for all
- Children
- Animals
- Fireworks and bonfires
- Bouncy castles.

Access for all

Like architects and designers, anyone planning a fundraising event to which all members of the public are invited should, by definition, make the event accessible to all. This means people with babies, elderly people and people with permanent or temporary disabilities.

Achieving this will not always be possible and no-one is going to jump down your throat if you have tried but been unsuccessful. The main point to remember is that if you don't make an effort to push aside some of the barriers that face disabled people then the problem will always remain and discrimination continue – even in fundraising. In addition, you and your organisation will be open to criticism, which at the very least is bad publicity.

When considering the following points during the planning stage of any event someone might say, 'There probably won't be any disabled people coming to this event anyway, so why go to all this trouble and expense?'. Your response to this is quite simple. 'If you don't make arrangements you definitely won't get people with disabilities to come and spend their money'. Plus, having made the event accessible you can advertise it as such which will add to your credibility; ensure you use an inclusive and factual phrase such as 'wheelchair friendly' rather than 'we welcome the disabled,' which can sound exclusive and patronising.

Access from outside

As an organiser it is up to you to be aware of potential difficulties and making your event accessible will not necessarily be impossible. For example, if the front entrance to your chosen venue has a flight of steps, then you must ask if the owners have an arrangement which overcomes the problem like a ramp or a side entrance. It is not ideal to be forced to use a side or back entrance but at least this method gets people to where they want to go.

If site-owners do not have an alternative access you will have brought the shortfall to their attention and they should feel compelled to make amends. Let them know that they have lost your business this time but if they can remedy the problem you will consider holding your event there another time.

Outdoor events are far from being problem-free but they normally present fewer problems where access is concerned. However, if you are considering a turnstile entry then you will need to make arrangements for a more appropriate entrance for wheelchair users to use. This will also make life easier for people with pushchairs. As a general guide, the dimensions of a standard wheelchair are around 76cms wide by 128cms long.

Access within the venue

Considerations do not stop at finding a venue where a wheelchair user can enter and exit freely. You will also need free movement inside the premises with no obstructions inside, such as steps to refreshment areas or inaccessible toilets. Choosing a public building is obviously a wise choice because all these needs should be covered.

One of the biggest headaches facing wheelchair users at outdoor events is pushing across grass or uneven surfaces. It may not sound like much of a problem but consider the difference between pushing an empty wheelbarrow around a show all day and one with a heavy load. Then you will get some idea of how off-putting some venues can be.

Many permanent show grounds have tarmac surfaces leading to stalls and attractions and in terms of easy access for disabled people this is probably the best arrangement that anyone could make. Most smaller-scale events are not so lucky and you would be well advised to make a plan which limits the amount of moving around between attractions and choose the most level area of your site to situate your stalls and stands. Again, imagine yourself pushing a heavy wheelbarrow around all day and you should get an idea of how to lay out your event.

I talked about toilet facilities in Chapter 10 but the essentials to remember are that, again, they need to be sited on level ground and never near mud, deep gravel or spongy grass. Make sure the entrances are wide enough for a chair or someone with seeing difficulties to have a guide walking beside them – about one metre's width should do. If your event takes place at night make sure that all steps, ramps and car parks are illuminated – this makes sense for able-bodied people also – or provide a guide with a torch.

> **Checkpoint**
>
> A useful point to remember is that wheelchair accessible toilets can be used by non-disabled people but non-accessible toilets cannot be used by disabled people. So, if in doubt, get an extra accessible toilet and don't site it too far away from the action. There is no real reason for this, but it has become the norm, so give clear instructions to whoever is responsible.

Seated shows

For seated shows it is not enough to remove a seat for a wheelchair; you must also ensure that the space is level and has enough leg room. Able-bodied people do not appreciate falling over hard foot plates in the dark and for the owner of the chair it can be very painful. Traditionally people with walking difficulties are situated near an exit for their convenience and to help clear the auditorium quickly in an emergency but do make sure they will be able to see the performance adequately.

Anybody who is hard of hearing and wears a hearing aid will tell you how effective a hearing loop system is in a theatre. It can make all the difference to an evening's entertainment and is well worth enquiring about when you hire a building.

Parking

Parking is an issue for everyone these days and it is a particularly controversial subject for people with disabilities so you should ensure that suitable parking arrangements are made.

Aim to section off an area of your car park which is near to the entrance, again with the terrain being as level as possible. A simple sign bearing the international symbol of disability and the words 'Disabled Drivers Only' should do the trick and demonstrates that the organisers are professionally minded.

If you can arrange a steward to be available should anyone need assistance, so much the better, but a word of warning: disabled people, like everyone else, will ask for help if they need it, so don't instruct your helpers to give assistance automatically when none is requested. If in doubt, just ask.

Key points:

- Always consider the needs of disabled people and ask if venue arrangements are not immediately apparent.
- A level site or floor is crucial.
- Don't site toilets too far from the action.
- Use the heavy wheelbarrow analogy to imagine how a wheelchair user might feel.
- Hearing loops make all the difference to people using hearing aids.
- Check there is adequate lighting at night-time events.
- Use discrete parking areas.

Children

You should think about providing a cordial atmosphere at any event where you expect families or even unaccompanied older children. We have an unfortunate reputation in this country for not providing enough facilities to enable the 'family outing' to be a pleasurable affair but perhaps with a little thought we can begin to make amends in this area.

Here are some suggestions.

- At the lower end of the age group a small tent or caravan designated as a 'mother and baby' room is an unusual but welcome addition at any outdoor event. A low chair for nursing in private and a trestle table for baby-changing with a covered bin nearby for nappies is all that is needed.
- A soft drinks bar for under-18s to purchase their own refreshments means that the main bar is less crowded and allows children a little independence.
- At fairgrounds it can be helpful if an area is sectioned off for little ones to play. This can include a ball pond, bouncy castle (see below), and small roundabouts.
- For some events it may be worth considering opening a short-stay crèche (less than two hours or you will have to register with your local authority). A Christmas craft fair might be all the better for giving parents the opportunity to browse quietly for a precious hour knowing that their toddlers were being looked after by responsible carers. It is most important to employ qualified crèche leaders and assistants. You can hire a mobile care unit or you can talk to

your local social services department to get advice on setting up one of your own. They will also advise you on the number of children per carer, which varies with the age of the children.

Remember, also, to fix a place for lost children to take refuge. The secretary's tent or front of house manager's office are good choices as they usually have access to a public address system.

Animals

There are several types of shows that involve working with animals or birds. They can be divided into three groups.

- The animals are demonstrating the way they work such as sheep dog displays, police dog handler demonstrations, ploughing exhibitions, carriage driving competitions or bird of prey demonstrations.
- Animals are on show or judged for their form and beauty such as stock classes at agricultural shows, cat and dog shows, horse shows or perhaps less of a formal nature, pens holding rabbits or goats for children to pet and stroke.
- Animals and birds provide the actual entertainment having been trained to do tricks or clever acts that are not part of their usual behaviour; these shows sometimes include the use of 'exotics' like big cats, seals, alligators, etc.

There are some shows where a combination of the above may be on offer.

There is one other way in which animals can become part of the attractions. This is where the event is held within their own environment, such as within a deer park or farm. Here, however, the animals are usually incidental and probably not the direct responsibility of the event organiser – although the safety of both animals and visitors will still be a consideration.

Professional clubs and associations

There are certain shows and competitions which you will not be able to hold without approval or permission from the appropriate association. You cannot, for instance hold an exemption dog show without first obtaining a licence from the Kennel Club; if you wish to hold an open dog show you would need to abide by its regulations and use its approved judges. The same goes for all sorts of other pedigree competitions where breed society regulations are concerned, including horse shows, cat shows and cage bird competitions. For example, you will be in trouble if you offer a best of breed cup at your heavy horse show but the judge is not on the approved list of the correct association.

Of course, if you are holding a children's gymkhana in a local field with apple bobbing races or bareback jumping classes the professional bodies are not going to mind because you are not holding your event up to be a serious competition, or yourself as an expert judge.

Clubs, associations and other relevant organisations can be of great assistance when working in a specialist field. They will often suggest the running order of the show for you, provide rosettes, prizes, programmes, numbers, cages and all sorts of other equipment sometimes free of charge. You will automatically have a listing in their newsletters or magazines and have the most valuable 'word-of-mouth' advertising.

Special facilities

The most obvious and vital facilities that you must make available if you are working with animals are water and shelter. Food will almost certainly be brought by the owners but they will expect fresh, clean water to be made easily available (see Chapter 10 on utilities).

Shelter need only be an area in shade for competitors to park their cars or trailers, but you might have to supply official show cages as at a cat show. Horse-owners will expect a grassed or hard-standing area for their animals to wait in; their horses are usually in the shelter of, or tied to, their own horseboxes. Sheep, however, may need a pen provided to keep them safe, sheltered and out of the crowd.

Make sure that you are aware of what animal owners expect from the organisers and supply the facilities to the highest standard that you can afford. A few extra buckets and the odd bale of straw are often useful for emergencies.

It is rare that a whole circus will be available for hire, but you may wish to employ one as part of another show or one or two circus acts by themselves. Circuses will need a certain amount of security both to keep the public out and the animals in. If you can supply a fenced off field or park, that helps; a grazing paddock and a safe place to exercise animals is even better.

Veterinary help

All animals are subject to disease and accident. For large animal shows you may be required by the relevant breed association to ensure that all animals coming to the show hold a current vaccination certificate. You will need to make this clear on the schedule that will go out in advance.

It is advisable to have made a prior arrangement with a veterinary practice nearby either to have a vet available at the show itself or to have a vet on call in case of accidents. The telephone number should be given to all stewards and officials.

Just once in my time I have been present when a horse had to be shot on site. It was a most unlikely and shocking experience but for one which contingency plans had been made. The animal panicked whilst being loaded into a horsebox and broke its leg. The club had a vet on site and he was able to examine the horse within minutes of the accident happening and announced that it had to be destroyed. A horse is a large and very heavy animal and it was impossible to move it to a less public area so the deed was done there and then. To prevent a curious crowd gathering, the animal was covered with a tarpaulin until the ground was cleared at the end of the show and only then was it removed. In retrospect, it was felt that because the decision had been taken quickly and acted on immediately a very unfortunate incident had the minimum of publicity and the distress of the animal and its distraught owner was not unnecessarily prolonged.

It is important to address the possibility of these potentially devastating accidents and at least decide on a plan or policy even if you do not go into great detail. Look at Chapter 8 on how to prepare a risk assessment.

Possible problems

Apart from the accident and injury problems as outlined above you may experience other difficulties peculiar to animal shows.

Animal rights groups are outspoken by nature and they are also well informed and aware of all types of animal shows in the area. If you choose to present a show that includes performing animals or circus acts you must not be surprised if they whirl into action. Whatever your own beliefs are there is, nevertheless, a growing number of the population who feel that it is wrong to allow animals the alleged indignity of performing for human beings' entertainment. Letters of a most inflammatory nature may appear in the press, pickets may hamper your ticket sales and groups bearing banners and leaflets may pervade your show ground. You have to decide whether it is worth it.

Tied into the above, you may well find that council-owned land is denied you if the local authority has a policy of either discouraging animal acts or banning them altogether.

Horse shows, in particular, are an added headache when it comes to clearing up. Your country farmer or city farm may be delighted at the offerings of fertiliser that are left, but the average park keeper will not be too thrilled unless it is near a compost heap next to the roses. Make sure that you know what will be required of you – perhaps you could make some extra money selling bags of manure!

> **Key points:**
>
> - Remember to ensure that you have covered all requirements made by the relevant professional body before you go ahead with any animal show.
> - Consider having veterinary help on hand.
> - Make sure that clean, fresh water is readily available and that you have provided all that is expected in the way of cages, pens, etc.
> - Think hard before agreeing to use animal circus acts. You may have problems from the local council and protesters.
> - Make arrangements to have animal waste disposed of properly.
> - Just occasionally you may be faced with unpleasant decisions involving injury or even death of an animal. Have a contingency plan ready.

Fireworks and bonfires

Modern fireworks provide a visually stunning display, and the combination of the sight, sound and smell of fireworks and bonfire turns an ordinary winter night out into an exciting event tinged with a thrilling sense of slight danger. Such firework displays are an ever-popular attraction.

Of course, firework displays can also take place in summer and during daylight. And there are some pyrotechnic companies that specialise in sound shows. For some reason they have not really taken off in the UK but should you go to some countries in the Middle East and southern Europe you will find that they are popular at all sorts of celebrations, particularly weddings and carnivals.

Overall safety guidelines

Fire is dangerous be it in a huge ball on the ground or raining out of the sky in a torrent of flaming droplets; it can cause horrendous injuries and even prove fatal. The number of people needing hospital treatment in the UK during the 2001 fireworks' season due to misuse of fireworks was 1,352, and every year families are devastated by accidents that will affect their children for a lifetime despite annual advice being widely advertised. They just will not be told. If you are organising a firework display or bonfire night you have to take responsibility for an element of highly irresponsible people. These shows can be more hazardous than other types of events as they are most usually held in November after sunset and often it is cold and damp which further encourages people to get as close as they can to the bonfire and displays. Darkness causes security and car parking concerns also.

So how do you keep a crowd safe from possible accident? You will need to think about a firing site, the wind direction, where the spectators are to watch from, crowd control and a host of other considerations.

If you proceed carefully and thoroughly using all the following guidelines you will have as safe a firework display as it is possible to organise but a lot of it is down to weather conditions, the mood of the crowd and Lady Luck. Above all, make yourself and your stewards familiar with the current RoSPA guidelines. You will find the RoSPA 'Guide to Firework Safety' on its website (see Resources at the back of the book).

Legal considerations

Control on the supply and acquisition of fireworks is covered by the Fireworks (Safety) Regulations 1997. This covers the sale of certain fireworks to restricted purchasers. Essentially this means that fireworks have been categorised according to power with BS category 1, and the smaller of categories 2 and 3 only being available to the public and then only to those over the age of 18.

We have been promised (or threatened, depending on your point of view) with a further tightening up of the regulations for several years. This could mean that fireworks, other than sparklers or indoor poppers, may be banned for sale to the general public. Already the stocking and purchase of fireworks is restricted to a few weeks in the year and it has been suggested that amateur displays might be outlawed.

The industry in general feels that these measures would be too unpopular and draconian and that we are still a few years away from their implementation. However, the future is in our own hands and if the annual accident rate starts to fall fireworks may be given a reprieve; if they continue to climb, the government cannot ignore it forever. Always obtain your fireworks from reputable companies and suppliers who can demonstrate that their products have been authorised and classified.

Professional or amateur firing?

For a large show it is sensible to leave the actual firing to the experts. Small shows may be easier on the pocket but with amateurs in charge they are no safer, and may be considerably more dangerous than large professionally-fired events. If you feel that you really cannot afford to bring in the professionals, then personally I feel that you should not be holding a public display at all. However I accept that there are situations when a group simply cannot afford to buy in a display or cope with the huge number of spectators necessary to make it viable.

It is fun to design and organise your own show but, remember, accidents do happen even to those who are trained and have happened to experienced members of well known companies.

The amateur firing team

Try to keep your firing team to a minimum; ideally they should have had some previous experience. Each operator should have a particular section or job allocated and the whole team should rehearse the show (using dummies, naturally) to familiarise themselves with the running order, the instructions and the fireworks themselves a couple of days in advance. If there is anything that they are not sure about you will have time to telephone the suppliers.

I could explain the varieties of fireworks and the design of a display here but fireworks frequently come ready packaged as set pieces with a suggested running order carefully explained. Unless you are very sure of what you are doing it is often better to take the advice offered – it comes from a background of professional experience.

Your team should read the instructions that are printed by law on every firework and obey these to the letter. It is easy to put a shell upside down into a mortar and when the fuse is lit the result can easily be an underground explosion which scatters hot debris at a horrifying rate over everybody within range.

You and the team should be aware that all fireworks released for sale to the public have to include a 5 to 8 second delay between ignition and firing. This is a British standard and you have the right to complain of any material that fails to give you this provision.

Choosing the venue

In choosing a venue you will need to consider the number of spectators that you expect. It is better to choose too large a field or park than one too small where the public are pressed up against the firing site. If you decide on a public area that is served well by public transport this can go a long way towards reducing the number of cars that need to be parked and, of course, it allows families without cars the opportunity of attending.

Two firing sites should be chosen. The first allows the spectators to stand with their backs to the prevailing wind and the second to be used in an emergency if the wind suddenly swings around from a less predictable direction: smoke and fallout need to be directed away from the crowd. The firing area needs to be at least 20m wide and 10m deep with a fallout area at the back of at least 50m (remember, casings and other debris can travel at least 50m in a brisk wind and will be hot). It is safer to cancel a display completely if the wind is above 30 to 35mph.

As a rough guide use the rule that if debris from a test rocket or shells blows out beyond your vision from the firing site, you should not proceed. You must ensure that all combustible materials are cleared and that there are no overhanging trees, long grass or undergrowth in the area.

Fallout can also cause serious damage to paintwork so make sure your car park is well away from the site or you could find yourselves with an insurance claim.

Keeping spectators away from fireworks

Before setting up the display you should already have erected the fence that is to keep the spectators away from the fireworks. Crowd control barriers or chestnut paling are ideal but if these are unavailable, rope and 4ft bumbling pins can be used, provided a second line of rope is used about 2ft from the ground. You may need two or three people walking up and down the fence to discourage people with a death wish, and especially children, from going round the sides or wriggling underneath.

The fence should be at least 40m from the nearest firework (some professional companies insist on 100m, but for the size of the fireworks available to the amateur market 40m should be adequate). You should not allow anybody, not even the firing team, to enter the fallout area to the rear of the display.

All high firing fireworks should be angled over the fallout area and well away from spectators so that the spent cases and materials can land where they can do least damage

Staff and stewards

You will need as many helpers as you can muster and they should be easily identified. Fluorescent waistcoats are ideal. The recommended minimum number of stewards is two for the first 50 spectators and one for each additional 100 but your site and type of event might dictate something different: your risk assessment (see Chapter 8) should tell you how many stewards you will need to employ.

Prior to the show you will need to make arrangements with the police and/or the Fire Service about how best to evacuate the site and how to bring emergency vehicles onto the site; each steward should know these procedures plus the layout of the site and the running order. This also should be part of your risk assessment plan. For a large display it may be necessary to have some stewards in contact with the firing team and the emergency crew.

You will need additional staff to supervise the bonfire if there is one and the exits and entrances. The latter should be observed to ensure that the general public do not bring their own fireworks onto the site; this prohibition should be well publicised in advance both on posters and again on signs at each entrance. There should be enough gates to facilitate evacuation should it become necessary.

Fire fighting

Allocate special duties to two or three of your stewards to provide a fire fighting team. They should have an adequate number of fire extinguishers and supplies of sand and water. It is prudent to provide training (the Fire Services can advise on this subject) in advance for the use of extinguishers and other fire fighting equipment.

First aid

The Red Cross or St John Ambulance should be invited to attend for half an hour before and during the whole display and remain until the site is cleared.

Although an independent first aid team should be available it is sensible to provide a fairly comprehensive first aid kit yourselves. Include a roll of cling film in the kit as this makes a perfect sterile, non-stick (to the surface of the wounds) protection for burns until they can be treated more conventionally. Clean burns, cuts and grazes well, using only clean water and – excluding the face – wrap gently in film and wait for medical assistance.

Public address (PA)

A public address system should be used at larger displays whereas a hand-held loud hailer or megaphone should be adequate for small shows. Make sure that all sections of the crowd can hear the PA as it might be vital if evacuation becomes necessary.

The choice of display

Various factors will determine the choice of fireworks. Budget will be a significant consideration and if money is tight today's sophisticated crowds far prefer a short but spectacular show, fired in quick succession than a long traditional display firing each firework one at a time.

Even if money is no object (and there cannot be many displays where the organisers are not carefully counting each penny), about 20 minutes is enough for an exciting and noisy display. It is uncomfortable standing in the cold looking up at the sky and being bombarded by loud explosions and after a while even the keenest firework enthusiast looks forward to the end.

Siting and igniting bonfires

Make sure that any bonfire is sited well away from the firing area and always down wind so that sparks cannot accidentally ignite the display. Ideally it should be well fenced off using metal interlocking crowd control barriers and continuously supervised.

Check the bonfire carefully for children, animals, aerosols, cans of paint, tyres or anything hazardous before it is lit, and ensure that is completely extinguished before you leave the site.

Unless you are holding a private display in your garden it is extremely unwise to cook anything in the embers. A large bonfire gives off a tremendous heat and takes a very long time to cool down; few people can be bothered to wait until the coals are safe enough for cooking.

Informing the authorities

The police, the fire and ambulance services all need to know where the display is being held, the date and time and which access will be used.

If an airport is near the site you should inform them of your display if it is a large one, and it is a courtesy to notify hospitals, sheltered housing, animal sanctuaries, farmers and other nearby residents if you think they may be affected.

> **Key points:**
>
> - Never forget that fireworks can and have killed.
> - If you can possibly afford it, hire the professionals.
> - Choose your venue with care. Consider the firing site, the prevailing wind directions, the estimated crowd numbers, what time of the evening, whether you have other activities, crowd control and emergency procedures.
> - Keep all spectators at least 40m from the nearest firework.
> - Ensure you have enough stewards.
> - For a large display you may need a meeting with the emergency services and possibly a dummy run of procedures.
> - Have adequate first aid facilities available.
> - Make sure that your public address system can be heard from all areas of the site.
> - A shorter, higher display is more satisfactory and safer than a longer, ground level display. Spend your money on quality rather than quantity and keep the rate of firing up.
> - Site bonfires well away from fireworks.
> - Remember to inform all interested parties well in advance.
> - NEVER angle a firework over the heads of spectators.

Bouncy castles

At present there are no laws governing what the HSE describes as 'Passenger carrying amusement devices: Inflatable bouncing devices' but that is not to say they are safe and I feel it will not be long before this is looked at. There have been some truly appalling accidents in recent years – over 4,000 children need hospital treatment every year in the UK – through negligence and thoughtless use; absolutely anybody can buy an inflatable castle and set themselves up as a hire company with no training or registration.

Inflatable castles or flatbeds should be secured with guy ropes, as in even the lightest of breezes they can take off, scatter children or crash into other visitors or buildings. Use should always be cancelled completely in rain due to slippery surfaces. One adult should be present within the castle to help children if they panic or are jumped on. Times restricted to certain age groups and limiting numbers on the castle at any one time can help keep accidents to a minimum, but the children still need supervision.

If there seems to be any problem at all with the blower or the possibility of damage to the fabric, the castle should be cleared until it is certain that the castle is fully inflated and likely to stay that way.

The relatively new 'bar jump' or 'sticky castles' that are now available provide a popular alternative, especially to teenagers and adults. These involve donning a velcro suit and hurling yourself at the 'sticky' rear wall of the castle and hanging there like a fly caught in a spider's web. It is great fun and reasonably safe so long as no more than one or two jumpers are taking part at a time. Restrict times to about five minutes each. In my experience people, especially adults, will have had enough long before the time is up. It is one of the most exhausting activities that I have ever tried!

Legal considerations

Whilst there are no statutory regulations as yet the HSE have issued detailed safety guidelines and remember that, as in all cases, you have a duty of care to your public. HSE *Guidance Note PM76* is available from the HSE website or the Stationery Office (see Publications at the back of the book).

Key points:

- Tie all inflatables down with guy ropes.
- Don't use bouncy castles in rain, if you are experiencing problems with the blower or if there is a risk of puncture.
- Don't mix ages or risk overcrowding.
- Read the HSE safety guidelines.

13

Winding up

How you cope with winding up your event can be almost as important as getting it off the ground. If you are planning another show on the same lines next year your attitude at the end of this year can make a big difference to the help and services that you can expect subsequently.

This chapter covers the following topics:

▶ Coping with end-of-event emotions
▶ Clearing up
▶ Final budgets and the presentation to the charity
▶ Thank you letters and staying in touch
▶ Planning for next year.

Coping with end-of-event emotions

The end of an event can bring satisfaction, realisation of a job well done and a sense of achievement. This is how one imagines it should feel but often these positive emotions are delayed and overcome by weariness, a feeling of anti-climax and occasionally disappointment if things have not gone according to plan.

Tempers can be frayed towards the end of the day and sometimes the organiser feels let down by fellow helpers who drift away leaving him or her to deal with the final arrangements. It is important to have invited volunteers for clearing up jobs before the event starts so that volunteers know the extent of their duties or have an opportunity to warn you that they can only stay until an appointed hour.

Don't worry if you feel depressed when it is all over, the elation will soon be there especially after a good night's sleep. After all, you have been running on extra adrenaline and under tremendous pressure all through the show and probably for several days before; your body is worn out. Because of these feelings it is important to hold a debriefing session a few days later and not straight away (I dislike calling these post mortems, it sounds so negative). During this session you will of course discuss your final tasks but you should also allow yourselves time to go through the good and the bad points of the event, to have a laugh and to commiserate if necessary, to give oodles of praise where it is due. Be gracious enough to accept a few pats on the back; you will have deserved them.

Clearing up

Leaving a site or venue clean always takes longer than you think and if you have a large show to tidy up after it is wise to make arrangements to leave things secure on site, if possible, so that you can finish off the next day.

Certain jobs should, however, be done as soon as possible.

- Removing money to a more secure place, even before it has been counted, is vital after a large outdoor event.
- All food waste and wrappers should be collected and disposed of either to the local tip or in a skip hired for the purpose.
- Loos should be cleaned or at the very least locked until they can be dealt with hygienically.
- Unless you are very sure of the weather, tents and marquees should be taken down.
- PA systems, sound mixing desks, loud speaker towers and lighting rigs should all be disconnected and, if not removed immediately, made secure; there is a very real risk of overnight vandalism.
- All electrical supplies, generators and their fuel should also be made secure.

It is helpful if you can find out when the next booking is due, if you have hired a hall, and whether a cleaner will be coming in. You may be expected to sweep up yourselves and you will not want to be left doing all the dirty work by yourself.

If your event is outside you will need to organise a thorough check on foot to ensure that there are no fence posts, tent pegs, piles of rubbish or other hazards left on site. I once found an abandoned car in a field that we had to have towed away at our expense and more than once I have had to beg a favour from a local diver to pull all manner of things out of the river. Why do people bring supermarket trolleys to outdoor events and how do they get them there?

Your main problem will be litter but if you read Chapter 10 you should be well prepared.

Final budgets and the presentation to the charity

At your final meeting you should go through the accounts and complete your actuals. If you have been fundraising you will have to agree, if you have not already made a decision, as to what part of the proceeds will be passed over. The treasurer can draw a cheque – the bank will be happy to prepare a giant-sized copy if you warn them in advance – so that you can present your donation at a pre-arranged reception having made sure that the press and the rest of the media will be there. You should milk the publicity as much as you can, it will please the charity and any sponsors as well as giving your group credibility for future endeavours.

If you have opened a bank account peculiar to this show, keep it open for another month just in case other expenses filter through. Then close it or, if you intend to run your event again next year, ask if you can keep the account open but suspended (so you don't pay charges) until you need it again.

Thank you letters and staying in touch

Thank you letters are very welcome and really help to make people feel positively enthusiastic about assisting on future occasions. If you have used the skills of many people all from one club then individual letters will not be necessary. A single letter addressed to the senior member but expressing gratitude to all those who gave their time will be much appreciated.

For those who lent their property, firstly ensure that they received their belongings back in good order and then thank them individually. Any damage or loss must be made good immediately.

Some organising groups may decide to help a specific organisation exclusively or for an allotted span of time. These groups or clubs may very well welcome a newsletter from their chosen charity or appreciate an invitation for one of their members to join the organising committee next time.

Sometimes a very labour-intensive event just has so many individuals to thank it can be worth inviting everyone who participated to the charity presentation or to a separate 'thank you' party. This is a lovely way to celebrate months and months of hard work and ends the whole business on a really memorable note.

Planning for next year

Some events are purely one-offs and some finish as a once only but many are planned as or evolve into annual shows.

If your show has gone well and the community really becomes part of it or you succeed in raising several hundred pounds for your cause, you will be wondering whether to repeat the work for next year.

For a community event the surest way of guaranteeing success again is to hold an open meeting to discuss if the neighbourhood wishes to repeat the exercise or if they prefer to wait a few years before having to commit themselves so thoroughly a second time.

Charity events may work well as an annual occurrence especially if they have been largely organised by a group or club prepared to take them on year after year. Much of the hard work is in setting up a show for the first time and you will be able to draw on past experience and perhaps have some spare capacity to develop the event into a large-scale show over the next few years if that is what is wanted. Annual events work best if they are held around the same date each year and become an established part of the calendar.

Some events appear, on the face of it, to be 'one day only', never to be held again, but with a little ingenuity even those can take on a new lease of life in further years. For instance several years ago events all around the country were held to mark the 400th anniversary of the vanquishing of the Spanish Armada. A once-in-a-hundred years celebration we all thought. However many groups enjoyed running their events so much that annual Elizabethan shows have risen from the ashes giving a much appreciated platform for early dance groups, Elizabethan instrument players and creative chefs.

Having run a show once you will know what you need as a basic structure for your event and you may well still have an organising committee in place.

Allowing enough time to plan the next event

Try not to be complacent about the time needed to plan your next year's event. Even if your event is not until late summer you will still need to get moving early on if only to preclude the panic that you experienced last year! Have at least one meeting to consolidate your committee, perhaps elect a new chairperson, and get the feel for who would be interested in taking on specific duties. After the Christmas and New Year celebrations are behind you the real work should begin. If you plan a Christmas event it is hard to think about winter activities in the heat of the summer but you will really need to start planning in May or June at the latest.

Whatever the date your event is planned for allow at least six months to get things organised, and if your event is medium- to large-scale or includes many elements you may have to allow a little longer.

Good luck!

Events are a wonderful way to involve a wider audience and for communities to come out of their little boxes and meet and mingle together for the common good.

If you are the catalyst to make the whole event work, then congratulations to you. I hope there are many more reading this who are prepared to give their time and energy to making fun, and a little money, for those that need it. If this book helps to make that possible then I am delighted.

Resources

Publications

Many relevant titles are available from and published by the Directory of Social Change (DSC). Call 020 7209 5151 for a free publications list or consult the DSC website: www.dsc.org.uk/charitybooks

Prices where given were correct at time of going to press, but may be subject to change.

Health and safety

The Health and Safety Handbook
Published by DSC
Al Hinde & Charlie Kavanagh, 2001.
Price £12.50.
ISBN: 1-903991 01 3

The Event Safety Guide: Essentials of Health and Safety at Work
Published by The Stationery Office (see website below)
ISBN: 0717 624 536
and
HSE Guidance Note PM76 – Inflatable Castles
Published by The Stationery Office
Website: www,tso.co.uk/bookshop

Food hygiene

Industry Guide to Good Hygiene Practice
Published by Chadwick House Group
ISBN: 0900 103 558
Tel: 020 7827 6319
Website: www.cieh.org/pubs/

The Food Safety (General Food Hygiene) Regulations 1995 and the Food Safety (Temperature Control) Regulations 1995

Published by Eaton Publications,
Eaton House,
PO Box 34, Walton-on-Thames,
Surrey
Tel: 01932 229001

Law

Charitable Status
Published by DSC
Andrew Phillips with Bates, Wells & Braithewaite, 2003. Price: £9.95
ISBN: 1-900360 83 7

Finance

The Charity Treasurer's Handbook
Published by DSC
Gareth G Morgon, 2002. Price: £9.95
ISBN: 1-900360 89 6

Finance of Voluntary Organisations
Published by Croner Publications Ltd
Tel: 020 8547 3333 (advice line)
Website: www.croner.co.uk
This is a large publication, loose-leaf for easy update. Due to its high cost probably best looked for in a library. It is well worth studying on all sorts of topics.

A Practical Guide to Charity Accounting
Published by DSC in association with Sayer Vincent
Edited by Kate Sayer, 2003.
Price: £14.95
ISBN: 1-903991 21 8

A Practical Guide to Financial Management
Published by DSC in association with Sayer Vincent
Kate Sayer, 2002. Price: £14.95
ISBN: 1-903991 29 3

Fundraising information

The Complete Fundraising Handbook
Published by DSC
Nina Botting & Michael Norton, 2001. Price: £16.95
ISBN: 1-900360 84 5

FunderFinder
Website: www.funderfinder.org.uk
Software to help individuals and not-for-profit organisations in the UK to identify charitable trusts.

A Guide to the Major Trusts Vol. 1
Published by DSC
Luke FitzHerbert & Jo Wickens, 2003.
Price: £20.95
ISBN 1-903991 27 7
Concentrating on the top 300 trusts, this guide is an essential aid for all those seeking to raise money for charity from grant-making trusts and foundations.

Also available are Volume 2, a further 700 trusts and Volume 3, a further 400 trusts. DSC also publishes guides to local trusts in England in four volumes and separate guides to Scottish Trusts and *The Welsh Funding Guide.*

All our trusts information, covering over 4,000 trusts, is also available on CD-ROM or via our website *www.trustfunding.org.uk*

General information

The White Book
Published by Inside Events
ISBN: 1-874494 67 3
Tel: 02476 559590
Website: www.whitebook.co.uk
Over 40,000 listings of event organisers' resources i.e. equipment, venues, infrastructure, professional bodies, etc. Offers invaluable information for the events industry.

The Showman's Directory
Published by Lance Publications
ISBN: 0-946 509 57 3
Tel: 01730 266624
Website: www.showmans-directory.co.uk
Lists entertainments, contractors, services and equipment.

Marketing

Arts Marketing
Keith Diggle
Published by Rhinegold Publishing
ISBN 0-946 890 58 7

Event Marketing: how to successfully promote events, estivals, conventions and expositions
Published by John Wiley & Sons
ISBN: 0-471 401 79 X

Promoting Your Cause
Published by DSC
Karen Gilchrist, 2002. Price: £10.95
ISBN: 1-900360 95 0

Writing a constitution

Voluntary but not Amateur
Published by DSC
Jacki Reason, Ruth Hayes & Duncan
Forbes, 2000. Price: £22.95.
ISBN 1-872582 71 0

Voluntary Sector Legal Handbook
Published by DSC
Sandy Adirondack & James Sinclair
Taylor, 2001. Price: £42.00 for
voluntary organisations.
ISBN: 1-900360 72 1

Preparing sponsorship applications

*Finding Company Sponsors for Good
Causes*
Published by DSC
Chris Wells, 2000. Price: £9.95.
ISBN: 1-900360 37 3

Regulations

The Gaming Board for Great Britain
Berkshire House,
168–173 High Holborn,
London WC1V 7AA
Tel: 020 7306 6200
Website: www.gbgb.org.uk
*Advice and registration for all forms of
lotteries where prizes are offered over
£2,000, and useful links.*

Customs and Excise
Tel: 0845 010 9000
Website: www.hmce.gov.uk
*National Advice Service for VAT or
contact your local office (listed on
the site).*

The Charity Commission
Tel: 0870 333 0123
Website: www.charity-
commission.gov.org
*Comprehensive advice about all
aspects of setting up charities,
registering as a charity, charities
and the law, charities and tax, list
of publications.*

Inland Revenue
Website:
www.inlandrevenue.gov.uk/leaflets
Website: www.taxcentral.co.uk
*List of leaflets and publications giving
advice about charitable giving, trading
by charities, tax position of voluntary
organisations, etc.*

The Performing Right Society
19 Church Lane
Peterborough
PE1 2UZ
Tel: 0800 068 4828
Website: www.prs.co.uk
*Local music adviser and advice on fees
that may be payable for live or
recorded music.*

Insurance

*There are very few event insurance
companies around these days. It
would be useful to look at these two
websites to see what is on offer,
compare and negotiate.*

Ansvar
Ansvar House
St Leornard's Road
Eastbourne, East Sussex
BN21 3UR
Tel: 01323 737541
Website: www.ansvar.co.uk

Event Insurance Services
20a Headlands Business Park
Ringwood
Hampshire
BH24 3PB
Tel: 01425 4703905
Website: www.events-insurance.co.uk

General contacts

The National Outdoor Events Association
7 Hamilton Way,
Wallington, Surrey SM6 9NJ
Tel: 020 8669 8121
Website: www.noea.org.uk
The industry forum representing buyers (local authorities, show organisers, etc.) and suppliers of equipment and services for outdoor events. Yearbook and members directory.

Community Matters
12–20 Baron Street,
London N1 9LL
Tel: 020 7837 7887
The national association of community organisations.

The National Association of Councils for Voluntary Service
177 Arundel Street,
Sheffield S1 2NV
Tel: 0114 2786636
Website: www.nacvs.org.uk
Can provide you with the address of your local voluntary service council which is a good starting point for information on local charities and voluntary organisations. Some offer DSC directories and FunderFinder

software giving details of funding from trusts.

The National Council for Voluntary Organisations
Regent's Wharf, 8 All Saints St
London N1 9RL
Tel: 020 7713 6161
Helpdesk: 0800 2 798 798
Website: www.ncvo-vol.org.uk

The National Federation of Women's Institutes
104 New King's Road,
London SW6 4LY
Tel: 020 7371 9300
Website: www.womens-institute.co.uk
Information on campaigns and local groups.

The National Gardens Scheme Charitable Trust
Hatchlands Park
East Clandon, Guildford
Surrey GU4 7RT
Tel: 01483 211535

St Johns Ambulance (national headquarters)
27 St John's Lane
London EC1M 4BU
Tel: 0870 010 49 50
Website: www.sja.org.uk

British Red Cross (national headquarters)
9 Grosvenor Crescent
London SW1X 7EJ
Tel: 020 7235 5454
Website: www.redcross.org.uk

Online directories

Events and Conference Directory Online
Website: www.ecd-online.uk
Everything (so they say!) for events and conferences, AV equipment, acts, agents, attractions, childcare, discos, fencing, mobile WCs, staging, venues.

Event Services Directory
Website: www.eventservicenet.co.uk

A few funding sources

The Arts Council of England
14 Great Peter Street,
London SW1P 3NQ
Tel: 020 7973 6517
Grants line: 0207 9736517

The Arts Council of Northern Ireland
MacNeice House,
77 Malone Road,
Belfast BT9 6AQ
Tel: 02890 285200
Website: www.artscouncil-ni.org

ArtsWales
9 Museum Place,
Cardiff CF1 3NX
Tel: 0292 0376500
Website: www.artswales.org.uk

Awards for All
Tel: 0845 600 20 40
Website: www.awardsforall.org.uk
A Lottery grants programme aimed at local communities.

The Crafts Council
44a Pentonville Road,
Islington,

London N1 9BY
Tel: 020 7278 7700
Website: www.craftscouncil.org.uk

The London Chamber of Commerce and Industry
33 Queens Street,
London EC4 1AP
Tel: 020 7248 4444
Website: www.londonchamber.co.uk

The Scottish Arts Council
12 Manor Place,
Edinborough EH3 7DD
Tel: 0845 603 6000
Website: www.sac.org.uk

Information on charity issues

Central Register of Charities
Tel: 0870 333 0123
Website:
www.charitycommission.gov.uk/registeredcharities
Register of all charities.

Charities Aid Foundation
Kings Hill
West Malling
Kent ME19 4TA
Website: www.cafonline.org
More charity advice and services links.

The Charity Commission
Harmsworth House
13–15 Bouverie Street,
London EC4Y 8DP
Tel: 0870 3330123
Website:
www.charitycommission.gov.uk
Advice and numerous leaflets on all charitable concerns.

The Directory of Social Change
24 Stephenson Way
London NW1 2DP
Tel: 020 7391 4848
E-mail: info@dsc.org.uk
Website: www.dsc.org.uk
Information and training for the
voluntary sector; comprehensive
publications list; training courses and
events; Charityfair.

Safety

Health and Safety Executive (HSE)
Website: www.hse.gov.uk

**RoSPA (Royal Society for the
Prevention of Accidents)**
Tel: 0121 2482000
Website: www.rospa.org.uk
Leaflets and online guide to
safety issues including those
concerning fireworks.

Signage

AA Signs
Lister Point,
Sherrington Way,
Basingstoke, Hampshire RG22 4DQ
Tel: 0800 731 7003
Website: www.theaa.com/aasigns
Highway signs and planning
permissions.

RAC Signs Service
Tel: 0845 601 0000
Website: www.racsigns.co.uk
Highway signs and planning
permissions.